THE 2013–2016 UNITED METHODIST DIRECTORY

THE 2013–2016 UNITED METHODIST DIRECTORY

Copyright © 2013 by Cokesbury

All rights reserved.

No part of this work may be reproduced or transmitted in any form or by any means, electronic or mechanical, including photocopying and recording, or by any information storage or retrieval system, except as may be expressly permitted by the 1976 Copyright Act or in writing from the publisher. Requests for permission should be addressed to Cokesbury Permissions, P.O. Box 801, 201 Eighth Avenue South, Nashville, TN 37202-0801 or e-mailed to permissions@umpublishing.org.

ISBN 978-1-4267-6614-5

This book is printed on acid-free, elemental chlorine-free paper.

The Councils, Boards, Commissions, and Conferences sections refer to official agencies of The United Methodist Church. Many affiliated groups officially relate to at least one of the general agencies of The United Methodist Church and are listed with the acronym of that agency. Other groups, caucuses, and ecumenical groups are listed for your convenience but do not necessarily have an official connection to The United Methodist Church.

This directory includes changes from Boards and Agencies through May 2013. Changes made after that date will be available at http://cokesbury.com/unitedmethodistdirectory. Changes can be sent to umdirectory@umpublishing.org.

Those who purchase *The 2013-2016 United Methodist Directory* have access to the digital edition of the book. When you visit the site, please click on the link to the digital edition, and when prompted, enter the following password: **UMD2013**. The web page will provide instructions on either viewing the digital edition in your browser or downloading it to your computer.

13 14 15 16 17 18 19 20 21 22—10 9 8 7 6 5 4 3 2 1

MANUFACTURED IN THE UNITED STATES OF AMERICA

Contents

THE UNITED METHODIST CHURCH
Facts and Figures 1

COUNCIL OF BISHOPS
Officers 5
Council of Bishops (active) 5
Council of Bishops (retired) 9
Episcopal Assignments 13

CONNECTIONAL TABLE 21

COUNCILS
General Council on Finance and Administration 25
    Staff 25
Audit and Review Committee 29
Judicial Council 30

BOARDS
General Board of Church and Society 31
    Staff 34
General Board of Discipleship 36
    Staff 37
General Board of Global Ministries 43
    Staff 45
General Board of Higher Education and Ministry 47
    Staff 48
General Board of Pension and Health Benefits 51
    Staff 53
Board of The United Methodist Publishing House 54
    Staff 56

COMMISSIONS
General Commission on Archives and History 61
    Staff 63
General Commission on Communication 64
    Staff 65
Commission on the General Conference 70
    Committee on Correlation and Editorial Review 72
General Commission on Religion and Race 73
    Staff 74

Contents

General Commission on the Status and Role of Women 76
    Staff 78
General Commission on United Methodist Men 79
    Staff 80
United Methodist Women, National Office 80
    Staff 80
JustPeace 84
    Staff 85

CONFERENCES
Jurisdictional Officers in the U.S. 87
Annual Conferences in the U.S. Jurisdictions
    (information as provided as of May 2013) 92
    Conference Office Address, Contact Information, Website
    Episcopal Office Staff
    District Superintendents (alphabetically by district)
    Conference Officers and Leaders (as provided): Director of
        Connectional Ministries or equivalent, Lay Leader, Treasurer,
        Secretary, Director of Communications
    Publications
    Foundation
Central Conference Episcopal Areas 155
    Regional Office Address, Contact Information, Website
    Conferences in the Area

GROUPS AND CAUCUSES
Affiliated and Related Groups 165
Caucuses 176
Ecumenical Groups 178

SCHOOLS, COLLEGES, UNIVERSITIES, SEMINARIES
Schools of Theology 181
Professional School 182
Senior Colleges and Universities 182
Two-Year Colleges 193
College Preparatory Schools 193
University Senate Approved Seminaries 194
Commission on Theological Education 200

INDEX 201

NOTE: This directory includes changes from boards and agencies through May 2013. Changes made after that date will be available online at http://www.cokesbury.com/umdirectory/2013. Changes can be sent to umdirectory@umpublishing.org.

The United Methodist Church
Facts and Figures

(as of December 31, 2011, most recent figures available)

GENERAL INFORMATION
InfoServ: www.umc.org/infoserv
United Methodist www.umc.org

OFFICIAL UNITED METHODIST RESOURCES
Available through www.cokesbury.com; toll-free Cokesbury Call Center (1/800/672-1789); Community Resource Consultants across the U.S.

U.S. MEMBERSHIP 7,526,642
- Lay 7,481,383
- Total Clergy 45,259
- Retired 14,833
- Clergywomen (under appointment) 8,601

U.S. MEMBERSHIP BY JURISDICTION
- North Central 1,295,640
- Northeastern 1,279,809
- South Central 1,717,265
- Southeastern 2,837,330
- Western 351,339

GENERAL CHURCH MEMBERSHIP ROLL 32

U.S. MEMBERSHIP BY ETHNIC GROUPS
(reporting incomplete)
- Asian 91,159
- African American 444,943
- Hispanic 72,811
- Native American 23,229

Pacific Islander 13,185
Multi-Racial 51,000
White 6,742,092

Lay Membership Outside the U.S. 4,400,510

Africa 4,191,108
Europe 63,760
Philippines 145,642

Active Clergy Outside the U.S. 11,979

Africa..9,209
Europe...1,058
Philippines 1,712

Congregations by Ethnicity in the U.S.

(estimate)

Asian..361
African American..2,282
Hispanic...312
Native American 148
Pacific Islander..38
Multi-Racial 84
White..29,796

Clergy Members of Annual Conferences in the U.S.—Ethnicity/Gender

Asian...1,202
African American..2,877
Hispanic...584
Native American 180
Pacific Islander..109
Multi-Racial 151
White..39,812
Female..11,302
Male..33,614

The United Methodist Church: Facts and Figures

ACTIVE BISHOPS IN THE U.S 46
(11 African American, 2 Hispanic, 6 Asian American, 11 Women)

ACTIVE BISHOPS OUTSIDE THE U.S............20

Africa 13
Eurasia 1
Europe 3
Philippines 3

RETIRED BISHOPS (ALL NATIONS) 98

AVERAGE ATTENDANCE AT WEEKLY WORSHIP SERVICES IN THE U.S. 3,021,494

AVERAGE ATTENDANCE AT SUNDAY CHURCH SCHOOL IN THE U.S. 1,127,916

PASTORAL CHARGES IN THE U.S. 25,539

DISTRICTS IN THE U.S. 426

Council of Bishops
cob@umc.org

OFFICERS

President: **Wenner, Rosemarie**,
President-Designate: **Brown Warner H., Jr.**,
Secretary: **Hayes, Robert E., Jr.**, PO Box 60467, Oklahoma City, OK 73146-0467, 405/530-2025 fax: 405/530-2040, rhayes@okbishop.org
Executive Secretary: **Weaver, Peter D.**,
Ecumenical Officer: **Swenson, Mary Ann**,
Past President: **Goodpaster, Larry M.**,
Administrative Assistant: **McClain, Jo Ann**, 100 Maryland Ave NE, Ste. 320, Washington, DC 20002, 202/547-6270 fax: 202/547-6272, jmcclain@umc-cob.org

ACTIVE

Alsted, Christian, (Nordic and Baltic Area) Rigensgade 21A, DK-1316 Copenhagen, Denmark, 45/5133 1477, office@umc-ne.org

Arichea, Daniel C. Jr., (Manila Area) United Methodist HQ, PO Box 756, 900 United Nations Ave., 1000 Ermita, Metro Manila, Philippines, 63/2 523 0297 fax: 63/2 532 2278, aricheadaniel@gmail.com

Bickerton, Thomas J., (Pittsburgh Area) PO Box 5002, Cranberry Twp, PA 16066-4914, 724/776-1499, 724/776-1599 fax: 724/776-1683, bishopsoffice@wpaumc.org

Bledsoe, W. Earl, (Northwest Texas-New Mexico Area) PO Box 866188, Plano, TX 75086-6188, 972/526-5015 fax: 972/526-5014, bishopbledsoe@ntcumc.org

Boni, Benjamin, (Côte D'Ivoire) 41 Blvd. de la Republique, Abidjan Plateau, Côte D'Ivoire, West Africa, +225/20 21 17 97 fax: +225 20 22 52 03, bishopboni@emu-ci.org

Brown, Warner H. Jr., (San Francisco Area) PO Box 980250, West Sacramento, CA 95798-0250, 916/374-1510 fax: 916/372-9062, bishop@calnevumc.org

Carcaño, Minerva G., (Los Angeles Area) PO Box 6006, Pasadena CA 91102-6006, 626/568-7312 fax: 626/568-7377, bishopmc@cal-pac.org

Carter, Kenneth H. Jr. (Florida Area) 450 MLK Jr. Ave., Lakeland, FL 33815, 863/688-5563 x151 fax: 863/687-0568, bishop@flumc.org

Cho, Young Jin (Richmond Area) 10330 Staples Mill Rd., PO Box 5606, Glen Allen VA 23058, 804/521-1102 fax: 804/521-1171, bishopcho@vaumc.org

Coyner, Michael J., (Indiana Area) 301 Pennsylvania Pkwy. #300, Indianapolis, IN 46280, 317/564-3239 fax: 317/735-4225, bishop@inumc.org

Davis, G. Lindsey (Louisville Area) 7400 Floydsburg Rd., Crestwood, KY 40014-8202, 502/425-4240 fax: 502/425-9232, bishop@kyumc.org

Devadhar, Sudarshana (Boston Area) PO Box 249, Lawrence, MA 01842-0449, 978/682-7555 x250 fax: 978/682-9555, bishop@neumc.org

Domingos, Gaspar Joao, (West Angola Area) Caixa Postal 68, Rua de N. S. Da Muxima 12, Luanda Angola, 244 222 33 2107, gdomingos61@yahoo.com

Dorff, James, E., (San Antonio Area) 16400 Huebner Rd., San Antonio, TX 78248, 210/408-4502 fax: 210/408-4501, bishop@umcswtx.org

Dyck, Sally, (Chicago Area) 77 W. Washington St. Ste. 1820, Chicago, IL 60602, 312/346-9766 x102 fax: 312/214-9031, bishop.dyck@umcnic.org

Goodpaster, Larry M., (Charlotte Area) PO Box 18750, Charlotte, NC 28218, 704/535-2260 fax: 704/535-9160, bishop@wnccumc.org

Hagiya, Grant J., (Greater Northwest Area) PO Box 13650, Des Moines, WA 98198-1009, 206/870-6810 fax: 206/870-6811, bishop@pnwumc.org

Harvey, Cynthia Fierro (Louisiana Area) 527 North Blvd., Baton Rouge, LA 70802, 225/346-1646 x212 fax: 225/387-3662, enixmore@bellsouth.net

Hayes, Robert E. Jr., (Oklahoma Area) PO Box 60467, Oklahoma City, OK 73146-0467, 405/530-2025 fax: 405/530-2040, rhayes@okbishop.org

Holston, L. Jonathan (Columbia Area) 4908 Colonial Dr. #121, Columbia, SC 29203, 803/786-9486 fax: 803/754-9327, bishop@umcsc.org

Hopkins, John L., (Ohio East Area) PO Box 2800, North Canton, OH 44720-0800, 330/499-3972 fax: 330/497-4911, bishop@eocumc.org

Hoshibata, Robert T., (Phoenix Area) 1550 E. Meadowbrook Ave., Phoenix, AZ 85014-4040, 602/266-6955 x209 fax: 602/279-1355, bishop@desertsw.org

Huie, Janice Riggle, (Houston Area) 5215 S. Main St., Houston, TX 77002-9792, 713/528-6881 fax: 713/529-7736, bishop.huie@txcumc.org

Innis, John G., (Liberia Area) PO Box 10-1010, Tubman Blvd. @ 13th St., Monrovia Liberia, West Africa, 011231886517192 U.S. Address: 819 Franklin St., Worcester, MA 01604 774/454-1437, b.innis123@gmail.com

Johnson, Peggy A., (Philadephia Area) PO Box 820, Valley Forge, PA 19482 610/666-9090 fax: 610/666-9181, peggy.johnson@epaumc.org

Jones, Scott J., (Great Plains Area) 9440 E. Boston, Ste. 160, Wichita, KS 67207-3603, 316/686-0600 fax: 316/684-0044, bishop@greatplainsumc.org

Juan, Rodolfo Alfonso, (Baguio Area) Methodist Mission Center, 10 Marcos Hwy., PO Box 87, 2600 Baguio City, Philippines, 6374-442-2879 fax: 6374-304-2653, chapsrudy@yahoo.com

Jung, Hee-Soo, (Wisconsin Area) 750 Windsor St. Ste. 303, Sun Prairie, WI 53590, 608/837-8526 fax: 608/837-0281, hsjung@wisconsinumc.org

Katembo, Kainda, (Southern Congo Area) 960 Av. Mzee Laurent Kabila, Lubumbashi, Democratic Republic of Congo, 243 88 47256 fax: 243 23 41191, akatembokainda@yahoo.fr

Keaton, Jonathan D., (Illinois Area) PO Box 19215, Springfield, IL 62794-9215, 217/529-3820 fax: 217/529-4190, jkeaton@igrc.org

Kiesey, Deborah L., (Michigan Area) 2164 University Park Ste. 250, Okemos, MI 48864, 517/347-4030 fax: 517/347-4003, bishop@miareaumc.org

King, James R., Jr., (South Georgia Area) 3370 Vineville Ave., Ste. 101, Macon, GA 31204-2331, 478/475-9286 fax: 478/475-9248, jking@sgaumc.com

Kulah, Arthur F., (Nigeria Area) UMCN Secretariat, Mile Six, Jalingo-Numan Rd., PO Box 148, Jalingo, Taraba State, Nigeria, 234-806-347-5207, 234-708-656-9911, afkulah@yahoo.com

Leeland, Paul L., (Alabama-West Florida Area) 100 Interstate Park Dr., Ste. 120A, Montgomery, AL 36109, 334/277-1787 fax: 334/277-0109, bishop@awfumc.org

Lowry, J. Michael, (Fort Worth Area) 464 Bailey, Fort Worth, TX 76107-2153, 817/877-5222 fax: 817/332-4609, bishop@ctcumc.org

Matthews, Marcus, (Washington Area) 11711 East Market Pl., Fulton, MD 20759, 410/290-7300 fax: 410/309-1159, BishopMarcusMatthews@bwcumc.org

McAlilly, William T. (Nashville Area) 520 commerce St. Ste. 201, Nashville, TN 37203-3714, 615/742-8834 fax: 615/742-3726, bishop@nashareaumc.org

McKee, Michael (Dallas Area) PO Box 866188, Plano, TX 75086-6188, 972/526-5015 fax: 972/526-5014, bishopmck@ntcumc.org

McLee, Martin D. (New York Area) 20 Soundview, White Plains, NY 10606, 914/615-2221 fax: 914/615-2246, bishop@nyac.com

Mueller, Gary E. (Arkansas Area) 800 Daisy Gatson Bates Dr., Little Rock, AR 72202-3770, 501/324-8001 fax: 501/324-8021, bishop@arumc.org

Nhanala, Joaquina F., (Mozambique Area) Rua D. Francisco Barreto 229, Caixa Postal 2640, Maputo, Mozambique, 258 21 49 3568 fax: 258 21 49 35 68, jnhanala@yahoo.com

Ntambo, Nkulu Ntanda, (North Katanga Area) UMC, Batiment Mokador Ave. Mobutu, Lubumbashi, Democratic Republic of Congo, 243 81 408 1120 fax: 243 971 08 9792, nntambo7@hotmail.com

Ough, Bruce R., (Dakotas-Minnesota Area) 122 West Franklin Ave. #200, Minneapolis, MN 55404-2472, 612/870-4007 fax: 612/870-3587, bishop@dkmnareaumc.org

Palmer, Gregory V., (Ohio West Area) 32 Wesley Blvd., Worthington, OH 43085, 614/844-6200 x215 fax: 614/781-2625, wocbishop@wocumc.org

Park, Jeremiah J., (Harrisburg Area) 303 Mulberry Dr. Ste. 100, Mechanicsburg, PA 17050-3198, 717/766-7871 fax: 717/766-3210, bishoppark@susumc.org

Quipungo, Jose, (East Angola Area) Rua Comandante Dangereux No. 46, C.P. No. 9, Malange, ANGOLA, Phone/fax: 244 2512 30063 cell: 244 92 354 1594, bishopquipungo@gmail.com

Schnase, Robert C., (Missouri Area) 3601 Amron Ct., Columbia, MO 65202 573/441-1770 fax: 573/441-0765, rschnase@moumethodist.org

Schol, John R., (New Jersey Area) 1001 Wickapecko Dr., Ocean, NJ 07712-4733, 732/359-1010 fax: 732/359-1019, bishopjohnschol@gnjumc.org

Soriano, Leo A., (Davao Area) United Methodist Center, 104 Recto Ave., 8000 Davao City, Philippines Phone/fax: 63 82 222 4474, bishopsoriano@yahoo.com

Stanovsky, Elaine J. W., (Mountain Sky Area) 6110 S. Greenwood Plaza Blvd., Greenwood Village, CO 80111, 303/733-0083 fax: 303/733-5047, bishop@mountainskyumc.com

Steiner Ball, Sandra L. (West Virginia Area) 900 Washington St. E., Charleston, WV 25301 Phone/fax: 304/344-8330, wvareaumc@aol.com

Streiff, Patrick, (Central & Southern Europe Area) Badener Strasse 69, PO Box 2239 CH-8026, Zürich, Switzerland, 41/44-299 30 60 fax: 41/44-299 30 69, bischof@umc-europe.org

Swanson, James E., Sr., (Mississippi Area) PO Box 931, Jackson, MS 39205-0931, 601/948-4561 fax: 601/948-5981, bishop@mississippi-umc.org

Taylor, Mary Virginia, (Holston Area) PO Box 850, Alcoa, TN 37701-0850, 865/293-4146 fax: 865/690-7112, bishop@holston.org

Trimble, Julius C., (Iowa Area) 2301 Rittenhouse St., Des Moines, IA 50321-3101, 515/974-8902 fax: 515/283-8672, jc.trimble@iaumc.org

Unda, Gabriel Yemba (New Congo Area) Ave de la Justice 75B, Combe-Kinshasa, Democratic Republic of Congo, 243 998127204, gabrielunda@hotmail.com

Växby, Hans, (Eurasia Area) Khamovnicheskiy Val 24, Stroenie 2, Moscow, 119048 Russia, 7/495-961-3458, bishop@umc-eurasia.ru

Wallace-Padgett, Debra (Birmingham Area) 898 Arkadelphia Rd., Birmingham, AL 35204-5011, 205/226-7991 fax: 205/226-7998, dpadget@northalabamaumc.org

Wandabula, Daniel, (East Africa Area) PO Box 12554, Plot No. 1259, Kampala, Uganda, 256 41 533978 fax: 256 41 533982, residentbishop aacumc@gmail.com

Ward, Hope Morgan, (Raleigh Area) 700 Waterfield Ridge Pl., Garner, NC 27529, 919/779-6115 fax: 919/773-2416, bishop@nccumc.org

Watson, B. Michael, (North Georgia Area) 4511 Jones Bridge Cir., NW, Norcross, GA 30092-1406, 678/533-1360 fax: 678/533-1361, bishop@ngumc.org

Webb, Mark J. (Upper New York Area) 324 University Ave. 3rd Fl., Syracuse, NY 13210, 315/422-5027 fax: 315/422-5304, bishopwebb@unyumc.org

Wenner, Rosemarie, (Germany Area) Ludolfusstrasse 2-4, D-60487 Frankfurt, Germany 49 69 24 25 210 fax: 49 69 24 25 2129, bischoefin@emk.de

Yambasu, John K., (Sierra Leone Area) 31 Lightfoot Boston St., PO Box 523, Freetown, Sierra Leone, 232 22 226625, 232 22 220212 fax: 232 22 224439, bishopyambasu@gmail.com

Yemba, David K., (Central Congo Area) 2867 Ave. des Ecuries, Ngaliema, B.P. 4727, Kinshasa II, Democratic Republic of Congo, 243-810806614, bishopccongo@yahoo.com

RETIRED

Bashore, George W., 2409 Broadlawn Dr., Pittsburgh, PA 15241-2407, 412/854-2389, bishgeocar@comcast.net

Blake, Bruce P., 3100 Cabrillo Dr., Winfield, KS 67156 620/221-6924, karbru@cox.net

Bolleter, Heinrich, Grenzweg 9, CH-5036, Oberentfelden, Switzerland, 41/62-723 02 71, h.bolleter@bluewin.ch

Carder, Kenneth, 536 Village Church Dr., Chapin, SC 29036, 803/932-0266, kcarder@div.duke.edu

Chamberlain, Ray W., Office: Bishop in Residence, Shenandoah University, 1460 University Dr., Winchester, VA 22601-5195, 540/665-1284 x540, rchamber@su.edu Home: 1521 Nester Dr., Winchester, VA 22601, 540/662-0009, raycan7777@aol.com

Chamness, Benjamin, 319 Elkins Lake, Huntsville, TX 77340, 936/293-8577, brchamness@att.net

Choy, Wilbur W. Y., 11 W. Aloha St., Apt. 830, Seattle, WA 98119-4746, sansui3@aol.com

Christopher, Sharon A. Brown, 4040 Woodlawn Dr., #30, Nashville, TN 37205, 615/385-1695, sab.christopher@comcast.net

Clark, Roy C., 500 Elmington Ave., #229, Nashville, TN 37205, Phone/fax: 615/383-3047, mscrcc20@gmail.com

Clymer, Wayne K., (May-Oct.) 2850 Inner Rd., Wayzata, MN 55391, 952/473-2812; (Nov.-Apr.) Pkwy. Villas, 6054 Coral Way, Bradenton, FL 34207, 941/727-7875, wclymer2000@yahoo.com

Colaw, Emerson S., 9840 Montgomery Rd. #2224, Cincinnati, OH 45242, 513/247-1854, emersoncolaw@gmail.com

Craig, Judith, 3699 Orchard Way, Powell, OH 43065, 614/761-0855, jcraig@columbus.rr.com

Crutchfield, Charles N. 2916 Charing Cross Rd., Oklahoma City, OK 73120, 405/286-6330, cncrutch@aol.com

De Carvalho, Emilio J. M., Rua Oliveira Martins, 29, Bairro de Alvalade, C. P. 2648, Luanda, Angola, 244 2 32 4431, emarcar@netangola.com

DeWitt, Jesse R., 3497 Huron View Ct., Dexter, MI 48130, 734/424-2860, ajdewitt@provide.net

Eutsler, R. Kern, 7090 Covenant Woods Dr., Apt. F-304, Mechanicsville, VA 23111, 804/569-8053, rkeeve@residents.com

Fannin, Robert E., 2065 Athenia Way, Lakeland, FL 33813, 863/647-9630, rfannin@flsouthern.edu

Fernandes, Moises Domingos, Rua de Liberdade 154-156, Vila Alice, Luanda, Angola

Fisher, Violet, 125 Berry Dr., Wilmington, DE 19808, 302/740-9379, L82839@aol.com

Galván, Elias G., 9845 E. Desert Cove, Scottsdale, AZ 85260, 480/361-6484, galvan222@msn.com

Gamboa, José C., Jr., 72 Virgo St., Camella Homes, Baccor 2, Cavite, PHILLIPINES, 63 46 472 1937

Grove, William Boyd, 109 McDavid Ln., Charleston, WV 25311-9708, 304/344-1384, wboydgrove@aol.com

Gwinn, Alfred Wesley Jr. 8301 Southwind Bay Cir., Fort Myers, FL 33908, 919/623-4999, bishopgwinn@gmail.com

Hancock, Charles W., 5300 Zebulon Rd., Apt. 1129, Macon, GA 31210, 478/757-0791, bishopcwh@cox.net

Hardt, John Wesley, 4833 W. Lawther Dr., Overlook 416, Dallas, TX 75214, 972/591-1938, hardt.j.w@gmail.com

Hassinger, Susan W., 57 Broadlawn Park 2B, Chestnut Hill, MA 02467, 617/325-9937, swhassinger@earthlink.net

Hearn, J. Woodrow, (Oct. 26-May 14) 62 Campeche Cir., Galveston, TX 77554-9361, 409/741-0350; (May 15-Oct. 25) PO Box 75, Friendship, ME 04547, 207/832-7518, bishopjwh@sbcglobal.net

Hicks, Kenneth W., 3909 S. Lookout, Little Rock, AR 72205-2027, 501/663-9670, kenhicks23@gmail.com

Hughes, H. Hasbrouck, Jr., 113 S. Stocker Ct., Williamsburg, VA 23188-6307, 757/258-0538, h3mgh@aol.com

Humper, Joseph C., 72 Old Wharf Rd., Wellington Freetown, Sierra Leone, West Africa, 076/76-602230, cjhumper77@yahoo.com

Hutchinson, William W., 1685 Stone Mountain Ln., Las Cruces, NM 88001, 225/205-4488, lahutchs@aol.com

Irons, Neil L., 5250 Meadowbrook Dr., Mechanicsburg, PA 17050, 717/580-5899, nlirons@aol.com

Ives, S. Clifton, 10 Quaker Ln., Portland, ME 04103, 207/797-8930, cives37@aol.com

Job, Rueben P., 300 Wheatfield Cir., #B322, Brentwood, TN 37027, 615/376-6096, dakotajob@aol.com

Johnson, Alfred, 201 W. 13th St., New York, NY 10011, 212/243-5470, 646/678-0464; 4 Inglewood Ln., Matawan, NJ 07747, 732/583-4740, bishopj@churchofthevillage.org

Jones, L. Bevel III, 2977 Blackwood Rd., Decatur, GA 30033-1011, 404/636-4401, lbjones@emory.edu
Jordan, Charles Wesley, 1014 Deborah St., Upland, CA 91784, 909/946-6785, bishop.jordan@iaumc.org
Justo, Benjamin A., bajusto@yahoo.com
Kammerer, Charlene P., 529 Crum Dr., Lake Junaluska, NC 28745, 828/452-0574
Klaiber, Walter, Albrechtstrasse 23, D-72072, Tuebingen, Germany, 49/7071-763451, walterklaiber@web.de
Knox, J. Lloyd, 205 Beechwood Pass, Gadsden, AL 35901, 256/547-8212, senorobispo@yahoo.com
Lee, Clay F., Jr., 5033 Forest Hill Rd., Byram, MS 39272, 601/373-3449, cflee5@aol.com
Lee, Linda, 115 Arbury Ct., Cottage Grove, WI 53527, 608/839-0048, lindaleetol@gmail.com
Lewis, William B., 916 University Dr., Edwardsville, IL 62025-2962, 618/656-1357, wmblewis@dcwis.com
Looney, Richard C., 1617 Old State Rd. 34, Telford, TN 37690, 423/753-6583, richardclooney@aol.com
Lyght, Ernest S., 77 Shipps Way, Delanco, NJ 08075, 856/764-1784, eslight@aol.com
Machado, João Somane, Estrade Nacional No. 1, PO Box 15, Inhambane, Mozambique, 258/293-61080, j.somane@yahoo.com
Martinez, Joel N., 14710 Kinsem, San Antonio, TX 78248, 210/764-0167, joelnmartinez@yahoo.com
May, Felton Edwin, 777 W. State St. #118, Trenton, NJ 08618, 501/352-1377, fepe2328@comcast.net
McCleskey, J. Lawrence, PO Box 164, Lake Junaluska, NC 28745, 828/456-5078, jlmccleskey@bellsouth.net
McConnell, Calvin D., 1630 S.E. River Ridge Dr., Portland, OR 97222, 503/353-2754, cvmcconnell@comcast.net
Meadors, Marshall L. Jr., 110 Midlake Heights, Anderson, SC 29626-6920, 864/261-3737, jackmeadors@aol.com
Middleton, Jane Allen, 53 Laurel Hill Dr., Woodstock Valley, CT 06282, 860/974-3808, bishop.jane.middleton@gmail.com
Minnick, C. P. Jr., 4480 Springmoor Cir., Raleigh, NC 27619, 919/848-7480, cminn27@aol.com
Minor, Ruediger R., Hochlandstrasse 28, D-01328 Dresden-Borsberg, Germany 49/351-284-3509, ruediger.minor@gmx.de
Morgan, Robert C., 1295 Malibu Pl., Birmingham, AL 35216, 205/979-7244
Morris, William W., 800 Harris Dr., Gallatin, TN 37066, 615/452-3002, bishopwmmorris@bellsouth.net

Morrison, Susan Murch, 518 School Ln., Rehoboth Beach, DE 19971, 302/227-4097, ogn509@aol.com

Mutti, Albert Frederick, 7909 NE 75th Terr., Kansas City, MO 64158-1087, 816/415-2838, fritzmutti@kc.rr.com

Nacpil, Emerito P., #4 Gardenia St., Dona Manuela Subdv., Pamplona Las Pinas, Metro Manila, Philippines 63 2 872 0309, emynacpil@yahoo.com.ph

Norris, Alfred L., 726 Lexington Ave., Jonesboro, GA 30236, 678/610-9239, bishopnorris@bellsouth.net

Oden, William B., 417 Kachina Ct., Santa Fe, NM 87501, 505/992-8622, wbo83@earthlink.net

Olsen, Øystein, Wessels Vei 7B, N-2005 Rælingen, Norway, 47 6480 1122 fax: 47/2263 1389, oeol@online.no

Onema, Fama, 64 Ave. Kutu, O Kinsuka-Ngaliema Kinshasa, B.P. 4669, Kinsha II, Democratic Republic of Congo, 243-998575407, bishoponema@yahoo.fr

Ott, Donald A., N22W24040 Cloister Cir. 3D, Pewaukee, WI 53072-4677, 262/523-2624, bishdott@aol.com

Pennel, Joseph E. Jr., 119 Richards Glen Dr., Franklin, TN 37067, 615/503-9752, jdpennel@att.net

Rader, Sharon Z., 1230 N. State Pkwy. 5B, Chicago, IL 60610, 312/255-8544, szrader@aol.com

Russell, John W., 8037 Misty Trail, Ft. Worth, TX 76123-1935, 817/292-2086, jmjrussell@sbcglobal.net

Sano, Roy I., 400 Elysian Fields Dr., Oakland, CA 94605, 510/635-7916, bishoprsano@earthlink.net

Schäfer, Franz W., Tannenrauchstrasse 102, CH-8038 Zurich, Switzerland +41/44-481 64 28, f.schaefer@bluewin.ch

Shamana, Beverly, 1525 Hill Dr., Los Angeles, CA 90141, 323/478-9999, bjsnewlife@aol.com

Sherer-Simpson, Ann B., 2501 S. 78th St., Lincoln, NE 68506, 402/483-7099, asherer@umcneb.org

Skeete, F. Herbert, 2765 Edgehill Ave., Riverdale, NY 10463, 718/549-1784, fhsblkrck@gmail.com

Solomon, Dan E., 3534 Riomar Ct., Abilene, TX 79606, 325/691-9716 Office: 325/793-4899, bishsol@mcm.edu

Spain, Robert H., Office: 201 Eighth Ave., So., PO Box 801, Nashville, TN 37202, 615/749-6377 fax: 615/749-6704; Home: 6031 Wellesley Way, Brentwood, TN 615/661-5565, rspain@umpublishing.org

Sprague, C. Joseph, 4846 Shackleford Ct., Columbus, OH 43220, 614/947-0304, csprague2@columbus.rr.com

Sticher, Hermann L., Untere Wengert-Str 16, D-72622 Nuertingen, Germany, 49 7 022 495 16, hermannsticher@alice.de

Stith, Forrest C., 13506 Leesburg Pl., Upper Marlboro, MD 20774, 301/249-5584, fcpreach@aol.com

Stockton, Thomas B., 1244 Arbor Rd., Winston-Salem, NC 27104, 336/464-1921, livalive@northstate.net

Stokes, Mack B., 13597 Perdido Key Dr., #16C, Pensacola, FL 32507, 850/492-1142, bishopmack@gmail.com

Swenson, Mary Ann, 101 Melrose Ave., Pasadena, CA 91105, 626/390-3239, bishopmas@gmail.com

Talbert, Melvin G., 1394 Moonlight Trail, Brentwood, TN 37027, 615/309-8096, 1bishopme@gmail.com

Toquero, Solito K., 930 Risaya St., Springfield Subdivision Biga I, Silang Cavite, Philippines 4118, 63 920 914 5271, bishopskt@yahoo.com

Tuell, Jack M., 816 S. 216th St. #637, Des Moines, WA 98198-6331, 206/870-8637, marjac@wesleyresident.org

Weaver, Peter D., 5269 Rockingham Dr., Williamsburg, VA 23188, 757/871-4569, pdweaver45@gmail.com

Wertz, Frederick, 1 Longsdorf Way #1, Carlisle, PA 17013, 717/240-2515

Whitaker, Timothy W., PO Box 219, Keller, VA 23401, 757/787-1081

White, C. Dale, 117 Eustis Ave., Newport, RI 02840-2865, 401/847-3419, cdwhite12@cox.net

White, Woodie W., Bishop in Residence, Candler School of Theology, Box 35, Emory University, Atlanta, GA 30322, 404/727-0734, wwwhite@emory.edu

Wilke, Richard B., 904 N. Clyde Dr., Winfield, KS 67156-1517, 620/221-0307; (Part Time): PO Box 88, Lake Junaluska, NC 28745 828/452-3068, rwilke@sckans.edu

Willimon, William H., 139 Pinecrest Rd., Durham, NC 27705, 919/699-2960, will@duke.edu

Wills, Richard J. Jr., 3325 Bridgefield Dr., Lakeland, FL 33803-5972, 863/709-8161, dwills60@mac.com

Wilson, Joe A., 132 Melissa Ct., Georgetown, TX 78628-2769, 512/868-2553, jwbish@verizon.net

Yeakel, Joseph H., 201 Quincy Ct. Unit D, Waynesboro, PA 17268, 717/387-5791, jhyeakel@yahoo.com

EPISCOPAL ASSIGNMENTS BY AREA

Central Conferences

Angola East Area—**Quipungo, Jose**
Eastern Angola Annual Conference

Angola West Area—**Domingos, Gaspar Joao**
Western Angola Annual Conference

Baguio Area—**Torio, Pedro M. Jr.**
Central Luzon Philippines Annual Conference
North Central Philippines Annual Conference
Northeast Luzon Phillipines Annual Conference
Northeast Philippines Annual Conference
Northern Philippines Annual Conference
Northwest Philippines Annual Conference
Pangasinan Philippines Annual Conference
Tarlac Phillipines Annual Conference

Central and Southern Europe Area—**Streiff, Patrick**
Austria Provisional Annual Conference
Bulgaria/Romania Provisional Annual Conference
Czech and Slovak Republics Annual Conference
Hungary Provisional Annual Conference
Poland Annual Conference
Serbia-Montenegro-Macedonia Provisional Annual Conference
Switzerland-France Annual Conference

Central Congo Area—**Yemba, David K.**
Central Congo Annual Conference
Kasai Annual Conference
Western Congo Annual Conference

Côte D'Ivoire—**Boni, Benjamin**
Côte D'Ivoire Annual Conference

Davao Area—**Francisco, Ciriaco Q.**
Bicol Provisional Philippines Annual Conference
East Mindanao Philippines Annual Conference
Mindanao Philippines Annual Conference
Northwest Mindanao Philippines Annual Conference
Visayas Philippines Annual Conference

East Africa Area—**Wandabula, Daniel**
East Africa Annual Conference (includes Burundi, Kenya,
   Rwanda, Sudan and Uganda)

East Congo Area—**Unda, Gabriel Yemba**
Eastern Congo Annual Conference
Kivu Annual Conference
Oriental and Equator Annual Conference

Germany Area—**Wenner**, **Rosemarie**
East Germany Annual Conference
North Germany Annual Conference
South Germany Annual Conference

Liberia Area—**Innis**, **John G.**
Liberia Annual Conference

Manila Area—**Juan**, **Rodolfo Alfonso**
Bulacan Philippines Annual Conference
Middle Philippines Annual Conference
Palawan Philippines Annual Conference
Pampango Annual Conference
Philippines Annual Conference
Philippines Annual Conference East
Philippines Annual Conference - Cavite
Quezon City Philippines Annual Conference
Southern Tagalog Provisional Annual Conference
Southwest Philippines Annual Conference
West Middle Philippines Annual Conference

Moscow (Eurasia) Area—**Khegay**, **Eduard**
Central Russia Annual Conference
East Russia and Central Asia Provisional Annual Conference
Northwest Russia Provisional Annual Conference
South Russia Provisional Annual Conference
Ukraine and Moldova Provisional Annual Conference

Mozambique Area—**Nhanala**, **Joaquina F.**
North Mozambique Annual Conference
South Mozambique Annual Conference
South Africa Provisional Annual Conference

Nigeria Area—**Yohanna**, **John Wesley**
Gwaten Nigeria Annual Conference
Pero Nigeria Annual Conference
Southern Nigeria Annual Conference

Nordic-Baltic Area—**Alsted**, **Christian**
Denmark Annual Conference
Estonia Annual Conference
Finland-Finnish Provisional Annual Conference
Finland-Swedish Provisional Annual Conference

Norway Annual Conference
Sweden Annual Conference

North Katanga Area—**Ntambo, Nkulu Ntanda**
North Katanga Annual Conference
Tanganyika Annual Conference
Tanzania Annual Conference

Sierra Leone Area—**Yambasu, John K.**
Sierra Leone Annual Conference

Southern Congo Area—**Katembo, Kainda**
Lukoshi Annual Conference
North-West Katanga Annual Conference
South Congo Annual Conference
South-West Katanga Annual Conference
Zambia Annual Conference

Zimbabwe Area—**Nhiwatiwa, Eben**
East Zimbabwe Annual Conference
Malawi Missionary Conference
West Zimbabwe Annual Conference

North Central Jurisdiction

Chicago Area—**Dyck, Sally**
Northern Illinois Conference

Dakotas/Minnesota Area—**Ough, Bruce R.**
Dakotas Conference
Minnesota Conference

Illinois Area—**Keaton, Jonathan D.**
Illinois Great Rivers Conference

Indiana Area—**Coyner, Michael J.**
Indiana Conference

Iowa Area—**Trimble, Julius C.**
Iowa Conference

Michigan Area—**Kiesey, Deborah L.**
Detroit Conference
West Michigan Conferences

Ohio East Area—**Hopkins, John L.**
East Ohio Conference

Ohio West Area—**Palmer, Gregory V.**
West Ohio Conference

Wisconsin Area—**Jung, Hee-Soo**
Wisconsin Conference

Northeastern Jurisdiction

Boston Area—**Devadhar, Sudarshana**
New England Conference

Harrisburg Area—**Park, Jeremiah J.**
Susquehanna Conference

New Jersey Area—**Schol, John R.**
Greater New Jersey Conference

New York Area—**McLee, Martin D.**
New York Conference

Philadelphia Area—**Johnson, Peggy A.**
Eastern Pennsylvania
Peninsula-Delaware Conferences

Pittsburgh Area—**Bickerton, Thomas J.**
Western Pennsylvania Conference

Upper New York Area—**Webb, Mark J.**
Upper New York Conference

Washington Area—**Matthews, Marcus**
Baltimore-Washington Conference West

West Virginia Area—**Steiner Ball, Sandra L.**
West Virginia Conference

South Central Jurisdiction

Arkansas Area—**Mueller, Gary E.**
Arkansas Conference

Dallas Area—**McKee, Larry Michael**
North Texas Conference

Fort Worth Area—**Lowry, J. Michael**
Central Texas Conference

Great Plains Area—**Jones, Scott J.**
Kansas East Conference
Kansas West Conference
Nebraska Conference

Houston Area—**Huie, Janice Riggle**
Texas Conference

Louisiana Area—**Harvey, Cynthia Fierro**
Louisiana Conference

Missouri Area—**Schnase, Robert C.**
Missouri Conference

Northwest Texas /New Mexico Area—**Bledsoe, W. Earl**
New Mexico Conference
Northwest Texas Conference

Oklahoma Area—**Hayes, Robert E. Jr.**
Oklahoma Conference
Oklahoma Indian Missionary Conference

San Antonio Area—**Dorff, James E.**
Rio Grande Conference
Southwest Texas Conference

Southeastern Jurisdiction

Alabama/West Florida Area—**Leeland, Paul L.**
Alabama-West Florida Conference

Birmingham Area—**Wallace-Padgett, Debra**
North Alabama Conference

Charlotte Area—**Goodpaster, Larry M.**
Western North Carolina Conference

Columbia Area—**Holston, L. Jonathan**
South Carolina Conference

Florida Area—**Carter, Kenneth H. Jr.**
Florida Conference

Holston Area—**Taylor, Mary Virginia**
Holston Conference

Louisville Area—**Davis, G. Lindsey**
Kentucky Conference
Red Bird Missionary Conference

Mississippi Area—**Swanson, James E. Sr.**
Mississippi Conference

Nashville Area—**McAlilly, William T.**
Memphis Conference
Tennessee Conference

North Georgia Area—**Watson, B. Michael**
North Georgia Conference

Raleigh Area—**Ward, Hope Morgan**
North Carolina Conference

Richmond Area—**Cho, Young Jin**
Virginia Conference

South Georgia Area—**King, James R. Jr.**
South Georgia Conference

Western Jurisdiction

Greater Northwest Area—**Hagiya, Grant J.**
Alaska Conference
Oregon-Idaho Conference
Pacific Northwest Conference

Los Angeles Area—**Carcaño, Minerva G.**
California-Pacific Conference

Mountain Sky Area—**Stanovsky, Elaine J. W.**
Rocky Mountain Conference
Yellowstone Conference

Phoenix Area—**Hoshibata, Robert T.**
Desert Southwest Conference

San Francisco Area—**Brown, Warner H. Jr.**
California-Nevada Conference

Office of Christian Unity and Interreligious Relationships

(Formerly the General Commission on Christian Unity and Interreligious Concerns)
475 Riverside Dr., Rm. 1300, New York, NY 10115
212/749-3553, fax: 212/662-7045
http://www.ocuir.org/

Chair: **Devadhar, Sudarshana**
Secretary: **Watson, Michael**
Ecumenical Officer: **Swenson, Mary Ann**
Ecumenical Staff Officer: **Sidorak, Stephen Jr.**, ssidorak@ocuir.org

Steering Committee

African Central Conference, **Domingos, Gaspar Joao**
African Methodist Episcopal Church, **Leath, Jennifer**
Christian Methodist Episcopal Church, **Bouknight, Jeanette**
Ecumenical Officer of the Council of Bishops, **Swenson, Mary Ann**
European Central Conferences, **Refsdal, Knut**
North Central Jurisdiction, **Park, Joon-Sik**
Northeastern Jurisdiction, **McCrae, Darlynn**
Philippines Central Conference, **Mangiduyos, Gladys**
South Central Jurisdiction, **Oliphint, Clayton**
Southeastern Jurisdiction, **McKinney, Sarah**
Western Jurisdiction, **Brower, Charles**

Staff

Executive Director of Finance and Administration: **Williams, Kathryn A.**, kawilliams@gccuic-umc.org
Office Assistant: **Diaz, Olga**, odiaz@gccuic-umc.org

The Connectional Table

Officers
Chairperson: **Ough**, **Bishop Bruce R.**, 122 West Franklin Ave. Ste. 200, Minneapolis, MN 55404-2472, 612/870-4007 fax: 612/870-3587, bishop@dkmnareaumc.org

Members

Name	Agency/Jurisdiction
Aguila, Pete	South Central Jurisdiction (Louisiana)
Alegría, Raúl	Methodists Associated to Represent Hispanic Americans
Alexander, Neil M.	UMPH (President and Publisher; (voice, no vote)
Arant, Andy	Southeastern Jurisdiction (Mississippi)
Barrow, Rev. Darryl	Northeastern Jurisdiction (North Central New York)
Birch, Rev. Ole	Northern Europe Central Conference
Birgham-Tsai, Kennetha	North Central Jurisdiction (West Michigan)
Birkhahn-Rommelfanger, Rachel	North Central Jurisdiction (Northern Illinois)
Boigegrain, Barbara	GBOPHB (General Secretary; voice, no vote)
Brady, Rev. Brad	Southeastern Jurisdiction (South Georgia)
Brewington, Fred	Northeastern Jurisdiction (New York)
Brown, Rev. Marc	Southeastern Jurisdiction (Virginia)
Brown, Rev. Tamara	Southeastern Jurisdiction (Kentucky)
Cape, Rev. Kim	GBHEM (General Secretary; voice, no vote)
Carcaño, Bishop Minerva	GCORR (President)
Clark, Doris	North Central Jurisdiction (Indiana)
Coyner, Bishop Mike	GCFA (President)
Deere, Josephine	South Central Jurisdiction (Oklahoma Indian Missionary)
Dopke, Cynthia	Connectional Table (Assistant Executive Secretary)
Dyck, Bishop Sally	UMCOM (President)
Finley, Margaret	Southeastern Jurisdiction (North Georgia)

Greenwaldt, Rev. Karen	GBOD (General Secretary; voice, no vote)
Hanke, Gil	GCUMM (General Secretary; voice, no vote)
Hare, Dawn	GCSRW (General Secretary; voice, no vote)
Harrison, Ricky	South Central Jurisdiction (North Texas)
Hawkins, Erin	GCORR (General Secretary; voice, no vote)
Hollon, Rev. Larry	UMCOM (General Secretary; voice, no vote)
Hoshibata, Bishop Robert	GBCS (President)
Innes, Emily	Southeastern Jurisdiction (North Carolina)
Jones, Beverly	South Central Jurisdiction (New Mexico)
Kemper, Thomas	GBGM (General Secretary; voice, no vote)
Kent, Cynthia	Native American International Caucus
Swanson, Bishop James	GCUMM (President)
Kumar, Moses	GCFA (General Secretary; voice, no vote)
Laishi, Rev. Dr. Bwalya	Congo Central Conference
Langford, Rev. Andy	Southeastern Jurisdiction (Western North Carolina)
Meekins, William	Northeastern Jurisdiction (Western Pennsylvania)
Miller-Yow, Rev. Ronnie	Black Methodists for Church Renewal
Nhambiu, Benedita Penicela	Africa
Olson, Harriett	UMW (General Secretary; voice, no vote)
Ough, Bishop Bruce	Connectional Table (Chair)
Park, Bishop Jeremiah	GCAH (President)
Rogers, Rev. Tim	Southeastern Jurisdiction (South Carolina)
Rückert, Rev. Harald	Germany Central Conference
Sauceda, Kevin	DMYP (Youth Member)
Sermonia, Jovita Jr.	Philippines Central Conference
Slaughter, Rev. Michael	North Central Jurisdiction (West Ohio)
Stanovsky, Bishop Elaine	GBOD (President)
Streiff, Bishop Patrick	Central/Southern Europe Central Conference
Swenson, Bishop Mary Ann	Ecumenical Officer
Tabelisma, Riva	DMYP (Young Adult)
Taiwo, Kunle	Western Jurisdiction (Rocky Mountain)
Thomas-Sano, Kathleen	National Federation of Asian American United Methodists
Tuitahi, Monalisa	Pacific Islanders National Caucus of UM
Wallace-Padgett, Bishop Deborah	GCSRW (President)
Ward, Bishop Hope Morgan	GBGM (President)
Williams, Matthew Theo, I Esq.	West Africa Central Conference
Williams, Rev. Robert	GCAH (General Secretary; voice, no vote)

Williams, Thomas   South Central Jurisdiction (Texas)
Winkler, James   GBCS (General Secretary; voice, no vote)

STAFF

8765 W. Higgins Rd., Ste. 404
Chicago, IL 60631
773/714-1517, fax: 866/324-6325
connectionaltable@umc.org
http://connectionaltable.umc.org

Executive Secretary: **Barker, Amy Valdez**, 706/540-9865, avaldez_barker@umc.org
Assistant Executive Secretary: **Dopke, Cynthia**, 773/777-7133, 773/301-0857 (cell), fax: 866/324-6325, cdopke@umc.org
Administrative Coordinator: **Tournoux, Joy**, connectionaltable@umc.org

Councils

General Council on Finance and Administration
www.gcfa.org

OFFICERS
President: **Coyner**, **Michael J.**
Vice President: **Vargo**, **Jessica**
Recording Secretary: **Argue**, **James**
General Secretary and Treasurer: **Kumar**, **A. Moses Rathan**

DIRECTORS
Bishops
Coyner, Michael J., 301 Pennsylvania Pkwy., Ste. 300, Indianapolis, IN 36280, 317/564-3239 fax: 317/924-4859, bishopcoyner@inumc.org
Hayes, Robert E. Jr., PO Box 60467, Oklahoma City, OK 73146-0467, 405/530-2025 fax: 405/530-2040, rhayes@okumc.org

Members
Argue, James Jr., 5300 Evergreen Dr., Little Rock, AR 72205-1814 501/664-8632, jargue@umfa.org
Bishop, John W., 110 W. Saddle River Rd., Saddle River, NJ 07458 201/934-7438, jbishop111@msn.com
Bjornevik, Per Endre, Kaprifolveien 34, Stavanger N-4022, NORWAY, +47 51874372 fax: +47 51875200, per-endre.bjornevik@lyse.net
Bush, Elizabeth, 1504 Lakewood Dr., Bainbridge, GA 39819, 229/246-0461 fax: 229/248-1108, kaybush5505@yahoo.com
Coyner, Bishop Michael J., 301 Pennsylvania Pkwy., Ste. 300, Indianapolis, IN 36280, 317/564-3239 fax 317/924-4859, bishop@inumc.org
Davis, Ryan C., 102 S. Shawgo Ave., Havana, IL 62644, 309/357-0829 (cell), ryducks@yahoo.com
Dodson, Christine, 700 Waterfield Ridge Pl., PO Box 1970, Garner, NC 27529, 919/779-6115 fax: 919/773-2308, christine@nccumc.org

Hayes, Bishop Robert E. Jr., PO Box 60467, Oklahoma City, OK 73146-0467, 405/530-2025 fax 405/530-2040, rhayes@okumc.org

Hundley, Stephen, 4502 Starkey Rd., Ste. 101, Roanoke, VA 24018, 540/989-3335, roanoked@vaumc.org

Jerusalem, Rose Beverly, 900 United Nations Ave., Manila, Philippines, +63.922.865.3791 fax: +63.252.567.778, pccumctreasurer@yahoo.com

Moore, Charles E., 3483 Olympia Rd. Davidsonville, MD 21035, 410/974-8080 fax: 410/956-6496, cmoore@telatlantic.net

Museu, Joseph Tunda, 2867 Ave. des Ecuries, BP 4727 Kinshasa, Ngaliema, Democratic Republic of Congo, +24 (315) 10 4776, tundajoseph@yahoo.fr

Ragland, Sharon, 8887 N. Treasure Mountain Dr., Tucson, AZ 85742, 520/297-2062 fax: 520/297-1058, sharon@umcstmarks.org

Riddle, W. Zac, 4339 Wilderness Ct., Birmingham, AL 35213, 205/297-5009 fax: 205/297-5747, zacriddle@hotmail.com

Robinson, Delmar, PO Box 4608, Biloxi, MS 39535, 228/348-2770 fax: 228/432-8899, drobinson@biloxihousing.org

Smith, Jodi S., PO Box 866128, Plano, TX 75086-6128, 972/526-5000 fax: 972/526-5033, Jodi@ntcumc.org

Stansell, Elijah, 5215 Main St., Houston, TX 77002-9752, 713/521-9383, 713/248-9042 (cell), eli@swbell.net

Vargo, Jessica, 8800 Cleveland Ave. NW, PO Box 2800, North Canton, OH 44720-0800, 800/831-3972 x123 fax: 330/966-7581, vargoj@eocumc.com

White, Mary, 312 Rockingham Rd., Rosemont, PA 19010, 215/236-0304, mwhite9891@aol.com

Willis, Valarie, 9698 Stonemasters Dr., Loveland, OH 45140, 513/677-5637 fax: 513/677-9945, vwillis@cinci.rr.com

Wood, Steve Doyle, 9820 Nesbit Ferry Rd., Johns Creek, GA 30020. 678/336-3124 fax: 678/336-3235, swood@mountpisgah.org

NON-VOTING MEMBERS (ADVISORS TO COMMITTEES)

Brown, Kelly (East Ohio)
Curry, Jodi (Alabama-West Florida)
Moots, Philip (West Ohio)
Stotts, David (Mississippi)
Sumner, Shannon (Alabama-West Florida)

COMMITTEE CHAIRS

Coordinating Committee: **Coyner, Michael J.**
Audit and Review: **Dodson, Christine**

Councils

Connectional Outreach: **White, Mary**
Fiduciary, Foundation and Property Matters: **Hundley, Stephen**
Legal and Corporate Governance: **Bishop, John W.**
Economic Advisory: **TBD**

STAFF

General Council on Finance and Administration
1 Music Cir. North, PO Box 340029
Nashville, TN 37203-0029
615/329-3393, Toll Free: 866/367-4232, fax: 615/329-3394
All Nashville phone numbers begin with 615/369-, unless otherwise noted.
gcfa@gcfa.org
www.gcfa.org,

Administration

General Secretary and Treasurer: **Kumar, A. Moses Rathan**, 2320, mkumar@gcfa.org
Executive Assistant: **Schuette, Natalie**, 2320 nschuette@gcfa.org
Deputy General Secretary/Administration: **Goolsbey, John T.**, 2319, jgoolsbey@gcfa.org
Deputy General Secretary-Operations: **Youngquist, Patricia H.**, 2318 phyoungquist@gcfa.org
Associate General Secretary-Connectional Outreach: **Brewer, Scott**, 2381, sbrewer@gcfa.org
Director, Records and Statistics: **Haralson, Cynthia J.**, 2386, charalson@gcfa.org
Director, Communications: **Dean, Sharon**, 2336, sdean@gcfa.org

Episcopal Services

Assistant General Secretary/Episcopal Services: **Sewell, Peggy**, 2327, psewell@gcfa.org

Financial Services

Chief Financial Officer: **Smith, Brent**, 2360, bsmith@gcfa.org
Director of Finance: **Conover, Matt**, 2360, mconover@gcfa.org
Assistant Controller: **Olson, Deena**, 2366, dolson@gcfa.org
Assistant Controller, Investments and UMC Foundation: **Redding, Elizabeth**, 2372, eredding@gcfa.org
Assistant Controller, General Agencies: **Moore, Susan**, 2362, smoore@gcfa.org

Information Technology

Director of Information Technology: **Cook, Michael**, 2375, mcook@gcfa.org
Marketing Coordinator/Technical Writer: **Arieux, Lauren**, 2377, larieux@gcfa.org
Senior Network Engineer: **Williams, Rick**, 2378, rwilliams@gcfa.org
Application Development Manager: **Owens, Dale**, 2380, dowens@gcfa.org

Legal Services

General Counsel: **Rettberg, Richard**, 2337, rrettberg@gcfa.org
Administrative Counsel: **Gary, Dan**, 2337, dgary@gcfa.org
Executive Asst.: **Niedziela, Dana**, 2337, dniedziela@gcfa.org
Tax exemption inquiries: 2395 fax: 866/246-2516, legal@gcfa.org

Personnel Services

Deputy General Secretary-Administration: **Goolsbey, John T.**, 2318, jtgoolsbey@gcfa.org

Support Services

Director, Support Services-Mtg. Planning, Facilities, Procurement: **Morrison, Alan J.**, 2350, amorrison@gcfa.org
Travel and Mtg. Planning, Business Manager for the General Conference: **Hotchkiss, Sara**, 2352, shotchkiss@gcfa.org
Building Services Manager: **Foust, Robert**, 2351, rfoust@gcfa.org

The United Methodist Church Foundation

Executive Director: **Bonner, Byrd**, 615/308-9178, BBonner@umcfoundation.org
Director of Giving and Development: **Logan, Rhodes**, 2383, rlogan@umcfoundation.org
Mgr. of Corporate Sponsorship & UMC Giving: **Smith, Bobby L.**, 2407, blsmith@gcfa.org

United Methodist Insurance

Chief Executive Officer: **Youngquist, Patricia H.**, 2381, pyoungquist@gcfa.org
New York Service Center: Assistant General Treasurer: **Fernandes, Roland**, 475 Riverside Dr., #1439, New York, NY 10115-0111, 212/870-3697 fax: 212/870-3697

Councils

Audit and Review Committee

MEMBERS

Chairperson: Dodson, Christine, 700 Waterfield Ridge Pl., Garner, NC 27529-3365, 919/779-6115, christine@nccumc.org (GCFA member)
Vice-Chairperson: Stotts, David, PO Box 1201, Jackson, MS 39215, 601/354-0515 x26, david@mississippi-umc.org
Brown, Kelly A., 2601 Link Dr., Franklin, TN 37064, 615/591-1744, kabrowncpa@gmail.com
Riddle, Zachary, 4339 Wilderness Court, Birmingham, AL 35213, 205/297-5009, zariddle@hotmail.com
Sumner, Shannon, 160 Carphilly Cir., Franklin, TN 37069-4358, 615/284-4756, SSumner@chanllc.com
Wood, Steven, 9820 Nesbit Ferry Rd., Johns Creek, GA 30020, 678/336-3124

STAFF

Demastus, Paul, 1 Music Cir. North, Nashville, TN 37203, 615/309-2229, pdemastus@lbmc.com
Schuette, Natalie, 1 Music Cir. North, Nashville, TN 37203, 615/369-2320, nschuette@gcfa.org

The 2013–2016 United Methodist Directory

Judicial Council

Officers

President: **Lawrence, William B.**, PO Box 750133, SMU, Dallas, TX 75275-0133, wblawren@smu.edu (if not confidential, CC dcoon@smu.edu)
Vice-President: **Brown, Angela**, 2251 Wimbledon Pl., San Leandro, CA 94577, jcumc2008@aol.com
Secretary: **Joyner, F. Belton, Jr.**, 1821 Hillandale Rd., Ste. 1B, PMB 334, Durham, NC 27705, judicialcouncil@umc.org or fbjjr2@msn.com

Members

Blackwell, Dennis L., Asbury UMC, 2220 Woodlynne Ave., Woodlynne, NJ 08107, Asbury.admin@gmail.com
Capen, Beth, 23 Rogers St., Kingston, NY 12401-6049, UMCmail@aol.com
Kiboko, Jeanne Kabamba, 22111 Morton Ranch Rd., Katy TX, 77449-7819, kabambak@aol.com
Mahle, Kathi Austin, 1410 Spring Valley Rd., Minneapolis, MN 55422, kaustinmahle@gmail.com
Reyes, Ruben T., Central UMC, 694 T.M. Kalow St., Ermita, Manila 1000, Philippines, jrtreyes@yahoo.com
Tweh, N. Oswald Sr., Pierra, Tweh & Assoc., Box 10-2536, Palm Hotel Building Ste., 101, Broad & Randall St., Monrovia, Liberia 1000, notweh@yahoo.com
First Clergy Alternate: **Bruster, Timothy Keith**, 120 Kristen Ct., Jackson, MS 39211 601/982-3997
First Lay Alternate: **Lutz, Sandra W.**, 4751 Helmsworth Dr., N.E., Canton, OH 44714, swlutz@sbcglobal.net
Clerk: **Askew, Sally Curtis**, 306 Providence Rd., Athens, GA 30606, sallyaskew40@gmail.com
Assistant to Secretary: **Smith, Lanella**, 1215 Shady Ln., Durham, NC 27712, del23sba@frontier.com
UM News Service: **Bloom, Linda**, 3530 Henry Hudson Pkwy., Apt. 4F, Bronx, NY 10463, lbloom@umcom.org

NOTE: Correspondence for the Judicial Council should be sent by postal service in care of the Secretary, 1821 Hillandale Rd., Ste. 1B, PMB 334, Durham, NC 27705 or electronically to judicialcouncil@umc.org.

Boards

General Board of Church and Society
www.umc-gbcs.org

Executive Committee
President: **Hoshibata, Bishop Robert**
Vice-Chair: **Phillips, Clarenda**
Secretary: **Calderon, Chelsea C.**
Personnel Chair: **Ivey, Dorothy**
Finance Chair: **Chafin, Lonnie**
Trustee Chair: **Ehrman, James W.**
Alcohol & Other Addictions Work Area: **Miller, Randall**
Biblical & Theological Chair: **Roth, Meghan**
Economic & Environmental Work Area: **Vetter, Molly E.**
Human Welfare Work Area: **Karandy, Kurt**
Peace with Justice & United Nations Work Area: **Pierson, Chris**
At-large Member: **Alsted, Bishop Christian**
At-large Member: **Knight, Jefferson**

Directors
Bishops
Alsted, Christian, (Nordic and Baltic Area) Rigensgade 21A, DK-1316 Copenhagen, Denmark, 45 5133 1477, office@umc-ne.org
Bledsoe, W. Earl, (Northwest Texas-New Mexico Area) PO Box 866188, Plano, TX 75086-6188, 972/526-5015 fax: 972/526-5014, bishopbledsoe@ntcumc.org
Cho, Young Jin (Richmond Area) 10330 Staples Mill Rd., PO Box 5606, Glen Allen VA 23058, 804/521-1102 fax: 804/521-1171, bishopcho@vaumc.org
Hopkins, John L., (Ohio East Area) PO Box 2800, North Canton, OH 44720-0800, 330/499-3972 fax: 330/497-4911, bishop@eocumc.org
Hoshibata, Robert T., (Phoenix Area) 1550 E. Meadowbrook Ave., Phoenix, AZ 85014-4040, 602/266-6955 x209 fax: 602/279-1355, bishop@desertsw.org
Johnson, Peggy A., (Philadelphia Area) PO Box 820, Valley Forge, PA 19482 610/666-9090 fax: 610/666-9181, peggy.johnson@epaumc.org

Members

Ahn, Sung Hoon, 1001Wickapecko Dr., Ocean, NJ 07712, 732/359-1000, gkaiser@gnj.umc.org

André, Manuel João, Bairro kilamba-kiaxi, Comuna de Camama I Angola, 934617271, manueljoao1965@hotmail.com

Bankston, L. James, 5501 Main St., Houston, TX 77004-6917, 713/528-0527, bankston@stpaulshouston.org

Calderon, Chelsea C., 5512 Don Felipe Pl. SW, Albuquerque, NM 87105, 505/328-3719, nov.chelsea11@yahoo.com

Campbell, Scott, 27 Avon Hill, Cambridge, MA 02140, 617/354-0837, campbellwscott@aol.com

Chafin, Lonnie, 77 W. Washington, Ste. 1820, Chicago, IL 60602, 312/346-9766, lchafin@umcnic.org

Christian, Solomon, 9871 Windward Slope Dr., Lakeland, TN 38002, 901/566-1414, schristiandds@aol.com

Clark, Philip Jayphen, 4823 Woodlawn, Little Rock, AR 72205, 501/944-8400, jclark@phumc.org

Cook, Karen, 1073 South Hague Ave., Columbus, OH 43204, 614/274-4929, pastorkmc@wowway.com

Cooper, Kurt J., 1406 Rural St., Emporia, KS 66801, 620/342-5854, umcmesu@yahoo.com

Denmark, John A., 8347 Banyan Blvd., Orlando, FL 30533, 407/876-4991, jad.denmark@gmail.com

Dick, Dan R., 750 Windsor St., Sun Prairie, WI 53590, 615/491-6319, ddick@wisconsinumc.org

Edgar, David N., 1370 South 5th St., Columbus, OH 43207, 614/271-1811, david.n.edgar@gmail.com

Ehrman, James W., 1375 East 9th St., 20th Floor, One Cleveland Center, Cleveland, OH 44114-1793, 216/736-7298, james.w.ehrman@gmail.com

Farnell, Emily, 1103 S Walnut Dr., Smithfield, NC 27577, 919/631-1200, efarnell90@gmail.com

Garibay, Haniel Robles, 2785 Fariba Court, Vienna, VA 22181, 757/354-9903, h_garibay@hotmail.com

Garvin, Lisa, PO Box 1147, Jackson, MS, 601/354-0515, lisa@mississippi-umc.org

Hanshew, Don, 174 Church St., Weber City, VA 24290, 276/386-3142, dhanshew@holstonviewumc.org

Hearne, Richard, 5130 Vickery, Dallas, TX 75206, 214/505-2324, rbhearne@sbcglobal.net

Henry, Tyler A. R., 5929 Dabney Dr., Jackson, MS 39206, 601/842-8923, tylerarhenry@aol.com

Boards

Howell, James, 1501 Queens Rd., Charlotte, NC 28207, 704/376-8584 fax: 704/295-4847, james@mpumc.org
Ivey, Dorothy, 11780 Wexwood Dr., Richmond, VA 23236, 804/897-4060, ivey1961@verizon.net
Jacinto, Ranny, Rm. 205, UMC Building, 900 United Nations Ave., Ermita, Manila 1000, 63 920 832 9806, ranny_jacinto@yahoo.com
Johnson, Cynthia A., 5593 Birders Cove, Brownsville, TX 78526, 956/459-4006, mc2dogs@sbcglobal.net
Jones, Richard A., 102 Donald Preston Dr., Wolfforth, TX 79382-5400, 806/866-4200, rich@wolfforthumc.org
Karandy, Kurt F. II, 105 Bishop St., New Haven, CT 06511, 315/506-0174, kurt.karandy@gmail.com
Karges, Cynthia B., 1832 West 9th, Hastings, NE 68901, 402/239-9508, Ckarges02@umcneb.org
Kind, Kathleen E., 3939 Park Rd., Selins Grove, PA 17870, 814/693-9220, kkind@susumc.org
Knight, Jefferson, UMC, PO Box 10-1010, 13th St., Sinkor, 1000 Monrovia 10, Monrovia, Liberia, +231886572914, jboyeknight@hotmail.com
Leonard-Ray, Susan, 108 Keller Blvd., Clemson, SC 29631, 864/226-6640, spleonard-ray@umcsc.org
Luna, Pat, 110 Eve Cir., Santa Rosa Beach, FL 32459, 334/202-9440, patluna@charter.net
Martinez, Luisa C., 163 E. 111th St., New York, NY 10029, 212/289-5690, laurakeppis@yahoo.com
Miller, Randall, 8001Sterling Dr., Oakland, CA 94605, 510/435-7560, randall4015@hotmail.com
Muhota, Joseph Mazawu, The UMC, 960 Ave. Mzee Laurent Kabila, Lipamu Center, Lubumbashi, Democratic Republic of Congo, 00243993269391, mazawumuhota@yahoo.fr
Nelson, Kenneth L., 4908 Colonial Dr. Ste. 101, Columbia, SC 29203, 803/786-9486 x315, klnelson@umcsc.org
Nibbelink, Jim, 63327 E. Desert Crest Dr., Tucson, AZ 85739, 520/818-6766, jnibbelink@msn.com
Niederer, Jörg, Oberwiesenstrasse 64, CH-8500, Frauenfeld, Switzerland, 41 52 720 51 10, Jniederer@bluewin.ch
Nowling, Lisa Schubert, 230 W. Spruce St., Princeton, IN 47670, 812/385-2910, hillsideschubert@gmail.com
Obergfell, Daniel, Im Bosseldorn 23, D-69126, Heidelberg, Germany, +49/17640103545, dobergfell@emk-jugend.de
Parker, Michael A. II, 711 Baker St., Baltimore, MD 21217, 410/900-3535, mparker.umc@gmail.com
Parris, Mark D., 700 Main Ave., Northport, AL 35476, 205/758-4703, markparris216@gmail.com

Patterson, J. Liz, PO Box 5564, Spartanburg, SC 29304, 864/582-1970, lizpatterson@charter.net

Phillips, Clarenda, 3670 Walden Dr., #2, Lexington, KY 40517, 606/783-2434, dr.clarenda@gmail.com

Pierson, Chris, 217 Division St., Elgin, IL 60120, 847/931-0710 x15, cpierson@umcnic.org

Quick, Beth, 945 Comstock Ave., Syracuse, NY 13210, 315/729-7099, bethquick@gmail.com

Roth, Meghan, 6215 Rolling Rd., Springfield, VA 22152, 703/569-9862 x102, meroth@messiahumc.org

Santiago, Maria Teresa, Oasis Gardens, B16 Hondures, Guaynabo, Puerto Rico 00969, 787/938-8346, eirenesofia@yahoo.com

Stewart, Sharon S., 208 North Church, Goliad, TX 43085, 361/645-2546, sharonsstewart@hotmail.com

Stikes, Bill, 805 Rhodes Ln., Griffin, GA 30224, 678/688-8040, whstikes@gmail.com

Strickland, Daphine, 1223 Guilford College Rd., Jamestown, NC 27282, 336/292-6796, yellowbird55@triad.rr.com

Tobey, Briana Nicole, 1108 E. Eighth St., Cushing, OK 74023, 405/406-1350, tobey.brie@gmail.com

Trinidad, Saul C., GBGM, 475 Riverside Dr., Rm. 350, New York, NY 10115-0111, 212/679-9736, strinidad@juno.com

Vetter, Molly E., 243 S. Broadway, Redondo Beach, CA 90277, 310/728-8445, mollyvetter@gmail.com, pastormolly@beachfaith.com

Williams, Andrew Ponder, 3518 North College Ave., Kansas City, MO 64117, 816/853-6808, pleaseponder@gmail.com

Yebuah, Lisa, 228 West Edenton St., Raleigh, NC 27603, 919/832-7535 x227, lyebuah@esumc.org

STAFF

Washington DC Office
100 Maryland Ave., NE, Washington, DC 20002
202/488-5600
All Washington phone numbers begin with 202/488-, unless otherwise noted.
www.umc-gbcs.org

United Nations Office
Church Center for the United Nations
777 UN Plaza
New York, New York 10017
212/682-3633 fax: 212/682-5354

General Secretary's Office

General Secretary: **Winkler**, **James**, 5620, jwinkler@umc-gbcs.org
Assistant General Secretary for Administrative/Human Resources, **Roberts**, **Frances J.**, 5658, froberts@umc-gbcs.org
Building Receptionist/Administrative Assistant: **Smith**, **Wilma**, wsmith@umc-gbcs.org

Business Office

Controller: **Gong**, **Leigh Ann**, 5627, lgong@umc-gbcs.org
Accounts Payable/Office Manager: **Owens**, **Regina D.**, 5624, rowens@umc-gbcs.org

Communications

Director: **Whittaker**, **Michelle C.**, mwhittaker@umc-gbcs.org
Director: **Rhodes**, **Wayne**, 5630, wrhodes@umc-gbcs.org

Advocacy and United Nations (UN)

Assistant General Secretary for UN Ministry: **Bautista**, **Liberato C.**, 212/973-1702 x3125, lbautista@umc-gbcs.org
Director, Alcohol, Other Addictions, and Health Care: **Abrams**, **Cynthia J.**, 5636, cabrams@umc-gbcs.org
Director, Children's Advocacy: **Kim**, **Joseph**, 5649, jkim@umc-gbcs.org
Director, Civil and Human Rights: **Mefford**, **Bill**, 5657, bmefford@umc-gbcs.org
Director, Economic and Environmental Justice: **Hill**, **John S.**, 5654, jhill@umc-gbcs.org
Director, Peace with Justice Program: **Harrison**, **Mark**, 5645, mharrison@umc-gbcs.org
Director, Women's Advocacy: **Paparella**, **Amee**, 5631, apaparella@umc-gbcs.org
Administrative Assistant: **Brandyberry**, **Donna**, 5641, dbrandyberry@umc-gbcs.org
Consultant, Healthy Families, Healthy Planet: **Zeh**, **Katey** 704/604-6770, kateyzeh@gmail.com

Education and Leadership Formation

Assistant General Secretary: **Christie**, **Neal**, 5611, nchristie@umc-gbcs.org
Director, Seminar Designer: **Burton**, **Susan**, 5609, sburton@umc-gbcs.org
Administrative Assistant: **Scott**, **Marvlyn B.**, 5643, mscott@umc-gbcs.org
US-2 Program-Seminar: **Larson**, **Alex**, 202/488-5651, alarson@umc-gbcs.org

General Board of Discipleship
www.gbod.org

Officers
President: **Stanovsky, Elaine J. W.**
Vice President: **Park, Eric**
Secretary: **Carter, Brenda**
Treasurer: **Carnahan, Charles**

Directors
Bishops
Juan, Rodolfo Alfonso, 10 Marcos Highway, PO Box 87, Baguio City 2600, Philippines, 6374/442-2879 chapsrudy@yahoo.com

Stanovsky, Elaine J. W., 6110 South Greenwood Plaza Blvd., Greenwood Village, CO 80111 303/733-0083, fax 303/733-5047 bishop@mountainskyumc.org

Members
Angoran, Yed, 01 BP 1282, Abidjan 01, Côte d'Ivoire, 225/0506-0001 angoran.yed@alum.mit.edu

Bilog, Francisco, 104 C.M. Recto St., Davao City 8000, Philippines +63/9194667914, fbilog@yahoo.com

Brown, Olu, 5628 Jamerson Dr., Atlanta, GA 30349, 404/577-2826, olubrown@impactded.org

Calderon, Lourdes, 5512 Don Felipe Pl. SW, Albuquerque, NM 87105 505/877-0632 louseb@juno.com

Carter, Brenda, 3505 Lytham Pl., Raleigh, NC 27604, 919/231-9154, bcarter.raleigh@att.net

Chumley, Maddie, 901 Arrowhead Dr., Prosper, TX 75078, 469/839-0561, maddiehatters@gmail.com

Entwistle, Dan, 3720 Roe Ave., Leawood, KS 66224, 913/897-2977, dan.entwistle@cor.org

Fenstermacher, Ed, 2435 S. Webster St., Fort Wayne, IN 46807, 260/744-4301, ed.fenstermacher@inumc.org

Grossman, Gail, 1585 Kathryn Ln., Bellingham, WA 98229 360/738-1970 grossmang@juno.com

Horton, Anne, PO Box 2053, Mechanicsburg, PA 17055, 717/766-7441 ahorton@susumc.org

Jacob, Ann, 114 Koegel Ln., Norristown, PA 19403, 570/573-1394 acjacob1@gmail.com

Mackintosh, Hugh, 2979 310th St., Sumner, IA 50674 563/578-5028 cmack@iowatelecom.net

Park, Eric, 153 Dyers Stone Dr., Eighty Four, PA 15330 412/559-6199 pewboy@gmail.com

Rivera-Báez, Glorymar, 1000 Carr. 877, Apartment 111, San Juan, PR 00926 787/220-4440 glorymar79@hotmail.com

Sim, Sam, Youth

Simpson, Kim, 3905 Lake Powell Dr., Arlington, TX 76016, 817/478-0869, kimsimpson1@tx.rr.com

Sloan, Barry, Erlöserkirche, Dresdner Str. 111a, Chemnitz, Germany 09131, 0049/170 8227084, barry.sloan@me.com

Stokes, Martha, PO Box 5606, Glen Allen, VA 23058, 804/262-1466, marthastokes@vaumc.org

Swetman, Michael, PO Box 443, Saint Hedwig, TX 78152 210/656-4933, michael_swetman@msn.com

Wilson, Robin, 1507 Dauphin St., Mobile, AL 36604, 251/471-1511, rwilson@dauphinwayuc.org

STAFF

1908 Grand Ave.
PO Box 340003
Nashville, TN 37203-0003
615/340-7200, 877/899-2780, fax: 615/340-7006
All phone numbers begin with 615/340- unless otherwise noted.
gbod@gbod.org
www.gbod.org

General Administration

General Secretary's Office

General Secretary: **Greenwaldt, Karen**, 7022, kgreenwaldt@gbod.org
  Executive Assistant to the General Secretary: **Lockhart, Brenda**, 7022, blockhart@gbod.org
Chief Administrative Officer/Treasurer: **Carnahan, Charles**, 7032, ccarnahan@gbod.org
Special Assistant to the General Secretary for Development of International Resources and Initiatives: **Bryant, Stephen D.**, 7150, sbryant@gbod.org
General Administrative Coordinator: **Winton, Suzanne**, 7018, swinton@gbod.org@gbod.org

Communications & Brand Strategy
Executive Director of Communications & Brand Strategy: **Horswill-Johnston, Steve**, 1726, shorswill-johnston@gbod.org
Communications Project Coordinator: **Dandridge, Carolyn W.**, 1793, cdandridge@gbod.org
Creative Services Manager: **Hamdorff, Sara**, 7597, shamdorff@gbod.org
Director of Web Development: **Sharpe, Dwayne**, 1725, dsharpe@gbod.org

Financial
Controller: **Bryant, Vonzella**, 7035, vbryant@gbod.org

Human Resources and Staff Services
Director of Human Resources: **Blankenship, Tina**, 7108, tblankenship@gbod.org
Information Technology Team Leader: **Johnson, Robert**, 1711, bjohnson@gbod.org

Office of Fund Development
Executive Director of Fund Development: **Gilpin, M. Scott**, 7166, sgilpin@gbod.org
Manager, Fund Development Office: **Paschke, Ruth**, 7166, rpaschke@gbod.org

New Church Starts, Path 1
Executive Director: **Lewis, Candace**, 7078, clewis@gbod.org
Administrative Assistant of Executive Director: **Escobar, Pax**, 7139, pescobar@gbod.org
Assistant Executive Director: **Ruffle, Douglas**, 7130, druffle@gbod.org
Strategist: **Nixon, Paul**, 7064, pnixon@gbod.org
Strategist: **Crossman, Bob**, bcrossman@gbod.org
Strategist: **Reece, Emily**, 7076, ereece@gbod.org
Coaching Network Coordinator: **Maynard, Phil**, phil.maynard@flumc.org
Director, Hispanic/Latino New Church Starts: **Rodriguez, Samuel**, 1706, srodriguez@gbod.org
Spanish Language Acquisitions Editor: **Peréz, Alma**, 7118, aperez@gbod.org
Bilingual Assistant, Hispanic/Latino New Church Starts: **Escobar, Pax**, 7139, pescobar@gbod.org
Communications Assistant: **Brooks, Philip**, 7120, pbrooks@gbod.org

Leadership Ministries
Associate General Secretary's Office
Associate General Secretary: **Pierce Norton, MaryJane**, 7170, mnorton@gbod.org

Assistant to the Associate General Secretary: **Dunlap, Nancy**, 7141, ndunlap@gbod.org
Director, Best Practices: **Smith, Deb**, 7135, dsmith@gbod.org
Director, Adult Formation and Discipleship : **Krau, Carol**, 7171, ckrau@gbod.org
Director, Black Congregational Ministries: **Walker, Cheryl L.**, 7167, clwalker@gbod.org
Director, Older Adult Ministries: **Gentzler, Richard H.**, 7173, rgentzler@gbod.org
Director: Camp and Retreat Ministries: **Witt, Kevin**, 7082, kwitt@gbod.org
Director, Evangelism Ministries: **Lear, Heather**, 7049, hlear@gbod.org
Director, Preaching Ministries: **Chesser, Dawn**, 7084, dchesser@gbod.org
Director, Korean, Asian American, and Pacific Islander Ministries: **Kim, David** 7050, dkim@gbod.org
Director, Leadership for Congregational Renewal : **Heavner, Betsey**, 7295, bheavner@gbod.org
Director, Music Resources: **McIntyre, Dean**, 7073, dmcintyre@gbod.org
Director, Pastoral Leadership: **Miller, Craig**, 7081, cmiller@gbod.org
Director, Stewardship Ministries: **Sloane, Ken**, 7165, ksloane@gbod.org
Director, Wesleyan Leadership: **Manskar, Steven**, 1765, smanskar@gbod.org
Director, Worship Resources: **Burton-Edwards, Taylor W.**, 7072, tburtonedwards@gbod.org
Director, Ministry with Children : **Gordon, Melanie**, 1762 ,mgordon@gbod.org
Director, Connectional Laity Development: **Jackson, Sandy**, 7179, sjackson@gbod.org

Upper Room Ministries (www.upperroom.org)

Editor/Publisher: **Wilke, Sarah**, 7235, swilke@upperroom.org
Administrative Assistant to the Publisher: **Redman, Elizabeth**, 7250, eredman@upperroom.org

Upper Rm. Information
Standing Orders/Books/Subscriptions: 800/972-0433
Living Prayer Center Prayer Line: 800/251-2468

Customer Care
To Order Resources: 800/972-0433
On Line Bookstore: www.upperroom.org/bookstore
Director of Fulfillment System Services: **Bass, Patrick**, 7039, pbass@gbod.org

Marketing
Director of Magazine Marketing: **Gaither, Stacy**, 1717, sgaither@upperroom.org
Director of Book Marketing: **Neely, Janice**, 1792, jneely@upperroom.org

Publishing
Executive Director of Publishing: **Deming, Lynne**, 7093, ldeming@upperroom.org

Upper Room Books
Editorial Director: **Velander, Peter**, 7270, pvelander@upperroom.org
Managing Editor: **Collett, Rita B.**, 7530, rcollett@upperroom.org
Permissions: **Bradley, Joanna**, 7256, jbradley@upperroom.org

Discipleship Resources
Project Manager: **Breeden, Andrew**, 7332, abreeden@gbod.org

Magazines
ALIVE NOW: **Richardson, Beth**, 7242, brichardson@upperroom.org
DEVOZINE: **Miller, Sandy**, 7089, smiller@upperroom.org
EL APOSENTO ALTO: **Abarca, David**, 7246, dabarca@upperroom.org
POCKETS: **Gilliam, Lynn**, 7333, lgilliam@upperroom.org
THE UPPER ROOM (daily devotional guide): **Gray, Lindsay**, 7237, lgray@upperroom.org
Stafford, James, 7259, jstafford@upperroom.org
King, Susan, 7203, sking@upperroom.org
WEAVINGS: **Deming, Lynne**, 7093, ldeming@upperroom.org

Production
Gregory, Debbie, 7224, dgregory@upperroom.org

Interpretation and Development
Executive Director of Interpretation and Development: **Elliott, Sherry** 7520, selliott@upperroom.org
Chaplain of The Upper Rm.: **Albin, Tom**, 7110, talbin@upperroom.org
Director of Interpretation Ministries: **Williams, Marti**, 7596, mwilliams@upperroom.org
E-Learning: **Conley, Sharon** 7525, sconley@upperroom.org

Program
Executive Director of Programs: **Engroff, Greg**, 7288, gengroff@upperroom.org
Africa Upper Rm. Ministries: **Waymack, Dale**, 7236, dwaymack@upperroom.org
International Editions Coordinator: **Floyd, Joan**, 7251, jfloyd@upperroom.org
Chapel/Museum: **Kimball, Kathryn**, 7206, kkimball@upperroom.org
Living Prayer Center Manager: **Perez, Migdiel**, 7215, mperez@upperroom.org
Academy for Spiritual Formation: **Sears, Johnny**, 7232, jsears@upperroom.org

Business Operations
Director of Financial Services: **Runyan, Jeff**, 7282, jrunyan@upperroom.org

Teaching and Study Resources (Church School Publications)

Administrative Offices
Editor of Church School Publications: **Pon, Marjorie M.**, 615/749-6219 fax: 615/749-6512 mpon@umpublishing.org
Manager of Publishing Administration: **Turner, Rachel**, 615/749-6584 fax: 615/749-6512 rturner@umpublishing.org

Editorial Staff Adult Resources
Lead Editor: **Dilmore, Pamela**, 615/749-6474 fax: 615/749-6512 pdilmore@umpublishing.org

Children's Resources
Senior Editor: **Stickler, LeeDell**, 615/749-6216 fax: 615/749-6512 lstickler@umpublishing.org

Church School Publications
Managing Editor: **Pon, Marjorie M.**, 615/749-6219 mpon@umpublishing.org

Korean and Spanish Language Resources
Editor of Church School Publications: **Pon, Marjorie M.**, 615/749-6219 fax: 615/749-6512 mpon@umpublishing.org

Youth and Adult Resources
Senior Editor: **Kidd, Ron**, 615/749-6921 fax: 615/749-6512 rkidd@umpublishing.org

Young People's Ministries

Associate General Secretary: **Ratliff, Mike**, 7079, mratliff@gbod.org
Assistant: **Rice, Lee Ann**, 1723, lrice@gbod.org
Director, Young People's Ministries Development: **Wilterdink, Chris**, 7058, cwilterdink@gbod.org
Events Coordinator: **Thornell, Blake**, 1780, bthornell@gbod.org
Grants & Scholarship Administrator: **Tinker, Kelsey** 7184, ktinker@gbod.org
Associate Developer-Web: **Le, Truong**, 7180, tle@gbod.org
Team Assistant: **Coppock, Diane** 7074, dcoppock@gbod.org

Regional Staff

North Central: **Gladstone, Carl** 586/295-3055 cgladstone@gbod.org
Northeastern: **Bonner, Hannah** 610/405-3333 hbonner@gbod.org
South Central: **Parker, Abby** 210/885-6901 aparker@gbod.org

Southeastern: **Blakeney, Rori** 404/753-0198 rblakeney@gbod.org
Western: **Newell, Kelly** 530/263-6751 knewell@gbod.org
Program Assistant: **Hodges-Batzka, John** 717/579-4493 jhodges@gbod.org

Central Conference Regional Staff

Africa: **Mapoissa, Armindo** amapoissa@gbod.org
Philippines: **Rasing, Mighty** mrasing@gbod.org

General Board of Global Ministries
www.gbgm-umc.org

OFFICERS
President: **Ward, Bishop Hope Morgan**
Vice President: **Yambasu, Bishop John K.**
Corporate Secretary: **Atnip, Scott D.**
General Treasurer (ex-officio): **Fernandes, Roland**
At Large, Executive Committee: **Odland, Tove**
At Large, Executive Committee: **Richards, Yvette K.**
Chair, Audit Committee: **Evans, Emily Rogers**
Chair, CEIR: **Crisler, Timothy E.**
Chair, Communications and Development: **Kuch, Marie**
Chair, Finance: **White, Sara Ann**
Chair, Personnel Committee: **Brown, Jay W.**
Chair, Policy, Bylaws and Legislation: **Riss, Timothy**
Chair, UMCOR: **Jung, Bishop Hee-Soo**

DIRECTORS

Bishops

Jung, Hee-Soo, (Wisconsin) 750 Windsor St., Ste. 303, Sun Prairie, WI 53590, 608/837-8526, hsjung@wisconsinumc.org
Ward, Hope Morgan, (North Carolina) 4017 English Laurel Ln., Raleigh, NC 27612, 919/779-6115, bishop@nccumc.org
Yambasu, John K., (Sierra Leone) 31 Lightfoot Boston St., PO Box 523, Freetown, Sierra Leone, 232/22-226625; 232/22-220212, bishopyambasu@gmail.com

Members

Aguirre, Sam, 2516 SW 124th St., Oklahoma City, OK 73170, 405/954-0359, shaguirre@ieee.org
Aichele, Frank, United Methodist Church-Germany Board of Mission Holländisches Heide 13 42113 Wuppertal Germany, 492027670190, frank.aichele@emk.de
Anderson, Ruby D., 25180 Thorndyke, Southfield, MI 48033, 248/352-9246, rbydandrs@aol.com

Atnip, Scott D., 99 Elkins Lake, Huntsville, TX 77340, 936/295-7459, scottatnip@yahoo.com

Brown, Jay W., 1145 S. Beecham Rd., Williamstown, NJ 08094, 856/728-3191, usn65@aol.com

Bryant, Dan C., PO Box 11260, Youngstown, OH 44511, 330/270-3400, dbryant485@sbcglobal.ne

Carter-Rimbach, Joan E., 6201 Belcrest Rd., Hyattsville, MD 10782, 301/927-6133 x17, pastorjcr@fumchy.org

Cazombo, Elvira Moises, Igreja Metodista Unida, Rua Nossa Senhora da Muxima 12, Cxp 68 – C, Luanda, Angola, 244 926393273, elvira-moises@hotmail.com

Crisler, Timothy E., 2 Pintail Cove, Raymond, MS 39154, 601/857-0401, tcrisler1@hotmail.com

Dayap, Efraim A., National Tobacco Administration, Calaoa-An, Candon City, Ilocos Sur., Philippines, 0777425604, efraimdayap@yahoo.com

Evans, Emily Rogers, 480 Reed Canal Rd., Apt. 48, South Daytona, FL 32119, 843/610-5802, emichele87@gmail.com

Kamara, Yeabu, 31 Lightfoot Boston St., PO Box 523, Freetown, Sierra Leone, 232/22 220212, yeabu2000@yahoo.co.uk

Kelemeni, Tupou Seini, 1218A Artesian St., Honolulu, HI 96826, 808/522-9555, ts_kelemeni@yahoo.com

Kuch, Marie, 2415 N 65th St., Seattle, WA 98103, 425/390-4309, pnw.marie@gmail.com

Lindsey, Allison Ross, 1807 Robin Ln., Douglas, GA 31533, 912/393-5524, allison@sgaumc.com

Mhone, Daniel Levson Ion, Malawi UMC, PO Box 150, Blantyre, Malawi, 668/768 767, dlmhone@gmail.com

Murphy, Tonya, 4224 Cascade Rd., Atlanta, GA 30331, 770/364-6351, tmmam@bellsouth.net

Mutombo, Stanislas Ilunga, 2 De La Dase St., Kamina, DRC, 00245815695789, ilungamutombo1@yahoo.fr (cc: revmaloba@yahoo.fr)

Myers, Ron, 10381 Tree Top Ln., Anchorage, AK 99507, 907/272-2112, rrpmyers@gmail.com

Nkonge, Jean-Marie, UMC DR Congo, Box 22037, Kitwe Zambia, 00243 9971 06518, jmnkonge@gmail.com

Odland, Tove, PO Box 2744, St. Hanshaugen, 0131 Oslo, Norway, 479/139-4443, toveodl@online.no (or) tove.odland@metodistkirken.no

Richards, Yvette K., 4012 East 16th Terrace, Kansas City, MO 64127, 816/304-9041, aggiesnc310@aol.com

Riss, Timothy, 130 W. Old Country Rd., Hicksville, NY 11801, 516/931-2626, UMHicks@optonline.net

Ruiz-Millan, Ismael A., 407 Chapel Dr., Box 90968, Durham, NC 27708, 919/660-3545, irmillan@div.duke.edu

Saufferer, Cindy, 6981 NW 97th Ave., Morristown, MN 55052, 507/835-1354, cindy.saufferer@gmail.com
Squires, Jessica, 38 Hoopes Rd., Newport News, VA 23602-5212, 757/877-2270, pastorjessiesquires@gmail.com
Staempfli, Andreas C., Connexio, Badenerstrasse 69, Postfach 1344, CH-8026 Zurich, Switzerland, +41/44 29930-70, a.staempfli@umc-europe.org
Stanton, Nathan D., 1600 W 27th St. N, Wichita, KS 67204, 316/838-1600, nathans@pvumc.com
Stickley-Miner, Deanna, 32 Wesley Blvd., Worthington, OH 43085, 614/844-6200, dstickley@WOCUMC.or
Vianese, Carmen, PO Box 156, Nuanda, NY 14517, 585/237-2230, vianese4@frontiernet.net
White, Sara Ann, 4908 Colonial Dr., Columbia, SC 29203, 803/786-9486, sawhite@umcsc.org

Liaison Representative

Acevedo-Delgado, German, Urb. Rio Piedras Heights, Calle Weser 163, San Juan, PR 00926, 787/765-3195, gacevedo2002@yahoo.com

STAFF

475 Riverside Dr.
New York, NY 10115
212/870-3600, fax: 212/870-3748
Mission Information Line: 800/UMC-GBGM or 862-4246
www.gbgm-umc.org

Board Leadership

General Secretary: **Kemper, Thomas**, 212/870-3606, tkemper@umcmission.org
Executive Secretary: **Mahaney, Deborah**, 212/870-3606, dmahaney@umcmission.org
Missionary in Residence: **Whitlatch, Cathy**, 212/870-3692, cwhitlatch@umcmission.org
Deputy General Secretary, Mission Theology and Evaluation: **Domingues, Jorge**, 212/870-3873, jdomingues@umcmission.org
Deputy General Secretary, Mission and Evangelism: **Howard, George**, 212/870-3885, ghoward@umcmission.org
Deputy General Secretary, Communications and Development: **Bakker, Shawn**, 212/870-3791, sbakker@umcmission.org
Deputy General Secretary, UMCOR: **Vacant**

The 2013–2016 United Methodist Directory

General Treasurer, Finance and Administration: **Fernandes**, **Roland**, 212/870-3637, rfernandes@umcmission.org
Ministry with the Poor Consultant: **Kris**, **Mary Ellen**, 212/870-3608, mkris@umcmission.org

General Board of Higher Education and Ministry
www.gbhem.org

OFFICERS

President: **Dorff, E. James**
Vice President, Chair of Division of Ordained Ministry: **Mills, Ianther Marie**
Vice President, Chair of Division of Higher Education: **Brown, Ted**
Secretary: **Wright, Rachel**

DIRECTORS

Bishops

Dorff, E. James, 16400 Huebner Rd., San Antonio, TX 78248, 210/408-4502 fax: 210/408-4501, bishop@umcswtx.org
Hagiya, Grant J., PO Box 13650, Des Moines, WA 98198, 310/995-5739 fax: 206/870-6811, granth@flash.net
Yemba, David K., 2867 AVE des Ecuries Ngaliema, PO Box 4727, Kinshasa II, Congo Democratic Republic), 243 81 0806614, 88 243 03723, dhyemba@yahoo.com

Members

Beach, Demetrio, 116 E Main St., Dover, DE 19709, 410/725-1821, demetriobeach@gmail.com
Beckley, David L., Rust College, 150 Rust Ave., Holly Springs, MS 38635, 662/252-2491, fax: 662/252-8863, dlbeckley@rustcollege.edu
Brown, Ted, 433 W Madison St., Pulaski, TN 38478, 931/363-9801, 931/363-9892, tbrown@martinmethodist.edu
Cataldo, Jodi, 1331 W. University Ave., PO Box 460, Mitchell, SD 57301, jodi.cataldo@dakotasumc.org
Copeland, Jennifer, PO Box 90974, Durham, NC 27708, 919/684-6735, jec16@duke.edu
Culbertson, Barry, Dept of Pastoral Care, Vanderbilt U Medical Center, D-2111 Med Cntr North, Nashville, TN 37232, 615/343-3535, barry.culbertson@vanderbilt.edu
del Rosario, DJ, 125 202nd St. SE, Seattle, WA 98012, 206/390-7717, pastordelrosario@gmail.com
Downs, Beth, P. O. Box 5606, Glen Allen, VA 23058, 804/521-1127, fax: 804/521-1176, BethDowns@vaumc.org

Fryer, **Christine**, 324 University Ave., 3rd Floor, Syracuse, NY 13210, 315/422-5027, doran.christine@ymail.com

Gearhart, **Amy**, 204 S Ninth St., Columbia, MO 65201, 573/443-3111, amy.gearhart@moumc.org

Ingram, **Kim**, P. O. Box 18005, Charlotte, NC 28218, 704/535-2260, fax: 704/567-6117, kingram@wnccumc.org

Matonga, **Forbes**, 27 Saint Patricks Rd., Hatfiled PO Box 33, Harare, Zimbabwe, 263 4 573 073, ma.tonga@hotmail.com

Mills, **Ianther Marie**, 11711 East Market Pl., Fulton, MD 20759, 410/309-3400, fax: 410/872-0203, imills@bwcumc.org

Minthorn, **Robin**, 9250 Eagle Ranch Rd. NW, Apt. 411 S, Albuquerque, NM 87114, 589/695-4688, rminthorn@unm.edu

Moreno Jackson, **María**, PO Box 23339, San Juan, PR, Puerto Rico, 00931, 787/765-3195, marita_79@hotmail.com

Niethammer, **Hans-Martin**, Friedrich-List-Straße 69, D-71032, Boeblingen, D-71032, Germany, 0049 7031 220570, fax: 0711 2578711, hans-martin.niethammer@emk.de

Sit, **Tyler**, 3110 Chestnut St. N., Unit #304, Chaska, MN 55318, 612/360-1593, tyler.sit@gmail.com

Tritle, **Barrie**, 214 E. Jefferson St., Iowa City, IA 52245, 319/338-9259, fax: 515/279-3523, btritle@icfirstchurch.org

Viuya, **Priscilla**, 4158 Chuchi Ave., San Sebastian Village, Tarlac City, 2300, Philippines, 045 982 5574, pcviuya@yahoo.com

Wright, **Rachel**, 1221 West Ben White Blvd., Ste. 201-A, Austin, TX 78704, 512/444-1983, Rachel@umcad.org

STAFF

1001 Nineteenth Ave., South
PO Box 340007
Nashville, TN 37203-0007
615/340-7400, fax: 615/340-7048
All phone numbers begin with 615/340- unless otherwise noted.
www.gbhem.org

General Secretary's Office

General Secretary: **Cape, Kim**, 7356, kcape@gbhem.org

Special Assistant to the General Secretary/Global Education and New Initiatives: **Nascimento, Amos**, 7398, anascimento@gbhem.org

Executive Assistant to the General Secretary: **Lord, Kimberly**, 7356, klord@gbhem.org

Administrative Assistant: **Allen, Eydie**, 7424, eallen@gbhem.org

Office of Administration

General Inquiries: 615/340-7400
Treasurer and Chief Financial Officer: **Lesesne, John**, 7359, jlesesne@gbhem.org
Human Resources Manager: **Stacker, Cheryl**, 7360, cstacker@gbhem.org

Division of Ordained Ministry (DOM)

(7389, dom@gbhem.org)
Associate General Secretary: **Purushotham, Gwen**, 7357 fax: 7395, gpurushotham@gbhem.org
Office Administrator/Administrative Assistant: **Knox, Jean**, 7357 fax: 7395, jknox@gbhem.org

DOM Clergy Life Team

Assistant General Secretary: **Wingfield, Myron**, 7365 fax: 7358, mwingfield@gbhem.org
Office Administrator & Endorsement Administrator: **Sturdivant, Sue**, 7362 fax: 7358, ssturdiv@gbhem.org
Endorsing Agent & Director of Endorsement: **Carter, Tom**, 7331 fax: 7358, tcarter@gbhem.org
Director of Extension Ministry & Pastoral Care: **Fenner, Bruce**, 7397 fax: 7358, bfenner@gbhem.org
Office Coordinator, UMEA (UM Endorsing Agency): **Flippen, Laura**, 7364 fax: 7358, lflippen@gbhem.org
Director of Provisional Members, Deacon Support & Specialized Ministries: **Wood, Anita**, 7371 fax: 7358, awood@gbhem.org
Coordinator, Provisional Members, Deacon Support & Specialized Ministries: **Heist, Linda**, 7335 fax: 7358, lheist@gbhem.org
Director of Clergy Lifelong Learning: **Park, HiRho**, 7391 fax: 7358, hpark@gbhem.org
Coordinator, Clergy Lifelong Learning: **Hestand, Joshua**, 7432 fax: 7358, jhestand@gbhem.org

DOM Clergy Formation Team

Assistant General Secretary: **Yocom, Rena**, 7527 fax: 7377, ryocom@gbhem.org
Office Administrator/Administrative Assistant: **Cheatham, Dena**, 7388, fax: 7377, dcheatham@gbhem.org
Director of Young Adult Ministry Discernment & Enlistment: **Lowery, Trip** 7405 fax: 7377, tlowery@gbhem.org

Division of Higher Education

(7402 fax: 7379)
Associate General Secretary: **Lord, Gerald D.**, glord@gbhem.org

Assistant General Secretary/Collegiate Ministry: **Young-Ross, Bridgette**, byoungross@gbhem.org
Assistant General Secretary/Black College Fund: **Hopson, Cynthia Bond**, chopson@gbhem.org
Assistant General Secretary/Schools, Colleges, and Universities: **Overton, Melanie**, moverton@gbhem.org
Director of Student Faith and Leadership Formation: **Ludlum, Beth**, bludlum@gbhem.org
Director of Campus Ministry Resources and Training: **McCord, Michael**, mmccord@gbhem.org
Director, Research and Data Management: **Pederson, Michelle**, mpederson@gbhem.org

Office of Interpretation
Executive Director: **Hiers, Terri J.**, 7383 thiers@gbhem.org

Office of Loans and Scholarships
Executive Director: **Collinsworth, Allyson**, 7342 acollinsworth@gbhem.org

Related Units

Africa University Development Office
PO Box 340007, Nashville, TN 37203
7438 fax: 7290, audevoffice@gbhem.org
www.support-africauniversity.org

Associate Vice Chancellor for Institutional Advancement: **Salley, James H.**, jsalley@gbhem.org
Director of Planned Giving: **Jenkins, Elaine**, ejenkins@gbhem.org

Africa University
Nyanga Rd. and Fairview Rd.
PO Box 1320
Mutare, Zimbabwe
263/20-60075 fax: 263/20-61785
info@africau.edu
www.africau.edu

United Methodist Higher Education Foundation
PO Box 340005
Nashville, TN 37203-0005
615/649-3990, toll free: 800/811-8110 fax: 615/649-3980
www.umhef.org
President/CEO: **Fletcher, Robert R.**, bfletcher@umhef.org

General Board of Pension and Health Benefits
www.gbophb.org

EXECUTIVE COMMITTEE
Chairperson: **Leeland, Paul L.**
Vice Chairperson: **Schnase, Robert**
Recording Secretary: **Schnase, Robert**
Chairperson, Appeals: **Haverstock, Zedna**
Chairperson, Audit: **Burton, Jennifer**
Chairperson, Bellwether/Services: **George, Gary**
Chairperson, Board Life and Governance: **Pinkerton, Jerry**
Chairperson, Fiduciary: **Brackey, Donald**
Chairperson, UMC Principles: **Tomlinson, Ed**

DIRECTORS
Bishops
Domingos, Gaspar Joao, Caixa Postal 68, Rua de N.S. Da Muxima 12, Luanda, Angola, 244/222-33-2107, gdomingos61@yahoo.com
Leeland, Paul L., 100 Interstate Park Dr., Ste. 120A, Montgomery, AL 36109, 334/277-1787, bishop@awfumc.org
Schnase, Robert C., 3601 Amron Court, Columbia, MO 65202, 573/777-1290, rschnase@moumethodist.org

Members
Bass, Tracy, 81 Devon Rd., Paoli, PA 19301, 610/644-5300, pastortracy1@verizon.net
Berner, Jim, PO Box 2469, Charleston, WV 25329, 304/344-8331, tresrr@aol.com
Biler, Brenda, 914 E. Jefferson St., Ste. 104, Charlottesville, VA 22902, 434/977-4254, charlottesvilleds@vaumc.org
Brackey, Donald, 1560 Sherman Ave., Evanston, IL 60201, 847/492-1640, donbrackey@cs.com
Bridgeforth, Cedrick, 8910 Denker Avenue, Los Angeles, CA 90047-3634, 818/882-8005, pastorcedrick@gmail.com
Bryan, Robert Lawson, 2416 West Cloverdale Park, Montgomery, AL 36106, 334/834-8990, lbryan@fumcmontgomery.org

Burton, Jennifer, PO Box 18005, Charlotte, NC 28218, 704/714-2323, jburton@wnccumc.org
Carmichael, Dan, 605 Ocean Club Ct., Amelia Island, FL 32034, danrcarmichael@gmail.com
Edin, Jean, 122 W. Franklin Ave., Rm. 400, Minneapolis, MN 55404, 612/230-6136, Jean.Edin@minnesotaumc.org
Emmert, Don, 1309 N. Ballenger Hwy., Ste. 1, Flint, MI 48504, 810/233-5500 x353, demmert@detroitconference.org
Flynn, Rachel, 401 E. Washington St., Lewisburg, WV 24901, flynnrachelm@gmail.com
George, Gary, 8800 Cleveland Ave., N.W., PO Box 2800, North Canton, OH 44720, 800/831-3972 x111, gary.george@eocumc.com
Goodwin, John, 7801 Academy Rd., NE2-101, Albuquerque, NM 87109, jwgood@swcp.com
Goodwin, Kevin, 440 Haystack Dr., Newark, DE 19711, 302/453-1169, kevin.g.goodwin@usa.dupont.com
Griffith, Janice, 4537 Barrington Dr., Springfield, IL 62711, 217/529-3820, Jgriffith@igrc.org
Hagan, Miriam, PO Box 52101, Macon, GA 31208-4313, 478/738-0048, miriam@sgaumcadmin.com
Haverstock, Zedna, 303 Mulberry Dr., PO Box 2053, Mechanicsburg, PA 17055-2053, 717/766-5275, zhaverstock@susumc.org
Junk, Bill, 4201 N. Classen Blvd., Oklahoma City, OK 73118, 405/525-6863, bjunk@okumf.org
Keese, Teresa, PO Box 574, Brady, TX 76825, 325/456-1489 (cell), tkeese@cebridge.net
Kymn, Gloria, 5600 64th St., NE, Marysville, WA 98270, 360/659-8521, umcpastorglo@yahoo.com
Long, Robert, 222 NW 15th St., Oklahoma City, OK 73103-3598, 405/232-1371 x104, blong@stlukesokc.org
Lowry, Robby, 2056 NC Highway 710 S., Rowland, NC 28383, robbylowry@gmail.com
Mariano, Feliza, 28 M. Jockson St., Varsity Hills, Loyola Heights, Queson City, Philippines, 63 918 935 3807, Lizpm18@gmail.com
Morris, Patricia A., 1204 Freedom Rd., Cranberry Twp., PA 16066, 724/776-9766, treasurer@wpaumc.org
Nessler, Paul, 12277 Cyrano Ave., Brooksville, FL 34601, 352/596-4242, paulnessler@bellsouth.net
Pinkerton, Jerry, 9327 Canter Dr., Dallas, TX 75231, 214/340-2042, jerry.pinkerton@sbcglobal.net
Selman, Scott, No. Alabama Conf, 898 Arkadelphia Rd., Birmingham, AL 35204, 205/226-7989, sselman@northalabamaumc.org

Southern, **Gray**, 5 Timbercreek Ct., Durham, NC 27712-9530, 919/362-7807, grays@nccumc.org

Tomlinson, **Ed**, 70 Mansell Court, Ste. 115, Roswell, GA 30062, 770/362-1002, ed.tomlinson@ngumc.net

Wilson, **Melba**, 110 5th St. (business), Port Arthur, TX 77640, highcottn@msn.com

STAFF

1901 Chestnut Ave.,
Glenview, IL 60025
847/869-4550
www.gbophb.org

Agency Management Staff

General Secretary: **Boigegrain, Barbara A.**, 847/866-4200 bboigegrain@gbophb.org

Senior Executive Assistant: **Figueredo, Mary**, 847/866-4201 mfigueredo@gbophb.org

Chief Operating Officer: **Busbia, Mark**, 847/866-4300 mbusbia@gbophb.org

Chief Financial Officer: **Koch, Tim**, 847/866-4900 tkoch@gbophb.org

General Counsel: **Hirsen, Sarah**, 847/866-4644 shirsen@gbophb.org

Chief Investment Officer: **Zellner, Dave**, 847/866-4698 dzellner@gbophb.org

Managing Director, Customer Service: **Reid, Debbie**, 847/866-4576 dreid@gbophb.org

Managing Director, Communications: **Nies, Colette**, 847/866-4296 cnies@gbophb.org

Board of The United Methodist Publishing House
www.umph.org

OFFICERS
Chair: **Frazier, Carl**
Vice Chair: **Clark, Connie**
Secretary: **Lee, Sunyoung "Sunnie"**
President and Publisher: **Alexander, Neil M.**

DIRECTORS

Bishops
Khegay, Eduard bishop.eduard@umc-eurasia.ru
Lowry, J. Michael, 464 Bailey Ave., Ft. Worth, TX 76107, 817/877-5222, MikeLowry@ctcumc.org
Palmer, Gregory V., 32 Wesley Blvd., Worthington, OH 43085, 614/601-1986, wocbishop@wocumc.org

Members
Alexander, Neil M., 201 Eighth Ave., South Nashville, TN 37203, 615/749-6510, nalexander@umpublishing.org
Alston, Ellen R., 2350-A Methodist Pkwy., Woodworth, LA 71485, 318/451-2970, ellen.alston@gmail.com
Balisi, Eliseo C., Purok 6, District 1, Maharlika Home SUBD., Cauayan City, Isabela 3305, Philippines, 639228646721, elic_balisi@yahoo.com.ph
Braddon, David V., PO Box 673, Johns Island, SC 29457, 4174 Chisolm Rd., (29455), 843/270-4978, dvbraddon@gmail.com
Burris, Todd, 800 Daisy Bates Dr. (PO Box 3611), Little Rock, AR 72202 (72203), 501/730-6710, tburris@arumc.org
Bushfield, James C., 301 Pennsylvania Pkwy., Ste. 300, Indianapolis, IN 46280, 317/564-3248, jim.bushfield@inumc.org
Christian, Monica S., 131 Big John Dr., Martin, TN 38237, 731/435-0890, monicachristian1981@hotmail.com
Chun, Young-Ho, 12851 Gooddard Ave., Overland, KS 66213, 816/245-4812, younghchun@spst.edu
Clark, Connie, 351 Fourth Ave. S., Franklin, TN 37064, 615/504-4712, connieclark06@comcast.net

Boards

Crane, David, (June 1–Dec. 27) 133 Brighton Close, Nashville, TN 37205, (Jan. 1–June 1) 55-417 Firestone, LaQuinta, CA 92253, 812/459-7220, dfcrane@dfcrane.com
Crowell, Linda Johnson, 6727 Chinkapin Court, Oakwood Village, OH 44146, 216/533-4101, lfchso@msn.com
DeLaunay, Janine, 919 SW 185 Ave., #11, Aloha, OR 97006, 503/754-6505, jandela51@comcast.net
Frazier, R. Carl Jr., 117 S. Academy St., Cary, NC 27511, 919/467-1861, cfrazier@nccumc.org
Garcia, Edward, 1707 Taylor Gaines St., Austin, TX 78741, 512/696-5333, usmc2umc@gmail.com
Goto, Shinya, 530 S. 14th St., San Jose, CA 95112, 209/628-9205, shinyag@sanjosefirst.org
Higginbotham, Robert W., Jr., 807 Megan Dr., Cranberry Township, PA 16066, 814/598-4499, pilgrim1@zoominternet.net
Kilpatrick, Joe W., 100 Crescent Centre Pkwy., Ste. 710, Tucker, GA 30084, 770/455-8706, joe@kilpatrickcpa.com
Lee, Sunyoung "Sunnie", 1410 Brett Pl. Unit 236, San Pedro, CA 90732, 424/222-9640, pastorsunnie@gmail.com
Maldonado, Carmilla, 401 B Turtle Court, Montgomery, AL 36117, 256/617-3125, carmilla_maldonado@yahoo.com
McKinney, Eric, 303 Shady Oak Dr. (PO Box 881), Georgetown, TX 78628 (78627), 512/635-0755, jem881@gmail.com
Milford, Brian K., 1201 East 7th St, Ste. #300, Atlantic, IA 50022, 712/243-8573, b.milford@iaumc.org
Mulenga, Maidstone, 238 Desmond Rd., Rochester, NY 14616, 585/455-5683, maidstonemulenga@unyumc.org
Myers, Greg C., 570 S. Huron Cir., Hazelton, PA 18202-9157, 570/384-7375 (home), gmyers@susumc.org
Oglesby, Dennis M., Jr., 3200 Carnation Ave., N. Brooklyn Park, MN 55443, 612/871-4684, dmojr@comcast.net, dennisoglesby@parkavechurch.org
Preston, James, 401 West Dundee Rd., Buffalo Grove, IL 60089, 312/285-9023, jcpumc@aol.com
Purushotham, Samuel, 1733 Hickory Bark Ln., Nashville, TN 37211, 615/844-3285 (home), spurushotham@comcast.net
Ray, Natasha, 1900 Stillhouse Hollow Dr., Prosper, TX 75078, 254/265-0757, nray@curves.com
Revels, Akwiasdi K., 201 Weisner Rd., Olin, NC 28660, 704/450-8329, akrevels@live.com
Ruof, Klaus Ulrich, Ludolfusstr.2-4, D-60487, Frankfurt, Germany, 49 176 83112093, leiter.medienwerk@emk.de
Ruth, Barbara J., 1201 Lavaca St., Austin, TX 78701, 512/769-9644, barbara@fumcaustin.org

Salsgiver, **Thomas L.**, 31 Baylor Blvd., Lewisburg, PA 17837, 570/523-9592, tsalsgiver@susumc.org

Travis, **Anne S.**, 217 S. Rankin Rd. (PO Box 850), Alcoa, TN 37701, 865/690-4080, annetravis@holston.org

Tumblin, **Thomas F.**, 500 LeBeau Dr., Nicholasville, KY 40356, 859/221-3883, tom.tumblin@asburyseminary.edu

Watts, **Michael B.**, KY Conference of the UMC, 7400 Floydsburg Rd., Crestwood, KY 40014, 502/509-2887, mwatts@kyumc.org

Wiatt, **Wayne**, 2125 E. South St., Orlando, FL 32803, 407/403-4367, ds-ec@flumc.org

Williams, **Heather**, 429 Fay Rd., Syracuse, NY 13219, 315/391-3500, pastorheather@twcny.rr.com

Wolf, **Susie**, PO Box 1077, 319 5th Ave. Kenbridge, VA 23944, 434/676-8936 (home), susieandrex@embarqmail.com

STAFF

201 Eighth Ave. South, Nashville, TN 37203
615/749-6000, fax:: 615/749-6079
All phone numbers begin with 615/749- unless otherwise noted.
www.umph.org

President and Publisher/Book Editor of The UMC: **Alexander, Neil M.**, 6327, nalexander@cokesbury.com

Associate to the President & Publisher: **Smith, Amy C.**, 6860, fax: 6510, asmith@umpublishing.org

Executive Assistant: **Sanders, Janet**, 6328, fax: 6510, jsanders@umpublishing.org

Administrative Assistant: **Greer, Chari**, 6862, fax: 6510, cgreer@umpublishing.org

Chaplain: **Spain, Bishop Robert H.**, 6377 rspain@umpublishing.org

Finance and Administrative Services

Senior Vice President, Finance and Administrative Services/Treasurer/CFO: **Wallace, Larry L.**, 6214, lwallace@umpublishing.org

Administrative Office Manager: **Bigach, Sheila**, 6215, fax: 6236, sbigach@umpublishing.org

Controller: **Mabry, Tim**, 6247, tmabry@umpublishing.org

Director, Distribution Services: **Orman, Gail**, 6188, gorman@umpublishing.org

Production & Property Services Director: **Scott, Alvin**, 6427, ascott@umpublishing.org

Human Resources

Vice President, Human Resources: **Meadors, Alyce**, 6367, fax: 7604 ameadors@umpublishing.org

Analyst: **Sansone**, **Amanda**, 6237, asansone@umpublishing.org
Director: **Thorpe**, **Robbie**, 6339, rthorpe@umpublishing.org

Revenue & Operations

Executive Vice President, Revenue & Operations: **Kidd**, **Audrey**, 6181, akidd@umpublishing.org
Executive Assistant: **White**, **Deborah**, 6221, fax: 6510, dwhite@umpublishing.org

Marketing & Sales

Senior Vice President, Marketing and Sales: **Kowalski**, **Edward**, 6044, ekowalski@umpublishing.org
Executive Assistant: **Ellis**, **Claudia**, 6045, fax: 6417, cellis@umpublishing.org
Executive Director: **Barnes**, **Jeffrey R.**, 6682, jbarnes@umpublishing.org
Director, Cokesbury.com: **Booher**, **Jody**, 6735, jbooher@umpublishing.org
Director, Creative Design: **Shaver**, **Kim**, 6144, kshaver@umpublishing.org
Director, Promotion Planning: **Blair**, **Alan**, 6466, ablair@umpublishing.org
Strategic Alliance Manager: **Bruner**, **Linda**, 6155, lbruner@umpublishing.org

Information Technology

Executive Director, Information Technology: **Cunningham**, **Mike**, 6554, mcunningham@umpublishing.org
Executive Director, Application Technology: **Cashion**, **Steve**, 6547, scashion@umpublishing.org
Executive Director, Publishing Systems: **McLoud**, **Kevin**, 6808, kmcloud@umpublishing.org
IT Planning & Projects Management Coordinator: **Armstrong**, **Holly**, 6006, harmstrong@umpublishing.org
Director, Database Management: **Heile**, **Dan**, 6566, dheile@umpublishing.org
Telecom System Manager: **Bess**, **David**, 6021, dbess@umpublishing.org

Business Operations

Vice President, Business Operations: **Gaines**, **Tammy**, 6271, tgaines@umpublishing.org
Executive Assistant: **Christie**, **Annaleigh**, 6615, achristie@umpublishing.org
Executive Director, Merchandising: **Hupp**, **Michael**, 6297, mhupp@umpublishing.org
Director, Publishing Business Management: **MacKendree**, **Bob**, 6581, bmackendree@umpublishing.org
Manager, Publishing Procurement: **Murphy**, **Marsha**, 6156, mmurphy@umpublishing.org

Abingdon Press Marketing & Sales

Executive Director: **Crabtree, Tamara**, 6640, tcrabtree@abingdonpress.com
Director: **Yeh, Mark**, 6451, myeh@abingdonpress.com
Manager, Web Content and User Experience, MinistryMatters.com: **Hall, Betsy**, 6507, betsy@ministrymatters.org,
Manager, Web Content and User Experience, MinistryMatters.com: **Raynor, Shane**, 6218, shane@ministrymatters.org

Teaching & Learning Resources

Associate Publisher, Teaching & Learning/Editor of Church School Publications: **Pon, Marjorie M.**, 6219, mpon@umpublishing.org
Executive Assistant: **Turner, Rachel**, 6404, rturner@umpublishing.org
Senior Editor, Children's Teaching & Learning: **Stickler, LeeDell**, 6216, lstickler@umpublishing.org
Editor, Youth: **Tinley, Josh**, 6819, jtinley@umpublishing.org
Lead Editor, Adult: **Dilmore, Pamela**, 6474, pdilmore@umpublishing.org
Korean and Spanish Resources: **Pon, Marjorie M.**, 6219, mpon@umpublishing.org
Director, Vacation Bible School Resources: **Robinson, Cathy**, 6584, crobinson@umpublishing.org

Bibles, Leadership, Theology

Associate Publisher, Bible, Leadership, Theology: **Franklyn, Paul**, 6733 paul.franklyn@commonenglish.com
Senior Editor: **Stephens, Michael**, 6719, mstephens@umpublishing.org
Senior Editor: **Stella, Connie**, 6816, cstella@umpublishing.org
Lead Editor: **Armistead, Kathy**, 6788, karmistead@umpublishing.org
Project Manager: **Teel, David**, 6416, dteel@umpublishing.org

Abingdon Fiction/Christian Living

Associate Publisher, Christian Living, Abingdon Fiction: **Clements, Pamela**, 6331 pclements@abingdonpress.com
Executive Assistant: **Merritt, Frances**, 6301, fmerritt@umpublishing.org
Senior Editor, Fiction: **Richards, Ramona**, 6715, rrichards@abingdonpress.com
Senior Editor, Christian Living: **Copan, Lil**, 6334, lcopan@abingdonpress.com
Editor: **Crowe, Joseph A.**, 6137, jcrowe@umpublishing.org

Ministry Resources

Associate Publisher, Ministry Resources: **Salley, Susan**, 6736 ssalley@umpublishing.org
Unit Administrator: **Worsham, Sonia**, 6758, sworsham@umpublishing.org

Senior Editor: **Kidd, Ron**, 6921, rkidd@umpublishing.org
Senior Editor: **Sharpe, Sally**, 6105, ssharpe@umpublishing.org

Worship, Music, Official, Abingdon Church Resources

Associate Publisher, Worship, Music, Official Congregational Resources/Editor-in-Chief: **Dean, Mary Catherine**, 6792 mdean@umpublishing.org
Executive Assistant: **Merritt, Frances**, 6301, fmerritt@umpublishing.org
Editor: **Hoosier, Regina**, 6789, rhoosier@umpublishing.org

Publishing Services

Editor-in-Chief: **Dean, Mary Catherine**, 6792 mdean@umpublishing.org
Contracts, Rights & Permissions: **Martin, Laurene**, 6387, lmartin@umpublishing.org
Editorial Services: **Johnston, Mada**, 6375, mjohnston@umpublishing.org

Cokesbury

Cokesbury Contact Center
201 Eighth Ave. S.
Nashville TN 37202-9931
800/672-1789, fax: 800/445-8189, TDD/TT 800/227-4091

Cokesbury.com
www.cokesbury.com

Cokesbury Resource Consultants
http://www.cokesbury.com/forms/CRClocator.aspxcokesbury

Commissions

General Commission on Archives and History
www.gcah.org

OFFICERS
President: **Park, Jeremiah J.**
Vice President: **Maenzanise, Beauty**
Secretary: **Watkins, Nancy**
Archives & Library: **Tang, Anthony**
Archives & Library: **Fergus, Judi**
Heritage Landmarks: **Homitsky, Larry**
Heritage Landmarks: **Huff, A. V. III**
History & Interpretation: **Laferty, Matthew A.**
History & Interpretation: **Miller, Diana**

BOARD
Bishops
Katembo, Kainda, 960 Av. Mzee Laurent Kabila, Lubumbashi, Democratic Republic of Congo, 243/88-47256, akatembofainda@yahoo.fr
Park, Jeremiah J., 303 Mulberry Dr., Ste. 100, Mechanicsburg, PA 17050-3141, 717/766-7871, fax: 717/766-3210, bishop@susumc.org

Members
Corbin, Ivan, Grace UM Church, 65 Needle Blvd., Merritt Island, FL 32953, 321/452-2420, 407/401-2388 (cell), IvanCorbin@bellsouth.net
Day, Alfred III, Historic St. George's UM Church, 235 North 4th St., Philadelphia, PA 19106, 215/925-7788, 215/266-6334 (cell), pastor@historicstgeorges.org
Fergus, Judi, Moore Methodist Museum, 100 Arthur Moore Dr., PO Box 24081, St. Simons Island, GA 31522, 912/638-4050, 912/230-9514 (cell), mmarchives@mooremethodistmuseum.comcastbiz.net

Flores, Daniel F., PO Box 64394, Fort Worth, TX 761654, 817/624-3242, 817/891-7778 (cell), dflores.phd@gmail.com

Homitsky, Larry, 971 Beech Ave., Pittsburgh, PA 15233, 412/231-2007 or 412/231-4900, 724/272-3486 (cell), churchunion@stargate.net

Huff, A.V. III, 30 Glenrose Ave., Greenville, SC 29617, 864/834-9726, 864/561-2216 (cell), av.huff@furman.edu

Laferty, Matthew A., Lomonosovsky Prospect 38, Apt. 59, 119330 Moscow, Russia, +7/499-143-35-62, +7/962-943-92-11 (cell), +1/419/557-2310 (from the USA), malaferty@gmail.com

Lakatos, Judit, 1141 Budapest, Vizakna utca 38/B, Hungary, +36/1-387-4692, +36/70-940-4192 (cell), lakatos.judit@metodista.hu

Loyer, Matthew J., 1495 Kunkles Mill Rd., Lewisberry, PA 17339, 717/292-5430, 85 York St., Wellsville, PA 17365, 717/432-5366, 717/357-0707 (cell), mloyer@susumc.org

Lusk, Bettie, (June through October), 3505 Lake View Dr., #208, Hazel Crest, IL 60429, 708/799-0530, (November through May), 4009 North 156th Ln., Goodyear, AZ 85338, 623/935-1684, 708/205-3763 (cell), dandblusk@prodigy.net

Maenzanise, Beauty, Africa University, P. O. Box 1320, Mutare, Zimbabwe, +263/20-66967, +263/20-772265629 (cell), rosebeau3@yahoo.com

McClain, William Bobby, Wesley Theological Seminary, 4500 Massachusetts Ave., NW, Washington, DC 20016, 202/885-8644, 301/509-5330 (cell), wbmcclain28@juno.com

Miller, Diana, 3352 West River Dr., Gladwin, MI 48624-9730, 989/436-2644, 989/418-8562 (cell), diana@ddmiller.net

Palomo, Manuel G. Sr., 105 Benigno St., Dona Adela Subdivision, Mabini Homesite, Cabanatuan City, Philippines, +63/917/505-1949, mannypal@yahoo.com

Rogers, Cornish, 840 West Orange Grove Ave., Arcadia, CA 91006, 626/355-3662, crogers@cst.edu

Schramm, Linda, 244 South Elk St., Sandusky, MI 48471, 810/648-4696, 810/404-4698 (cell), lars@greatlakes.net

Scott, George "Doug", PO Box 431, Holdenville, OK 74848, 405/205-3229 (cell), gdougscott@yahoo.com

Tang, Anthony, University UM Church, 4412 S. Maryland Pkwy., Las Vegas, NV 89119, 702/733-7155, 702/808-2353 (cell), anthony.j.tang@gmail.com

Walker, James, 950 Vineland Dr., #46, Clarkston, WA 99403, 509/758-8995, 208/791-9230 (cell), jkdwalk01@aol.com

Watkins, Nancy, SEJ Heritage Center, PO Box 1165, Lake Junaluska, NC 28745, 828/454-6781, 828/550-5927 (cell), nwatkins@lakejunaluska.com

Winegar, Grady C., 5503 Pinecrest Rd., Knoxville, TN 37912, 865/688-6448, 865/414-8506 (cell), winegars@bellsouth.net

Commissions

Wolf, Christina, Archives, Oklahoma City University, 2501 N. Blackwelder Ave., Oklahoma City, OK 73106, 405/208-5919, 405/250-5638 (cell), cwolf@okcu.edu

STAFF

36 Madison Ave.
PO Box 127
Madison, NJ 07940
973/408-3189, fax: 973/408-3909
rwilliams@gcah.org
www.gcah.org

General Secretary: **Williams, Robert J.**, rwilliams@gcah.org
Archivist/Records Administrator: **Patterson, L. Dale**, 973/408-3195, dpatterson@gcah.org
Administrative Assistant: **Merkel-Brunskill, Michelle K.**, mmerkel@gcah.org
Associate Archivist: **Shenise, Mark C.**, 973/408-3194, mshenise@gcah.org
Reference Archivist: **Lyons-Bristol, Frances**, 973/408-3196, fbristol@gcah.org
Methodist Librarian: **Anderson, Christopher J.**, 973/408-3910, cjanders@drew.edu
Methodist Library Associate: **Fick, Corey**, 973/408-3590, cfick@drew.edu

General Commission on Communication

www.umcom.org

OFFICERS

President: **Dyck, Sally**
Vice President: **Evans, Cashar**
Recording Secretary: **Dixon Hall, Maria**
Chair, Personnel: **Cox, Greg**
Chair, Finance: **Evans, Cashar Jr.**
Chair, Evaluation Committee: **Reisman, Kimberly**
Chair, Legislative Committee: **Vázquez-Garza, Virgilio**

BOARD

Bishops

Dyck, Sally, Chicago Area Episcopal Office, 77 W. Washington St., Ste. 1820, Chicago, IL 60602, 312/346-9766, x102, sdych@umcnic.org

Nhiwatiwa, Eben, UMC-163 Chinhoyi St. PO Box 3408, Harare, Zimbabwe, 263 4 751 508, umczim@africaonline.co.zw

Schol, John R., New Jersey Area Episcopal Office, 1001 Wickapecko Dr., Ocean, NJ 07712, 732/359-1010, bishopjohnschol@gnjumc.org

Members

Allen, Emily, 202 23rd Ave., San Francisco, CA 94121, 650/796-8461, ladyemilybug@gmail.com

Bailey, Marshall, 716 S. Pine St., Richmond, VA 23220 804/601-0274, MarshallSBailey@gmail.com

Bushart, Hannah, 408 Sunset, Herford, TX 79045 432/559-4277, hananahmarie@gmail.com

Calentine, Raggatha, 333164 Light House Rd., Shelbyville, DE 19975, 302/436-2492, RagghiRain@gmail.com

Colvin, Eleanor F., 4032 Rogers St., Houston, TX 77022, 713/695 2469, efcolvin@sbcglobal.net

Cox, Gregory D., 512 Sarah Dr., Cranberry Twp., PA 16066, 724/553-5161, preachercox@earthlink.net

Dixon Hall, Maria, 1718 McCosh Dr., Dallas, TX 75228, 214/768-3393, madixon@smu.edu

Evans, Cashar Jr., 69 Poteskeet Trail, Kitty Hawk, NC 27949, 252/261-3301, casharevansjr@gmail.com

Hahn, Wesley 4505 Stone Ridge Ct., Traverse City, MI 49684, 231/357-4676, wizardrooster@gmail.com

Lauber, Melissa 1215 East-West Highway, Apt. 910, Silver Springs, MD 20910, 410/309-3455, mlauber@bwcumc.org

Manning, Allison 111 Lake Hollingsworth Dr., Box 15960, Lakeland, FL 33801, 863/660-8312, allisonbmanning@gmail.com

Mowery, Don 2765 Telegraph Rd., St. Louis, MO 63125, 573/382-7408, drmowery46@hotmail.com

Page, Jonathan 4704 Wouthern Pines Dr., Virginia Beach, VA, 757/748-4785, jonathanjpage@gmail.com

Porter, Derrick 36 Talley Ct., Wilmington, DE 19802, 302/674-2626, dsdporter@gmail.com

Reisman, Kimberly 3072 Hamilton St., West Lafayette, IN 47906, 765/742-6502, kim.reisman@inumc.org

Rogers, Alice, 1309 Creekside Pl., Smyrna, GA, 404/727-3006, alice.rogers@emory.edu

Rooks, Jessica, 1600 S. Pearl St., Denver, CO 80210, 303/777-7638, revjessrooks@hotmail.com

Serdyukov, Pavel, Perovo United Methodist Church, Moscow, Russia, +7 915 190-3406, serdukov79@yandex.ru

Sison, Vida Grace, 900 United Nations Ave., Ermita, Manikla, Philippines, 63 919 442 3057, vidagracesison@yahoo.com

Steele, Rodney, 605 W. Sixth St., Mt. Home, AR 72653, 870/425-6036, rsteele@fumcmh.org

Strickland, Walter "Skip," 2280 Watersong Cir., Longmont, CO 80111, 800/536-3736, skip@rmcumc.com

Trefz, Rebecca, 316 River Oak St., Brandon, SD 57005, 605/201-5391, pastor_rebecca@alliancecom.net

Vázquez-Garza, Virgilio, 16400 Huebner Rd., San Antonio, TX 78248, 210/408-4520, RevDiver@aol.com

Wilson, Carol E., 3105 Eagle Dr., Maryville, TN 37803, 865/690-4080, carolwilson@holston.org

STAFF

United Methodist Communications Headquarters
810 Twelfth Ave., South, Nashville, TN 37203-4744
615/742-5400, fax: 615/742-5415
www.umcom.org

General Secretary's Office

General Secretary: **Hollon, Larry**, 615/742-5410, lhollon@umcom.org
Executive Assistant: **Saunders, Linda**, 615/742-5119, lsaunders@umcom.org

Core Leadership Team

Chief Operating Officer: **Thiel, Sherri**, 615/742-5484, sthiel@umcom.org
Executive Director of Content: **Tanton, Tim**, 615/742-5473, ttanton@umcom.org
Executive Director of Global Health Initiative: **Henderson, Gary**, 615/742-5768, ghenderson@umcom.org
Executive Director of Human Resources: **Allen, Helen**, 615/742-5412, hallen@umcom.org
Executive Director of New Media: **Panovec, Kay**, 615/742-5147, kpanovec@umcom.org

Communications Ministry Group

(Toll-free: 877/281-6535 fax: 615/742-5777)
Director of Communications Ministry & Brand Strategy: **Rodia, Jennifer**, 615/742-5134, jrodia@umcom.org
Assistant Director: **Hicks, Neelley**, 615/742-5444, nhicks@umcom.org
Project Coordinator: **Harrison, Sheila**, 615/742-5128, sharrison@umcom.org
Administrative Assistant: **Jarrett, Deborah**, 615/742-5769 fax: 615/742-5485, djarrett@umcom.org
Director, Media Services & Rethink Church Community Events: **Vaughan, Jackie**, 615/742-5140, jvaughn@umcom.org
Project Coordinator, Rethink Church Community Events: **Solomon, Lindsey**, 615/742-5418, lsolomon@umcom.org
Promotion and Event Assistant, Rethink Church Community Events: **Adair, Steven** 615/742-5106, sadair@umcom.org
Conference Relations: **James, Royya**, 615/742-5461, rjames@umcom.org
Manager, Communications Training and Technology: **Shownes, Patrick**, 615/742-5775, pshownes@umcom.org
Manager, Communications Training and Development: **Congdon, Caitlin**, 615/742-5142, ccongdonn@umcom.org
Project Coordinator, Training: **Gooding, Anthony** 615/742-5403, agooding@umcom.org
Site Administrator, Rethinkchurch.org: **Crawford, Susan**, 615/742-5418, scrawford@umcom.org
Minister of Online Engagement, Rethinkchurch.org: **Agtarap, Sophia** 615/742-5411, sagtarap@umcom.org

Commissions

Connectional Giving Team
Director of Marketing: **Cunningham**, **Elsie**, 615/742-5488, ecunningham@umcom.org

Content Team
Executive Director, **Tanton**, **Tim**, 615/742-5473, ttanton@umcom.org

Interpreter
Publisher: **Hollon**, **Larry**, 615/742-5410, lhollon@umcom.org
Editor: **Noble**, **Kathy**, 615/742-5441, knoble@umcom.org
Twitter: https://twitter.com/InterpreterMag

Young Adult Content Team
Editor: **Butler**, **Joey**, 615/742-5105, jbutler@umcom.org
Multimedia Reporter: **Gilbert**, **Kathy L.**, 615/742-5471, kgilbert@umcom.org

Internal Church Content
Editor: **Dunlap-Berg**, **Barbara**, 615/742-5489, bdunlap-berg@umcom.org

United Methodist News Service
News Writer (New York): **Bloom**, **Linda**, 646/369-3759, lbloom@umcom.org
News Writer (Nashville) **Hahn**, **Heather**, 615/742-5475, hhahn@umcom.org
News Editor: **Hillery**, **Maggie**, 615/742-5472, mhillery@umcom.org
Photographer: **DuBose**, **Mike**, 615/742-5150, mdubose@umcom.org
Manager, Digital Assets: **Barry**, **Kathleen**, 615/742-5112, kbarry@umcom.org
Facebook: UMNS
Twitter: https://twitter.com/UMNS

Central Conference Communications Initiative
Director: **Mudambanuki**, **Tafadzwa**, 615/742-5149, tmudambanuki@umcom.org

Korean Resources
Director, **Lee**, **Jacob**, 615/742-5118, jlee@umcom.org
Coordinator, **Kim**, **Young Joo**, 615/742-5765, ykim@umcom.org
Twitter: https://twitter.com/KoreanUMC

Hispanic UMC Communications
Director: 615/742-5113
Associate Director: 615/742-5490
Twitter: https://twitter.com/Hispanic_UMC

Facilities and Operations Team

Customer Service Center: Toll-free: 888/346-3862 (888-FINDUMC)
Team Leader: **Loney, Carlton**, 615/742-5493, cloney@umcom.org
Director of Customer Services: **Herity, Sheila**, 615/742-5402, sherity@umcom.org
Maintenance: **Byrd, Jeff**, 615/742-5495, jbyrd@umcom.org

Finance & Administration

Chief Operating Officer: **Thiel, Sherri**, 615/742-5484, sthiel@umcom.org
Administrative Assistant: **Erlandsson, MaryAnna**, 615/742-5407, merlandsson@umcom.org

Financial Services Team

Team Leader: **Dawson, Tangi**, 615/742-5486, tdawson@umcom.org
Accounts Payable Staff Accountant: **Janoe, Rhonnie**, 615/742-5480, rjanoe@umcom.org
Accounts Receivable Staff Accountant: **Blair, Karen**, 615/742-5487, kblair@umcom.org

Global Health Initiative

Executive Director of Global Health Initiative: **Henderson, Gary**, 615/742-5768, ghenderson@umcom.org
Project Coordinator: **Maloney, Diane**, 615/742-5419, dmaloney@umcom.org
Communication Coordinator: **Weaver, Sandra Long**, 615/742-5482

Imagine No Malaria Campaign

Manager: **Altland, Sheri**, 615/742-3594, saltland@umcom.org

Human Resources Team

Executive Director of Human Resources: **Allen, Helen**, 615/742-5412, hallen@umcom.org
Human Resources, General Information: _____, 615/742-5137, hr@umcom.org
Manager, Payroll & Benefits: **Beckman, Sheri**, 615/742-5498, sbeckman@umcom.org

InfoServ

Director of InfoServ: **Wallace, Vicki**, 615/742-5427, vwallace@umcom.org
Information Consultant: **Holly, Mary Lynn**, 615/742-5424, mholly@umcom.org

Commissions

New Media Team (UMC.org, UMTV, UM Productions)
Executive Director **Panovec, Kay**, 615/742-5147, kpanovec@umcom.org

UM Productions Team
Team Leader: **Leake, Harry**, 615/742-5477, hleake@umcom.org
Administrative Assistant: **Terry, Carol**, 615/742-5779, cterry@umcom.org
Special Projects Producer: **Snider, Jan**, 615/742-5474, jsnider@umcom.org
Supervising Editor: **Barrow, Ricky**, 615/742-5121, rbarrow@umcom.org
Video and Photography Assistant: **Perry, Ronny**, 615/742-5135, rperry@umcom.org
Studio Manager: **Holt, Andrew**, 615/742-5155, aholt@umcom.org

Web Ministry Team (UMC.org)
Web Team Leader: **Mayfield, Sheila**, 615/742-5453, smayfield@umcom.org
Project Manager: **Lewis, Julie**, 615/742-5457, jlewis@umcom.org
UMC.org Managing Editor: **Glass, Laurens**, 615/742-5405, lglass@umcom.org
UMC.org Web Producer: **Caldwell, Cindy** 615/742-5132, ccaldwell@umcom.org
Manager, Online Media: **Denson, Lane**, 615/742-5764, ldenson@umcom.org
Web Production Assistant: **Furtado, Jefferson**, 615/742-5153, jfurtado@umcom.org
UMCGiving.org Web Coordinator: **Carey, Lladale**, 615/742-5104, lcarey@umcom.org

UMTV
Supervising Producer: **Walsh, Fran**, 615/742-5458, fwalsh@umcom.org

Product Marketing and Research Team
Director: **Niedringhaus, Charles**, 615/742-5101, cniedringhaus@umcom.org

Public Relations
Director of Public Relations: **Degnan, Diane**, 615/742-5406, ddegnan@umcom.org

TechShop Team
Sales Representative: **Karima, Chilima**, 615/742-5139, ckarima@umcom.org
Sales Representative: **Clark, Scott**, 615/742-5478, sclark@umcom.org

Technology Team
Team Leader: **Mai, Danny**, 615/742-5156, dmai@umcom.org
Network and Data Operations and Security Director: **Fusco, John**, 615/742-5447, jfusco@umcom.org
Software Engineering Manager: **Bonner, Bruce**, 615/742-5448, bbonner@umcom.org

Commission on the General Conference

Officers

Chairperson: **Kenaston, Judi**, 201 Alderson St., Lewisburg, WV 24901, 800/788-3746 ext 23, judikenaston@aol.com
Vice Chairperson: **Beard, Frank J.**, 6428 Timber Walk Dr., Indianapolis, IN 46236, 317/855-7949, frank.beard@inumc.org
Secretary: **Lux, David**, 7221 Framton Rd, Lincoln, NE 68516, 402/477-6951, dlux@saintpaulumc.org

Members

Abdon, Reynaldo V., Dona Manuela Subdivision, Pamplona 3, Las Pinas City, 1740 Philippines, +63 2 873 4841, shiningrey@gmail.com
Beard, Frank J., 6428 Timber Walk Dr., Indianapolis, IN 46236, 317/855-7949, frank.beard@inumc.org
Bindl, Helene, Schubertstrasse 17, Linz, Austria 4020, bindl.helene@gmail.com
Charley, Francis B., 31 Lightfoot Boston St., Freetown, Sierra Leone, revcharl@yahoo.co.uk
Collier, T. Cody, 4240 Blue Ridge Blvd., Ste. 210, Kansas City, MO 64133, 816/737-1114, tcodycollier@att.net
Deckard, Stephanie, 4 Vinal St. Apt 6, Brighton, MA 02135, 315/729-5214, sdeckard@bu.edu
Eberhart, Diane Wasson, 916 5th Ave., Grinnell, IA 50112, 641/236-3757, deacondiane@iowatelecom.net
Elias, Joao Damiao, UMC—Rua Kibiriti Diwane 229, Maputo, Mozambique, 258/23-311670, muhale@rocketmail.com
Flick, Christine, Neuffenstrasse 37/1, Wendlingen, Germany D-73240, 49/7024.52381, christine.flick@emk.de
Haden, William R, 624 NW Westover Terrace, Portland, OR 97210, 503/946-8231, haden551@comcast.net
Hill, A. Lynn, 143 Fifth Ave. S, Franklin, TN 37064, 615/794-2734, lhill@franklinfumc.org
Holt, Gloria E., 6740 Clear Creek Cir., Trussville, AL 35173, gloriaholt1959@gmail.com
Kashala, Mujinga, UMC PO Box 22037, Kitwe, Zambia, 243/814825991, matmadima@yahoo.fr
Kassongo Ka Suedi, Stanislas, B.P. 4727, Kinshasa 2, RDC Congo, stanprenomkassongo@yahoo.fr

Commissions

Kenaston, **Judi**, 201 Alderson St., Lewisburg, WV 24901, 800/788-3746 ext 23, judikenaston@aol.com
Lockward, **Jorge A.**, 340 Have Ave #1M, New York, NY 10033, 212/870-3967, jorgelockward@yahoo.com
Lux, **David**, 7221 Framton Rd, Lincoln, NE 68516, 402/477-6951, dlux@saintpaulumc.org
McMillan IV, **Samuel D.**, 3301 Kentrye Dr., Fayetteville, NC 28303, sdmcmillan0727@email.campbell.edu, samuelmcmillan@ccs.k12.nc.us
Mulongo, **Ndala Joseph**, PO Box 20219, Kitwe, Zambia, Congo, 243/993194108, knmulongo@yahoo.fr
Natt, **Ellen J.**, UMC Central Office, 13th St. Box 1010, Sinkor Monrovia, Liberia, 231/886551896, ellenjnatt@yahoo.com
Pritchard, **Donna**, 1838 SW Jefferson St., Portland, OR 97201-2463, 502/228-3591 ext 226, dpritchard@fumcpdx.org
Rosario, **Ileana**, PO Box 2266, Suffolk, VA 23432, 757/255-4537, ilerosas@aol.com
Simpson, **Kim**, 3905 Lake Powell Dr., Arlington, TX 76016, 817/478-0869, kimsimpson1@tx.rr.com
Westad, **Audun**, Asbratstien 15, Oslo, Norway NO-1251, 0047/416-65-694, audunwestad@gmail.com

Ex-Officio

Secretary of the General Conference: **Reist, Fitzgerald**, 1292 Stony Fork Rd., Wellsboro, PA 16901-7367, 570/972-0537, freist@susumc.org
Business Manager of the General Conference: **Hotchkiss, Sara**, PO Box 340029, Nashville, TN 37203-0029, 615/369-2352 fax: 615/369-2355, shotchkiss@gcfa.org
Treasurer of GCFA: **Kumar, A. Moses Rathan**, PO Box 340029, Nashville, TN 37203-0029, 615/369-2320 fax: 615/369-2321, mkumar@gcfa.org
Council of Bishops Representative: **Carcaño, Minerva G.**, 110 S. Euclid Ave., Pasadena, CA 91101, 626/568-7312 fax: 626/796-7377, bishopmc@cal-pac.org

Observers

Alsted, **Christian**, Rigensgade 21A, DK-1316 Copenhagen, Denmark, +45/5133 1477, office@umc-ne.org
Brumbaugh, **Susan**, Coordinator of the Calendar, 2000 Thomas Dr., Las Cruces, NM 88001, 575/309-8872 (cell), 575/522-4845, susan@aphids.com
Cropsey, **Marvin W.**, DCA Editor, UMPH, 201 8th Ave., South, Nashville, TN 37203, 615/749-6292 fax: 615-749-6512, mcropsey@umpublishing.org

Degnan, Diane, Director of Public Relations, United Methodist Communications, 810 Twelfth Ave. S., Nashville, TN 37203-4744, 615/742-5406, ddegnan@umcom.org

Goodpaster, Larry M., PO Box 18750, Charlotte, NC 28218, 704/535-2260 fax: 704/535-9160, bishop@wnccumc.org

Graves, Gary W., Petitions Secretary, 305 West Main St., Princeton, KY 42445, 270/365-3528, gwg85@earthlink.net

Hauser, Joshua, Youth Observer Host Committee, joshua.w.hauser@gmail.com

COMMITTEE ON CORRELATION AND EDITORIAL REVIEW (CCER)

Chairperson: **Haigler, Anne**, 1600 Wm. E. Summers Dr. #100, Louisville, KY 40211, 502/485-8858, ahaig@netzero.net

Vice Chairperson: **Bartle, Naomi**, 1006 17th St., S., Fargo, SD 58103, 701/235-1276, dnbartle@cableone.net

Secretary: **Burkhart, J. Robert**, 2301 Rittenhouse St., Des Moines, IA 50321, 515/974-8903, Bob.burkhart@iaumc.org

Kohler, Rebecca, 170 Kenwood Ave., Oneida, NY 13421, 315/723-1643, rebeccakohler@unyumc.org

Caldwell, Linda, 1276 Halyard Dr., West Sacramento, CA 95691, 916/374-1517, linda@calnevumc.org

Schenk, Carl, 14975 Broadmont Dr., Chesterfield, MO 63017, 636/207-9259, cschenck@eden.edu

Secretary of the General Conference: **Reist, Fitzgerald**

Ex Officio: **Alexander, Neil M.**, Book Editor of The UMC 615/749-6327 fax: 615/749-6510, nalexander@umpublishing.org

Staff

Dean, Mary Catherine, 615/749-6792, mdean@umpublishing.org

Dick, Barbara, 608/658-4447, barbara.a.dick@gmail.com

Commissions

General Commission on Religion and Race

www.gcorr.org

OFFICERS

President: **Carcaño, Minerva**
Vice President: **Harris, Joseph**
Secretary: **White, Justin**

BOARD

Bishops

Carcaño, Minerva G., 110 South Euclid Ave., Pasadena, CA 91101, 626/568-7312 fax: 626/568-7377, bishopmc@cal-pac.org
Jones, Scott J., 9440 E. Boston, Ste. 160, Wichita, KS 67207-3603, 316/686-0600 fax: 316/684-0044 bishop@greatplainsumc.org
Wandabula, Daniel, Plot 6B Sturrock Rd, Kamwokya, PO Box 12554, Kampala, Uganda, 256 772 507173 or 256 41 533978, fax: 256/41-533982, residentbishopeaacumc@gmail.com

Members

Brown, David L., 5575 Seminary, Falls Church, VA 22041, 703/575-8353 brownbas@fastmail.fm
Finau, Sela E., 1608 Catalpa Rd., Flower Mound, TX 75028, 817/354-9038 x2202, s.finau@yahoo.com
Fukumoto, JoAnn Yoon, 1796 Hoolehua St., Pearl City, HI 96782, 808/371-7694, joumc@aol.com
Gonzales, Vince, 134 Sunburst Ct., Weatherford, TX 76087, 214/354-2337, dpmitigation@hotmail.com
Handy, Stephen E, 608 Logwood Briar Cir., Brentwood, TN 37027, 616/271-2600, mckendreestephen@gmail.com
Harris, Joseph, 1501 NW 24th St., Oklahoma City, OK 73106, 405/530-2077, jharris@okumc.org
Kurien, Christopher Jacob, 114 Koegel Ln., Norristown, PA 19403, 610/666-9080, christopherkurien@gmail.com
Locklear, Neffie Connie, 5717 Bramblegate, Greensboro, NC 27409, 336/273-2891, waterbird@triad.rr.com
Maguiraya Acdal, Rodel, 57 College Ave., Tuguegarao City, Philippines, 63/78-846-4084, rodelacdal@yahoo.com

Malone, **Tracy S.**, 77 W. Washington, Ste. 1820, Chicago, IL 60602, 312/346-9766, tmalone@umcnic.org

McClendon, **Tim**, 4908 Colonial Dr., Ste. 124, Columbia, SC 29206, 803/786-9486 x302, wtmcclendon@umcsc.org

McCray, **Marian B.**, 81 Northbrook Cir., Apt. 18, Fairview Heights, IL 62208, 618/332-0909, marianmccray@yahoo.com

McGhee, **Delaine**, 973 Mechanic St., Grafton, OH 44044, 440/926-2034, preacherlady@rocketmail.com

Nausner, **Asa Helene**, Hagstrasse 8, DE-72762 Reutlingen, Germany, +49/7121-205605, asa.nausner@gmx.de

Santiago, **Ali**, 4219A Arbutus, Raleigh, NC 27612 910/478-6546, jasantia@email.meredith.edu

Weatherspoon, **Dale**, 1509 Jasper Dr., Sunnyvale, CA 94087, 650/261-3830, fax: 650/261-3830, dmwspoon@aol.com

White, **Justin**, 4523 Kings Highway, Jackson, MS 39206, 601/573-4297, dawgwhite2@gmail.com

STAFF

100 Maryland Ave. NE, Ste. 400
Washington, DC 20002
202/547-2271, fax: 202/547-0358
info@gcorr.org
www.gcorr.org

Executive Staff

General Secretary: **Hawkins, Erin**, 202/547-2271, ehawkins@gcorr.org

Team Leader for Monitoring and Advocacy: **Arroyo, Giovanni**, 202/495-2943, garroyo@gcorr.org

Director of Annual Conference Relations: **Kim, Myungim**, 202/495-2945, mkim@gcorr.org

Team Leader for Finance and Administration: **Stapleton, Amy**, 202/495-2952, astapleton@gcorr.org

Team Leader for Program Ministries: 202/547-2271, info@gcorr.org

Team Leader for Communications and Media: 202/547-2271, info@gcorr.org

Administrative Staff

Web Content Manager: **DeBlaker-Gebhard, Kyra**, 202/495-2942 fax: 202/547-0358, kdeblaker-gebhard@gcorr.org

Production Support and Social Media Specialist: **Kim, Jeehye**, 202/495-2947, jpak@gcorr.org

Commissions

Financial Services Assistant and Administrative Assistant: **Tello, Michelle**, 202/495-2951, mtello@gcorr.org
Executive Assistant: 202/495-2941, info@gcorr.org
Director of Human Resources: **Jett-Roberts, Frances**, 202/488-5658, froberts@umc-gbcs.org

General Commission on the Status and Role of Women

www.gcsrw.org

Officers
President: **Wallace-Padgett, Debra**
Vice President: **Nhanala, Joaquina F.**
Secretary: **Russell, Ryan M.**

Board
Bishops
Nhanala, Joaquina F., jnhanala2@yahoo.com
Wallace-Padgett, Deborah, dwp@northalabamaumc.org

Members
Alschwede, Stephanie M., revsteph@bigmuddyumc.org
Cooper, Michelline, miki2@sc.rr.com
Crismo, Phebe, G., prgcrismo@yahoo.com
Dellinger, Lisa A., dellinger.lisa@yahoo.com
Fogle-Miller, Carlene R., carfm@aol.com
Gallo Seagren, Lilian, lilian.gallo-seagren@iaumc.org
Iliya, Eunice Musa, euniceiliya@yahoo.com
Kaleuati, Kaleuati, kkaleuat@umcneb.org
Kenaston, Diane M., rev.diane.kenaston@gmail.com
Leyva, Elizabeth elizzleyva@yahoo.com
Mitchell, Cathy D., ebonylocs@sc.com
Ransom, Opal G., kaylawill@aol.com
Russell, Ryan M., ryan.russell@garrett.edu
Schwaller, Tyler M., tyler.schwaller@gmail.com
Urda, Ana-Haydee, AHUrda@att.net
Wallace, William T., dinkyjr@myshorelink.com
Westad, Anne, Berit berit.westad@ebnett.no

Staff
77 W. Washington St., Ste. 1009
Chicago, IL 60602

Commissions

312/346-4900 or 800/523-8390, fax: 312/346-3986
gcsrw@gcsrw.org
www.gcsrw.org

General Secretary: **Wiggins Hare, Dawn**, dhare@gcsrw.org
Assistant General Secretary for Finance and Administration: **Moy, Elaine**, emoy@gcsrw.org
Assistant General Secretary, Advocacy and Sexual Ethics: **Stephens, Darryl W.**, dstephens@gcsrw.org
Director of Communication: **Keaton, Susan**, skeaton@gcsrw.org
Director of Gender Justice and Education: **Krumbach, Audrey**, akrumbach@gcsrw.org
Director of Monitoring and Research: **Kane, Erin**, ekane@gcsrw.org
Administrative Coordinator: **Goldman, LeeAnn**, lgoldman@gcsrw.org

General Commission on United Methodist Men

www.gcumm.org

OFFICERS

President: **Swanson, James E. Sr.**
Vice President: **Bickerton, Thomas**
Secretary: **Godwin, Gregory**
Treasurer: **Donley, Lee**
USA National President of UMM: **Ramsey, Dan**

BOARD

Bishops

Bickerton, Thomas J., PO Box 5002, Cranberry Township, PA 16066, 724/453-1258, bishopsoffice@wpaumc.org
Swanson, James E. Sr, 320 Briarwood Dr., Jackson, MS 39206, bishop@mississippi-umc.org
Yohanna, John Wesley, UMCN Secretariat, Mile Six, Jalingo-Numan Rd., PO Box 148, Jalingo, Taraba State, jywesley@yahoo.com

Members

Alegria, Richard, 2533 Wind Rose, Corpus Christi, TX 78414, 361/739-5056, church.musico@yahoo.com
Cage, John Bright, Mid-State Cardiology, 222 22nd Ave. N., Ste. 400, Nashville, TN 37203, 615/371-0885, jbcage@comcast.net
Donley, Lee, 1223 Brauer Rd., Oxford, MI 48371, 810/358-2091, leedonley2@aol.com
Dozier, Larry, 13112 S. Wilton Pl., Gardena, CA 90249-1844, 310/719-8974, lrrdz@att.net
Enstine, Ed, 363 W. King Rd., Ithaca, NY 14850-8601, 607/592-8276, eenstine@aol.com
Godwin, Gregory, PO Box 746, Athens, WV 24712, 304/384-9636, gagodwin@citlink.net
Grant, Reginald, 2411 6th Ave., Los Angeles, CA 90018, eplaybook1@mindspring.com
Lilleoja, Tarmo, Hamariku tee 13, 7690 Harku vald, Tabasula, 372/527-9095, tarmo@tarian.ee

Managuelod, Narciso Immanuel, 388 Rizal St., Barangay Onse, San Juan, Metro Manila 1500, nicmanaguelod@yahoo.com
Price, Larry, 2406 Ashford Dr., Albany, GA 31721, 229/883-3302, price2406@bellsouth.net
Ramsey, Dan, 18003 Wild Oak, Houston, TX 77090, 281/440-1253, dbramseyjr@sbcglobal.net
Shytle, Ed, 2200 Ranch Rd., Ashland, KY 41102, 606/329-0461, edshytle@roadrunner.com
Tielke, Kenneth, 4002 Meadowbend Dr., Richmond, TX 77469, 281/342-9677, Kenwtielke@aol.com
Trammell, Ben, 4600 FM 359, Richmond, TX 77406, ben.trammell@faithumc.org
Vogt, Amanda, 16041 Forest Valley Dr., Ballwin, MO 63021, 636/394-6809, venturingpresident@yahoo.com
Wilson, Jennifer A., 1711 Creve Coeur, LaSalle, IL 61301, billandjenwilson@comcast.net
Wright, Doug, 7772 N. Sun Flair Dr., Tucson, AZ 85741, dwright5@qwest.net

STAFF

1000 17th Ave. S.
PO Box 340006 (37203 zip)
Nashville, TN 37212
615/340-7145
gcumm@gcumm.org
www.gcumm.org

General Secretary: **Hanke, Gilbert C.**, 615/340-7145 ghanke@gcumm.org
National Director of Scouting and Youth-serving Ministries: **Coppock, Larry**, 615/620-7261 lcoppock@gcumm.org
Operations Manager: **Davis, Martha**, 615/620-7266 mdavis@gcumm.org
Scouting Ministry Assistant: **Stowe, Marc**, 615/620-7262, mstowe@gcumm.org
Financial and Web Services Assistant: **Eidson, Joshua**, 615/620-7263, jeidson@gcumm.org
Charter System Administrator: **Strausbaugh, Joseph**, jstrausbaugh@gcumm.org
Communication Coordinator: **Peck, Rich**, 615/620-7264, rpeck@gcumm.org

Deployed Staff
Arnold, Greg, garnold@gcumm.org
Boesch, Jim, jboesch@gcumm.org
Dehority, Mark, mdehority@gcumm.org
Lubbock, Mark, mlubbock@gcumm.org

United Methodist Women, National Office

www.umwonline.org

OFFICERS

President: **Richards, Yvette K.**
Vice President: **Kelemeni, Tupou Seini**
Secretary: **Thompson, Becky**
Chair, Finance Committee: **Guy, Nichea VerVeer**
Chair, Planning and Assessment Committee: **Kelemeni, Tupou Seini**
Chair, Governance Committee: **Pierre-Okerson, Judith**

STAFF

Interchurch Center
475 Riverside Dr., 15th Floor
New York, NY 10115

Office of the General Secretary/CEO

Fax: 212/870-3736
General Secretary/CEO: **Olson, Harriett Jane**, 212/870-3752, holson@unitedmethodistwomen.org
Executive Assistant: **Jaffary, Syed I.**, 212/870-3749, sjaffary@unitedmethodistwomen.org
Staff Recording Secretary: **Douglas, Linda C.**, 212/870-3753, ldouglas@unitedmethodistwomen.org
Director of Fund Development: **TBN**
Director of Mission Education and Enrichment: **Trent, Cheryl E.**, 212/870-3745, ctrent@unitedmethodistwomen.org
Reading Program Specialist: **Thompson, Brenda A.**, 212/870-3733, bathomps@unitedmethodistwomen.org
Assistant Assembly Chair: **Brockus, Sarah**, 212/870-3750, sbrockus@unitedmethodistwomen.org
Program Associate: **Craddock, Rashida**, 212/870-3760, rcraddock@unitedmethodistwomen.org
Program Associate: **Nurse, Denise**, 212/870-3746, dnurse@unitedmethodistwomen.org

Commissions

Communications

Director of Communications: **Ewing, Selby T.**, 212/870-3755, sewing@unitedmethodistwomen.org

Executive Secretary for Communications/*response* Editor: **Moore, Yvette L.**, 212/870-3822, ymoore@unitedmethodistwomen.org

Executive Secretary for Communications/Staff Editor: **Barnes, Tara**, 212/870-3628, tbarnes@unitedmethodistwomen.org

Executive Secretary for Communications/Creative Director: **Miller, Emily R.**, 212/870-3728, emiller@unitedmethodistwomen.org

Executive Secretary for Communications/Program Resource Editor: **Balasundaram, Praveena**, 212/870-3688, pbalasundaram@unitedmethodistwomen.org

Operations Manager: **Gibbs, Laurina**, 212/870-3757, lgibbs@unitedmethodistwomen.org

Web Content/Public Relations Associate: **Rogers, Leigh M.**, 212/870-3696, lrogers@unitedmethodistwomen.org

Senior Web Designer: **Wilbur, Margaret**, 802/233-9184, mwilbur@unitedmethodistwomen.org

Christian Social Action

Fax: 212/682-5354

Assistant General Secretary: **Lee, Sung-ok**, 212/682-3633 x3109, slee@unitedmethodistwomen.org

Chaplain: **TBN**

Executive Secretary for Community Action: **Barton, Carol A.**, 212/682-3633 x3104, cbarton@unitedmethodistwomen.org

Executive Secretary for Global Justice: **Dwyer, Tatiana**, 212/682-3633 x3108, tdwyer@unitedmethodistwomen.org

Executive Secretary for Economic and Environmental Justice: **Stone, Kathleen**, 212/682-3633 x3114, kstone@unitedmethodistwomen.org

Executive Secretary for Racial Justice: **Rosheuvel, Janis**, 212/682-3633 x3102, jrosheuvel@unitedmethodistwomen.org

Executive Secretary for Public Policy: **Johnson, Susie**, 202/488-5660 x103, johnsons@unitedmethodistwomenc.org

Executive Secretary for Children, Youth, and Family Advocacy: **Taylor, Julie A.**, 212/682-3633 x3106, jtaylor@unitedmethodistwomen.org

Finance & Administrative Services

Fax: 212/870-3736

Treasurer of the United Methodist Women: **Knight, Martha S.**, 212/870-3740, mknight@unitedmethodistwomen.org

Comptroller: **Mui, Halina**, 212/870-3743, hmui@unitedmethodistwomen.org
Manager of Accounting: **TBN**
Director Financial Systems: **Nedderman, Leslie**, 212/870-3739, lnedderm@unitedmethodistwomen.org
Senior Accountant: **Gadit, Farhan**, 212/870-3859, fgadit@unitedmethodistwomen.org
Data Manager: **Jolly, Donovan C.**, 212/870-3737, djolly@unitedmethodistwomen.org
Office Manager: **Jones, Zelda C.**, 212/870-3732, zjones@unitedmethodistwomen.org
Property Manager: **Spencer, Wanda**, 212/870-3708, wspencer@unitedmethodistwomen.org

Alma Mathews House

Fax: 212/870-727-9746
House Manager: **Nesbitt, Claretta**, 212/870-691-5931, cnesbitt@unitedmethodistwomen.org
Assistant Manager: **Peterson, Brian T.**, 212/870-691-5931, bpeterson@unitedmethodistwomen.org

Section on Ministry Opportunities

Assistant General Secretary: **Salter, Andris Y.**, 212/870-3843, asalter@unitedmethodistwomen.org
Director, Global Women's Leadership Center/Seoul, Korea: **Kim, Heasun**, 02-3276-3747 (Korea), hkim@unitedmethodistwomen.org
Executive Secretary for Office of Deaconess and Home Missioner: **Louter, Doris R. [Becky]**, 212/870-3850, dlouter@unitedmethodistwomen.org
Executive Secretary for Community Relations, Office of Deaconess and Home Missioner: **Vickery, Scott**, 212/870-3850, svickery@unitedmethodistwomen.org
Executive Secretary for International Ministries: **Akuamoah, Donna**, 212/870-3685, dakuamoah@unitedmethodistwomen.org
Executive Secretary for International Ministries: **Gittens, Betty E.**, 212/870-3719, bgittens@unitedmethodistwomen.org
Executive Secretary for International Ministries: **Van Gorp, Carol**, 212/870-3391, cvangorp@unitedmethodistwomen.org
Executive Secretary for National Ministries: **Cabrera, Bridget**, 212/870-3846, bcabrera@unitedmethodistwomen.org
Executive Secretary for National Ministries: **Cody, Ebony**, 212/870-3697, ecody@unitedmethodistwomen.org
Executive Secretary for National Ministries: **Tyrell, Hortense A.**, 212/870-3887, htyrell@unitedmethodistwomen.org

Commissions

Membership & Leadership Development

Fax: 212/870-3736

Assistant General Secretary: **Vonner, Sally L.**, 212/870-3723, svonner@unitedmethodistwomen.org

Executive Secretary/Language Coordinator: **Villareal, Marisa**, 212/870-3726, mvillarr@unitedmethodistwomen.org

Executive Secretary for Leadership Development: **Tulloch, Julia R.**, 212/870-3769, jtulloch@unitedmethodistwomen.org

Executive Secretary for Membership: **Usher-Kerr, Marva D.**, 212/870-3738, musherke@unitedmethodistwomen.org

Executive Secretary for Organizational Development: **TBN**

Executive Secretary for Spiritual Growth: **TBN**

Seminar Designer: **McCallum, Jennifer**, 212/682-3633 x3119, jmccallum@unitedmethodistwomen.org

Seminar Designer: **Godfrey, Jay**, 212/682-3633 x3117, jgodfrey@unitedmethodistwomen.org

JustPeace
Center for Mediation and Conflict Transformation
www.justpeaceumc.org

OFFICERS
President: **Ward, Hope Morgan**
Vice President: **Jung, Hee-Soo**
Secretary: **Kraybill, Ron**
Treasurer: **Sharpe, Calvin**

BOARD
Bishops
Jung, Hee-Soo, 750 Windsor St. Ste. 303, Sun Prairie, WI 53590-2100, 606/837-8526 fax: 608/837-2081 cchuran@wisconsinumc.org
Ward, Hope Morgan, 700 Waterfield Ridge Pl., Garner, NC 27529-3365, 919/779-6115 fax: 919/773-2416, bishop@nccumc.org

Members
Albin, Tom, PO Box 340003, Nashville, TN 37203-0003, 615/340-7110, talbin@gbod.org
Christie, Neal, *Advisory,* 100 Maryland Ave., NE, Washington, DC 20002, 202/488-5611 fax: 202/488-5639, nchristie@umc-gbcs.org
Day-Lewis, Kimberly G. W., 2200 2nd St. SW Stop 7000 US Coast Guard, Washington, DC 20593, kdaylewis@daylewis.com
Purushotham, Gwen, PO Box 340007, Nashville, TN 37203-0007, 615/340-7573, gpurushotham@gbhem.org
Johnson, Susie, 100 Maryland Ave., NE, Ste. 530, Washington, DC 20002, 202/488-5660, johnsons@unitedmethodistwomen.org
Kraybill, Ron, 2628 Eversole Rd., Harrisonburg, VA 22802, 717/826-0224, rk@riverhouseepress.com
Mawokomatanda, Shandirai Wesley United Methodist Church 114 Main St. Worcester, MA 01608, 508/799-4191, pastorshandi@wesleyworc.org
McIntyre, Ingrid, 210 Morton Ave., Nashville, TN 37211, 615/340-7573, ingrid.mcintyre@gmail.com
Parrish, Craig, 2112 Third Ave., Ste. 300, Seattle, Washington 98121, 206/728-7462, cparrish@pnwumc.org

Commissions

Rettberg, Richard, *Advisory*, PO Box 340029, Nashville, TN 37203-0029, 615/369-2331 fax: 866/246-2516, rrettberg@gcfa.org
Sharpe, Calvin, 11075 East Blvd., Cleveland, OH 44106, 216/368-4905 fax: 216/368-6144, cws2@po.cwru.edu
Siemens, Stan, 348 N. Carroll Rd., Nixa, MO 65714, 417/725-1753, jastsiemens@aol.com
Stead, Jerre, 10040 E. Happy Valley Rd., #674, Scottsdale, AZ 85255, jerreMJ@aol.com
White, Mary, 312 Rockingham Rd., Rosemont, PA 19010, 610/519-9812, mwhite9891@aol.com
Wolf, Janet, 1512 Cedar Ln., Nashville, TN 37212, 615/256-1463, jlwolf@comcast.net

STAFF

100 Maryland Ave., NE, Rm. 216
Washington, DC 20002
202/488-5647, fax: 202/488-5639
justpeace@justpeaceumc.org
www.justpeaceumc.org

Executive Director: **Hixon, Stephanie Anna**, Main Office, sahixon@justpeaceumc.org
Resources and Administration: **Bray, Adam B.**, Main Office, abray@justpeaceumc.org
Staff Collective: **Gilliam, W. Craig**, cgilliam@justpeaceumc.org
Staff Collective: **Hooker, David Anderson**, 607 Terry St. SE, Atlanta, GA 30312, 404/226-2246, dahooker@justpeaceumc.org
Staff Collective: **Porter, Thomas W.**, 50 Dover Rd., Wellesley, MA 02482, 781/416-7044 fax: 781/416-0931, tporter@justpeaceumc.org

Conferences

Jurisdictional Officers in the U. S.

NORTH CENTRAL JURISDICTION
Secretary: **Wiblin, Maria D.**, 759 Clarke Dr., Dubuque, IA 52001, 563/564-8226, maria.wiblin@gmail.com, www.ncjumc.org

Areas and Annual Conferences
Chicago Area—**Dyck, Sally**
Northern Illinois Conference

Dakotas/Minnesota Area—**Ough, Bruce R.**
Dakotas Conference
Minnesota Conference

Illinois Area—**Keaton, Jonathan D.**
Illinois Great Rivers Conference

Indiana Area—**Coyner, Michael J.**
Indiana Conference

Iowa Area—**Trimble, Julius C.**
Iowa Conference

Michigan Area—**Kiesey, Deborah L.**
Detroit Conference
West Michigan Conferences

Ohio East Area—**Hopkins, John L.**
East Ohio Conference

Ohio West Area—**Palmer, Gregory V.**
West Ohio Conference Area

Wisconsin Area—**Jung, Hee-Soo**
Wisconsin Conference

NORTHEASTERN JURISDICTION
Secretary: **Daugherty, Ruth**, 1936 N. Eden Rd., Lancaster, PA 17601, 717/299-2203, rdaugherty@mycyberlink.net, www.nejumc.org/

Areas and Annual Conferences

Boston Area—**Devadhar, Sudarshana**
New England Conference

Harrisburg Area—**Park, Jeremiah J.**
Susquehanna Conference

New Jersey Area—**Schol, John R.**
Greater New Jersey Conference

New York Area—**McLee, Martin D.**
New York Conference

Philadelphia Area—**Johnson, Peggy A.**
Eastern Pennsylvania
Peninsula-Delaware Conferences

Pittsburgh Area—**Bickerton, Thomas J.**
Western Pennsylvania Conference

Upper New York Area—**Webb, Mark J.**
Upper New York Conference

Washington Area—**Matthews, Marcus**
Baltimore-Washington Conference West

West Virginia Area—**Steiner Ball, Sandra L.**
West Virginia Conference

SOUTH CENTRAL JURISDICTION

Director of Mission and Administration: **Severe, David L.**, 3160 W. Britton Rd. Ste. F, Oklahoma City, OK 73120-2037, scjdirector@scjumc.org, www.scjumportal.org/

Areas and Annual Conferences

Arkansas Area—**Mueller, Gary E.**
Arkansas Conference

Dallas Area—**McKee, Larry Michael**
North Texas Conference

Fort Worth Area—**Lowry, J. Michael**
Central Texas Conference

Great Plains Area—**Jones, Scott J.**
Kansas East Conference
Kansas West Conference
Nebraska Conference

Houston Area—**Huie, Janice Riggle**
Texas Conference

Louisiana Area—**Harvey, Cynthia Fierro**
Louisiana Conference

Missouri Area—**Schnase, Robert C.**
Missouri Conference

Northwest Texas /New Mexico Area—**Bledsoe, W. Earl**
New Mexico Conference
Northwest Texas Conference

Oklahoma Area—**Hayes, Robert E. Jr.**
Oklahoma Conference
Oklahoma Indian Missionary Conference

San Antonio Area—**Dorff, James E.**
Rio Grande Conference
Southwest Texas Conference

SOUTHEASTERN JURISDICTION
Secretary: **Travis, Anne S.**, PO Box 850, Alcoa, TN 37701-0850, toll-free: 866/690-4080, 865/690-4080, fax: 865/690-3162, annetravis@holston.org, www.sejumc.org/

Areas and Annual Conferences

Alabama /West Florida Area—**Leeland, Paul L.**
Alabama-West Florida Conference

Birmingham Area—**Wallace-Padgett, Debra**
North Alabama Conference

Charlotte Area—**Goodpaster, Larry M.**
Western North Carolina Conference

Columbia ABook of rea—**Holston, L. Jonathan**
South Carolina Conference

Florida Area—**Carter, Kenneth H. Jr.**
Florida Conference

Holston Area—**Taylor, Mary Virginia**
Holston Conference

Louisville Area—**Davis, G. Lindsey**
Kentucky Conference
Red Bird Missionary Conference

Mississippi Area—**Swanson, James E. Sr.**
Mississippi Conference

Nashville Area—**McAlilly, William T.**
Memphis Conference
Tennessee Conference

North Georgia Area—**Watson, B. Michael**
North Georgia Conference

Raleigh Area—**Ward, Hope Morgan**
North Carolina Conference

Richmond Area—**Cho, Young Jin**
Virginia Conference

South Georgia Area—**King, James R. Jr.**
South Georgia Conference

WESTERN JURISDICTION

Secretary: **Debree, Susan K.**, 2330 E. Broadway St., Helena, MT 59601-4956, 406/370-9953, su@yacumc.org, www.wjcumc.org/

Areas and Annual Conferences

Greater Northwest Area—**Hagiya, Grant J.**
Alaska Conference
Oregon-Idaho Conference
Pacific Northwest Conference

Los Angeles Area—**Carcaño, Minerva G.**
California-Pacific Conference

Mountain Sky Area—**Stanovsky, Elaine J. W.**
Rocky Mountain Conference
Yellowstone Conference

Phoenix Area—**Hoshibata, Robert T.**
Desert Southwest Conference

San Francisco Area—**Brown, Warner H. Jr.**
California-Nevada Conference

Annual Conferences in the U. S.

ALABAMA–WEST FLORIDA (SE, ALABAMA–WEST FLORIDA AREA)

100 Interstate Park Dr. Ste. 120
Montgomery, AL 36109-5488
888/873-3127, 334/356-8014, fax: 334/356-8029
awfcrc@awfumc.org
http://www.awfumc.org/

Episcopal Office

Bishop: **Leeland, Paul L.**, 334/277-1787, bishop.awf@knology.net
Administrative Assistant to the Resident Bishop: **Ard, Megyn**, 334/277-1787, megyn@awfumc.org

District Superintendents

Smith, Cory R., Baypines District, 866/670-5600, 251/580-2021, bpdist@bellsouth.net
Bonner, John H., Demopolis District, 334/289-0519, umcddoff@bellsouth.net
Morris, Daniel W., Dothan District, 334/792-4259, umcdothan@graceba.net
Daniel, Gary A., Marianna-Panama City District, 850/482-4905, office@mariannapcdistrict.org
Elmore, Tonya L., Mobile District, 251/345-3313, admin@mobileumc.com
Ball, Ronald T., Montgomery-Opelika District, 334/239-7329, mtopds@knology.net
McVay, Philip, E., Montgomery-Prattville District, 334/239-7329, mtptds@knology.net
Pridgeon, Jeremy Kimble, Pensacola District, 850/434-0118, office@umcpensacoladistrict.org

Officers and Leaders

Director of Connectional Ministries: **McDavid, Robert Neil**, 334/356-8014, neil@awfumc.org
Conference Lay Leader: **Furr, Steve**, 251/246-4446, furrs@bellsouth.net
Conference Treasurer: **Dunnewind, Frank**, 334/274-1051,
Conference Secretary: **Epler, Neil**
Conference Communications Director: **Phillips, Mary Catherine**, 334/356-8014, marycatherine@awfumc.org

ALASKA MISSIONARY (W, GREATER NORTHWEST AREA)

Greater Northwest Area (Alaska Missionary, Oregon-Idaho, Pacific Northwest)
1660 Patterson St.
Anchorage, AK, 99504
907/333-5050
umc@gci.net
www.alaskaumc.org

Episcopal Office

Bishop: **Hagiya, Grant J.**, 800/755-7710, bishop@pnwumc.org
Assistant to the Bishop: **Engle, Gretchen**, 1/800/755-7710, gengle@pnwumc.org
Office Administrator: **n/a**

District Superintendent

Beckett, David, Alaska, 907/333-5050, aumcdave@gmail.com

Officers and Leaders

Director of Connectional Ministries: **n/a**
Conference Lay Leader: **Brooks, Lonnie**, 907/333-4529, lonnieb@acsalaska.net
Conference Treasurer: **Parrish, Craig**, 800/755-7710, cparrish@pnwumc.org
Conference Secretary: **Erbele, Terence**, 907/225-2487, erbele@gmail.com
Conference Communications Director: **Doepken, Jim**, 907/224-7368, pastorjim@gmail.com

Publications

e~Aurora (weekly; http://alaskaumc.org/?page_id=435)

Foundation

United Methodist Foundation of the Northwest
Address: PO Box 656, Cashmere, WA 98815
800/488-4179
umfnw@nwi.net
www.nwumf.org
Director: **Wilson, Thomas B.**

ARKANSAS (SC, ARKANSAS AREA)

800 W. Daisy Bates Dr.
Little Rock, AR 72202

501/324-8000
info@arumc.org
www.arumc.org

Episcopal Office

Bishop: **Mueller, Gary E.**, 501/324-8019, bishop@arumc.org
Office Administrator: **Kuonen, Rose**, 501/324-8019, rkuonen@arumc.org

District Superintendents

Reeves, Bud, Northeast District, 870/793-5247, breeves@arumc.org
Roberts, Dede, Central District, 501/329-5141, droberts@arumc.org
Morey, Mike, Southwest District, 870/230-1118, mmorey@arumc.org,
Ledbetter, Susan, Southeast District, 870/367-3365, sledbetter@arumc.org,
TBD, Northwest District

Officers and Leaders

Executive Director of Mission and Ministry: **Yokem, Mackey** 479/783-0385, myokem@arumc.org (as of 7/1/2013)
Conference Lay Leader: **Mann, Karon**, 501/225-7971, kmann@arumc.org
Conference Treasurer: **Burris, Todd**, 501/324-8004, tburris@arumc.org
Conference Secretary: **Crossman, Bob**, 501/908-8177, bcrossman@arumc.org
Conference Center for Technology Director: **Epperson, Mark**, 501/324-8013, mepperson@arumc.org

Publications

Arkansas United Methodist (monthly; http://www.arumc.org/arkansas_united_methodist_newspaper.php)

Foundation

United Methodist Foundation of Arkansas
5300 Evergreen Dr., Little Rock, AR 72205
501/664-8632
jargue@umfa.org
www.umfa.org
Director: **Argue, James**

BALTIMORE-WASHINGTON (NE, WASHINGTON AREA)

11711 East Market Pl.
Fulton, MD 20759

410/309-3400
www.bwcumc.org

Episcopal Office

Bishop: **Matthews**, **Marcus**, 410/309-3400, x311, BishopMatthewsoffice@bwcumc.org
Assistant to the Bishop: **Mulenga**, **Maidstone**, 410/309-3420, mmulenga@bwcumc.org
Office Administrator: **King**, **Joyce**, 410/309-3400, x311, BishopMatthewsoffice@bwcumc.org

District Superintendents

Easto, **Laura**, Baltimore Suburban District, 410/309-3430, leasto@bwcumc.org
Moore, **Cynthia**, Baltimore Metropolitan District, 410/309-3435, cmoore@bwcumc.org
Daniels, **Joseph**, Greater Washington District, 410/309-3432, jdaniels@bwcumc.org
Park, **J.W.** , Central Maryland District, 410/309-3422, jpark@bwcumc.org
Rivera, **Edgardo**, Frederick District, 410/309-3436, erivera@bwcumc.org
Link, **Conrad**, Cumberland-Hagerstown District, 410/309-3444, clink@bwcumc.org
Young, **Evan**, Annapolis District, 410/3090-3439, eyoung@bwcumc.org
Iannicelli, **Rebecca**, Washington East District, 410/309-3472, riannicelli@bwcumc.org

Officers and Leaders

Director of Connectional Ministries: **Ferguson**, **Sandra**, 410/309-3431, sferguson@bwcumc.org
Conference Lay Leader: **Martin**, **Delores**, 410/647-0218, littleone_martin@verizon.net
Conference Treasurer: **Eichelberger**, **Paul**, 410/309-3424, peichelberger@bwcumc.org
Conference Secretary: **Sims**, **Mary Jo**, 410/848-2313, mjsims@deerparkumc.net
Conference Communications Director: **Lauber**, **Melissa**, 410/309-3455, mlauber@bwcumc.org

Publications

UMConnection, monthly, www.bwcumc.org
e-connection, weekly, www.bwcumc.org

Foundation

MidAtlantic United Methodist Foundation
11711 East Market Pl., Fulton, MD 20759
410/309-3475
jackbrooks.mafoundation@gmail.com
http://www.midatlanticfoundation.org
Director: **Brooks, Jack**

CALIFORNIA–NEVADA (W, SAN FRANCISCO AREA)

1276 Halyard Dr.
PO Box 980250
West Sacramento, CA 95798-0250
916/374-1500
comm@calnevumc.org
www.cncumc.org

Episcopal Office

Bishop: **Brown, Warner H. Jr.**, 916/374-1510, bishop@calnevumc.org
Assistant to the Bishop: **Roberson, Laura**, 916/374-1510 laurar@calnevumc.org

District Superintendents

Rhodes, Schuyler, Bridges, 916/374-1503, Bridges@calnevumc.org
Yoshino, Mariellen, Central Valley, 916/374-1501, CentralValley@calnevumc.org
Olah, Kristie L., El Camino Real, 916/374-1501, ElCaminoReal@calnevumc.org
Samelson, David, Great Northern, 916/374-1503, GreatNorthern@calnevumc.org

Officers and Leaders

Conference Superintendent for Mission Collaboration: **Caldwell, Linda**, 916/374-1517, lindac@calnevumc.org
Conference Superintendent for Leadership Development: **Berquist, Greg**, 916/374-1506, gregb@calnevumc.org
Conference Superintendent for Congregational Vitality: **Agtarap, Bener**, 916/374-1581, benera@calnevumc.org
Conference Co-Lay Leader: **Shearman, Gayle**, 415/506-4196, gsherman@comcast.net
Conference Co-Lay Leader: **Yin, Burt**, 510/582-4368, byin@sbcglobal.net
Conference Treasurer: **Knudsen, Diane**, 916/374-1520, dianek@calnevumc.org
Conference Secretary: **Sachen, Kristin**, 415/647-8393, ksachen329@gmail.com

Conference Communications Director: **Hygh, Larry R. Jr.**, 916/374-1529, larryh@calnevumc.org

Publications

Instant Connection (E-newsletter, weekly; http://www.cnumc.org/enewsletterarchives)

Foundation

California Nevada United Methodist Foundation
1276 Halyard Dr.
West Sacramento, CA 95691
888/789-7374
umf@canvumf.org
www.canvumf.org
Director: **Peters, Susan**

CALIFORNIA–PACIFIC (W, LOS ANGELES AREA)

110 S. Euclid Ave.
Pasadena, CA 91101
Mailing Address: PO Box 6006, Pasadena, CA 91102
800/244-8622, 626/568-7300, fax: 626.796-7297
gkeene@cal-pac.org
www.cal-pac.org

Episcopal Office

Bishop: **Carcaño, Minerva G.**, 626/568-7300 x312, bishopmc@cal-pac.org
Administrative Assistant: **Kendall, Gail**, 626/568-7300 x313, gkendall@cal-pac.org
Secretary: **David, Wes**, 626/568-7300 x312, wdavis@cal-pac.org

District Superintendents

Dang, Bau N., East District, calpaceastdistrict@gmail.com
Choi, Thomas S., Hawaii District, 808/536-1864, calpachawaiidistrict@gmail.com
Bridgeforth, Cedrick, North District, 818/882-8005, calpacnorthdistrict@gmail.com
Stevens, Willard R. "Buzz" (interim), South District, calpacsouthdistrict@gmail.com
Wilborn, Kathey Michelle, West District, 562/429-1441, calpacwestdistrict@gmail.com

Officers and Leaders

Executive Director of Connectional Ministries (interim): **Keene, Gary**, 626/568-7314, gkeene@cal-pac.org
Conference Co-Secretary: **Lewis, Dan**, secretary@cal-pac.org
Conference Co-Secretary: **Nakanishi, Leanne**, secretary@cal-pac.org

CENTRAL TEXAS (SC, FORTH WORTH AREA)

464 Bailey Ave.
Fort Worth, TX 76107-2153
800/460-8622, 817/877-5222, fax: 817/338-4541
randy@ctcumc.org
www.ctcumc.org

Episcopal Office

Bishop: **Lowery, J. Michael**, 817/877-5222 x41, bishop@ctcumc.org
Executive Director and Assistant to the Bishop: **Adamson, Georgia**, 817/877-5222 x39, Georgia@ctcumc.org
Executive Secretary: **Wood, Pattie**, 817/877-5222 x36, pattie@ctcumc.org

District Superintendents

Scott, Donald F., Central District, 254/776-8740, centraldistrict@ctcumc.org
Holloway, Robert W., East District, 817/451-7796, eastdistrict@ctcumc.org
Lindley, Gary A., New Church Start District, 817/877-5222, newchurchstart@ctcumc.org
Bassford, Virginia O., North District, 817/599-9541, northdistrict@ctcumc.org
Koch, Rankin H., South District, 254/773-2481, southdistrict@ctcumc.org
Woods, Carol, West District, 254/965-2594, westdistrict@ctcumc.org

Officers and Leaders

Conference Lay Leader: **Simpson, Kim**, kimsimpson1@tx.rr.com
Conference Treasurer: **Stinson, David**, 817/877-5222 x12
Conference Communications Director: **Morton, J. Vance**, 871/877-5222 x34, vance@ctcumc.org

DAKOTAS (NC, DAKOTAS–MINNESOTA AREA)

1331 W. University St.
Mitchell, SD 57301
605/996-6552, fax: 605/996-1766

greg.kroger@dakotasumc.org
http://www.dakotasumc.org/

Episcopal Office

Bishop: **Ough, Bruce R**, 612/870-4007, bishop@dkmnareaumc.org
Administrative Assistant: **Kyburz, Sheilah**, sheilah.kyburz@dkmnarea.org

District Superintendents

Spurrell, Marilyn, Eastern Sunrise District, 701/364-1941, marilyn.spurrell@dakotasumc.org
Caudill, Roy, Glacial Lakes District, 605/334-5248, roy.caudill@dakotasumc.org
Cross, Randolph M., Prairie Hills District, 605/343-3172, randy.cross@dakotasumc.org
Nelson, Keith F., Sakakawea District, 701/255-0800, keith.nelson@dakotasumc.org

Officers and Leaders

Director of Ministries: **Kroger, Greg**, 605/996-6552, greg.kroger@dakotasumc.org
Conference Treasurer: **Pospisil, Jeff**, jeff.pospisil@dakotasumc.org
Communications Director: **Gosmire, Doreen**, doreen.gosmire@dakotasumc.org

Foundation

Dakotas United Methodist Foundation
1331 W. University Ave.
Mitchell, SC 57301
605/996-1766bblumer@dakotasumf.org
http://www.dakotasumf.org/
Director: **Blumer, Bruce**

DESERT SOUTHWEST (W, PHOENIX AREA)

1550 E. Meadowbrook Ave.
Phoenix, AZ 85014-4040
602/266-6956, 800/229-8622
communications@desertsw.org
desertsouthwestconference.org

Episcopal Office

Bishop: **Hoshibata, Robert T.**, 602/266-6956, Bishop@desertsw.org
Assistant to the Bishop: **O'Neil, Julie**, 602/266-6956, Julie@desertsw.org

District Superintendents

Lansberry, Candace, North District, 702/369-7055, Candace@desertsw.org
Vannoy, Karen, South District, 520/325-2775, Karen@desertsw.org
Burns, Robert, Central East District, 480/854-1217, Robert@desertsw.org
Kennedy, Gary, Central West District, 623/977-0701, Gary@desertsw.org

Officers and Leaders

Director of Connectional Ministries: **McPherson, David**, 602/266-6956, DaveM@desertsw.org
Conference Lay Leader: **Nibbelink, Jim**, 520/818-6766, jnibbelink@msn.com
Conference Treasurer: **Bowman, Randy**, 602/266-6956, Randy@desertsw.org
Conference Secretary: **Lyon, Louie**, 623/974-5821, Louie@desertsw.org
Conference Communications Director: **Hustedt, Steve**, 602/266-6956, Steve@desertsw.org

Publications

Transformation Ministry Magazine (quarterly)
Our Conference Bulletin (monthly)
The Desert Connection (bi-monthly)

Foundation

Desert Southwest United Methodist Foundation
1550 E. Meadowbrook Ave.
Phoenix, AZ 85014-4040
602/266-6956 x202
Lucille@desertsw.org
dsumf.org
Director: **Sterling, Lucille**

DETROIT (NC, MICHIGAN AREA)

1309 N. Ballenger Hwy., Ste. 1
Flint, MI 48504
810/233-5500
conferenceoffice@detroitconference.org
www.detroitconference.org

Episcopal Office

Bishop: **Kiesey, Deborah L.**, 517/347-4030, bishopsoffice@miareaumc.org
Assistant to the Bishop: **Dobbs, William D.**, 517/347-4030, bdobbs@miareaumc.org
Office Administrator: **Nelson, Deana**, 517/347-4030, dnelson@miareaumc.org

District Superintendents

Spaw, **Mark**, Ann Arbor District, 734/663-3939, aadisumc@sbcglobal.net
Bartelt, **Joanne**, Blue Water District, 810/385-8840, bluewaterdist@gmail.com,
Sutton, **Tara**, Crossroads District, 810/233-5500, crossroadsdistumc@gmail.com
Carey, **Melanie**, Detroit Reniassance District, 313/638-2390, drds@
    detroitconference.org
Dulworth, **Elbert**, Marquette District, 906/228-4644, umc@mqtdistrict.com
Maxwell, **Jeffrey**, Saginaw Bay District, 989/793-8838, sagbaydist@aol.com

Officers and Leaders

Director of Connectional Ministries: **DeVine**, **Jerome**, 810/233-5500, jdevine@
    detroitconference.org
Conference Lay Leader: **Bank**, **Wayne**, 810/359-7281, waynebank@sbcglobal.net
Conference Treasurer: **Dobbs**, **David**, 810/233-5500, ddobbs@
    detroitconference.org
Conference Secretary: **Huffman**, **Tracy**, 734/663-4164, revtracyhuffman@
    westside-umc.org
Conference Communications Director: **TBD**

Publications

Michigan Area Reporter (monthly)

Foundation

United Methodist Foundation of Michigan
Address: PO Box 6247, Grand Rapids, MI 49516
888/451-1929
www.umfmichigan.org
Director: **Bell**, **David**

EAST OHIO (NC, EAST OHIO AREA)

8800 Cleveland Ave. NW, North Canton, OH 44720
PO Box 2800
North Canton, marian@umfmichigan.org marian@umfmichigan.org, OH 44720
800/831-3972
www.eocumc.com

Episcopal Office

Bishop: **Hopkins**, **John L.**, 800/831-3972 x112
Assistant to the Bishop: **George**, **Gary**, 800/831-3972 x112
Office Administrator: **Eshleman**, **Julie**, 800/831-3972 x112, julie@eocumc.com

District Superintendents

Stultz, Valerie, Canal District, 330/252-0299, canaldistrictumc@neo.rr.com
Claycomb, Judy Wismar, Firelands District, 419/668-6115, firelandsdist@rrbiznet.com
Bryant, Dan C., Mahoning Valley District, 330/270-3400, mvdistumc@aol.com
Oehl, Karen, Mid-Ohio District, 419/522-3881, midohiodistumc@aol.com
Streiff, Peggy, North Coast District, 216/441-4527, northcoastdistrict@gmail.com
Winkler, James, Ohio Valley District, 740/264-1601, ovoffice@ovdumc.com
Court, Steven, Southern Hills District, 740/255-5691, office@shillsumc.com
Humphrey, James, Three Rivers District, 740/622-8880, 3riversdist@sbcglobal.com
Rollins, Benita, Tuscarawas District, 330/492-7817, tuscoffice@rrbiznet.com
Scavuzzo, David, Western Reserve District, 440/352-2083, jerri@wrdistrict.org

Officers and Leaders

Director of Connectional Ministries: **White, Paul**, 800/831-3972 x136, paulw@eocumc.com
Conference Lay Leader: **Rentsch, Greg**, 440/243-6526, gregrentsch@gmail.com
Conference Treasurer: **Vargo, Jessica**, 800/831-3972 x123, vargoj@eocumc.com
Conference Secretary: **Patterson, Cynthia**, 330/929-0015
Conference Communications Director: **Wolcott, Richard**, 800/831-3972 x118, wolcott@eocumc.com

Publications

Joining Hands, quarterly
Conference E-news, twice monthly

Foundation

East Ohio United Methodist Foundation
8800 Cleveland Ave. NW, North Canton, OH 44720
800/831-3972 x152
brian@eoumf.org
www.eastohiounitedmethodistfoundation.org
Director: **Sheetz, Brian**

Eastern Pennsylvania (NE, Philadelphia Area)

980 Madison Ave.
Norristown, PA 19403

Mailing Address: PO Box 820, Valley Forge, PA 19482-0820
800/828-9093, 610/666-9090, fax: 610/666-9093
skeenan@epaumc.org
http://www.epaumc.org/

Episcopal Office

Bishop: **Johnson, Peggy A.**, 610/666-1442, pjohnson@epaumc.org
Executive Secretary: **Botti, Amy**, 610/666-1442, abotti@epaumc.org

District Superintendents

Powell, Anita Adams, Central District, 215/878-4607, ddalton@epaumc.org
Tatem, Dorothy Watson, East District, 215/914-2130, clarita.krall@epaumc.org
Cotto, Irving, Northeast District, 610/395-6661, nesuper@rcn.com
Nicholson, Gary L., Northwest District, 570/624-1471, christine.eddy@epaumc.org
Haugh, Thomas C., Southeast District, 610/436-4277, lin.george@epaumc.org
Todd, James B., Southwest District, 717/569-2038, swdistrict@comcast.net

Officers and Leaders

Director of Connectional Ministries: **Kurien, Christopher Jacob**, 484/762-8230, ckurien@epaumc.org
Conference Lay Leader: **White, Mary**, 215/236-0304, mwhite9891@aol.com
Conference Treasurer: **Dinofia, Peter T.**, 484/762-8209, pdinofia@epaumc.org
Conference Communications Director: **Keenan, Suzy**, 484/762-8227, skeenan@epaumc.org

Foundation

MidAtlantic United Methodist Foundation
484/762-8247
jbrooks@epaumc.org
Director: **Brooks, Jack**

FLORIDA (SE, FLORIDA AREA)

450 Martin Luther King, Jr. Ave.
Lakeland, Florida 33815-1522
863/688-5563
www.flumc.org

Episcopal Office

Bishop: **Carter, Kenneth H. Jr.**, 863/688-4427, bishop@flumc.org
Assistant to the Bishop: **Dodge, David**, 863/688-4427, ddodge@flumc.org
Office Administrator: **Proferes, Joanna**, 863/688-5563, jproferes@flumc.org

District Superintendents

Spencer, Gary, Atlantic Central, 772/299-0255, DS-AC@flumc.org, www.acdistrictumc.org
Pendergrass, Annette, East Central, 407/896-2230, DS-EC@flumc.org, www.ecdistrictumc.org
Powers, John, Gulf Central, 727/585-1207, DS-GC@flumc.org, www.gcdistrictumc.org
Haupert-Johnson, Sue, North Central, 352/376-6353, DS-NC@flumc.org
Smiley, Tim, North East, 904/396-3026, DS-NE@flumc.org
Gibbs, Robert, North West, 850/386-2154, DS-NW@flumc.org, www.nwdfl.org
Monroe, Walter, South Central, 813/719-7270, DS-SC@flumc.org, www.flumc-scdist.org
Nelson, Craig, South East, 305/445-9136, DS-SE@flumc.org, www.flsedistrictumc.com
Hernandez, Rini, South West, 941/371-6511, flumc-sw@flumc.org

Officers and Leaders

Director of Connectional Ministries: **Austin, Sharon G.**, 863/688-5563, sharon.austin@flumc.org
Conference Lay Leader: **Graves, Russ**, 321/722-3660, russ.graves@flumc.org
Conference Treasurer: **Wilson, Milton "Mickey,"** 863/688-5563, mwilson@flumc.org
Conference Secretary: **Minton, Kenneth**, 813/782-1933, kminton@flumc.org
Conference Communications Director: **Hastings, Gretchen**, 863/688-5563, ghastings@flumc.org

Publications

Annual Conference Journal (annual, www.floridaconferenceconnnection.info

Foundation

The Florida United Methodist Foundation, Inc.
Address: PO Box 3549, Lakeland, Florida, 33802-3549
863/904-2970
Foundation@fumf.org

Conferences

www.fumf.org
Director: **Tan, Wee-Li**

GREATER NEW JERSEY (NE, NEW JERSEY AREA)

1001 Wickapecko Dr.
Ocean, NJ 07712
732/359-1000 or 877/677-2594
communications@gnjumc.org
www.gnjumc.org

Episcopal Office

Bishop: **Schol, John R.** , 732/359-1010, BishopJohnSchol@gnjumc.org
Episcopal Associate: **Bender, Charles**, 877/677-2594 x1052, Cbender@gnjumc.org
Administrative Assistant to the Bishop: **Mulligan, Nicola**, 732/359-1010, nmulligan@gnjumc.org

District Superintendents

Maliel, Paul, Cape Atlantic
Wright, Varlyna D., Capital
Nichols, Richard, Delaware Bay
Kwak, Jisun, Gateway North
Costello, Robert E., Gateway South
Noll, Fran Lawrie, Northern Shore
Plumbstead, Wayne J., Palisades
Rambach, Barbara, Raritan Valley
Bechtold, Steve G., Skylands

Officers and Leaders

Director of Connectional Ministries: **Ahn, Sung Hoon**
Conference Lay Leader: **Williams, Rosa**, 201/833-0352, rosamw@optonline.netl
Conference Treasurer: **Cardillo, John**, 732/359-1030, Treasurer2gnjumc.org
Conference Secretary: **Wiley, David E. III**, 973/464-9298, conferencesecretary@gnjumc.org
Conference Communications Director: TBD
Conference Media Specialist: **Fullerton, Heather**, 732/359-1020, hfullerton@gnjumc.org

Publications

GNJ Digest, weekly newsletter

The 2013–2016 United Methodist Directory

Greater Northwest Area *(see Alaska, Oregon–Idaho, Pacific Northwest)*

Great Plains Area *(see Kansas East, Kansas West, Nebraska)*

HOLSTON (SE, HOLSTON AREA)

217 S. Rankin Rd.
PO Box 850
Alcoa, TN 37701
865/690-4080, 866/690-4080 (toll-free)
Info@holston.org
www.holston.org

Episcopal Office

Bishop: **Taylor**, **Mary Virginia**, 865/293-4146, Bishop@holston.org
Executive Assistant to the Bishop: **Wilson**, **Carol E.**, 865/293-4145, CarolWilson@holston.org
Executive Secretary to the Bishop: **Sluder**, **Lori L.**, 865/293-4146, LoriSluder@holston.org

District Superintendents

Johnson, **Sandra G.**, Abingdon District, 276/628-4421, SandraJohnson@holston.org
Coppedge, **Archer I.**, Big Stone Gap District, 276/523-3025, ArcherCoppedge@holston.org
Hubble, **R. Michael**, Chattanooga District, 423/629-0333, MikeHubble@holston.org
Green, **Joseph S.**, Cleveland District, 423/476-8221, JoeGreen@holston.org
Weikel, **Walter P.**, Johnson City District, 423/926-7533, WalterWeikel@holston.org
Graves, **David W.**, Kingsport District, 423/224-1533, DavidGraves@holston.org
Malone, **Nathan A.**, Knoxville District, 865/470-7005, NathanMalone@holston.org
Maynard, **Charles W.**, Maryville District, 865/982-1427, CharlesMaynard@holston.org
Ballard, **Thomas T.**, Morristown District, 423/586-2942, TomBallard@holston.org
McKee, **Adam III**, Oak Ridge District, 865/482-3209, AdamMcKee@holston.org
Tabor, **J. David**, Tazewell District, 276/988-4891, DavidTabor@holston.org
Taylor, **Meg**, Wytheville District, 276/228-4922, MegTaylor@holston.org

Officers and Leaders

Director of Connectional Ministries: **Travis, Anne S.**, 865/690-4080, AnneTravis@holston.org
Conference Lay Leader: Holley, **James D. "Del,"** 865/215-2515, delholley@auburnalum.org
Conference Treasurer: **Cherry, F. Richard**, 865/609-4080, RickCherry@holston.org
Conference Secretary: **Taylor, Daniel H. Jr.**, 865/690-4080, DanielTaylor@holston.org
Conference Communications Director: **Wilson, Carol E.**, 865/293-4145, CarolWilson@holston.org

Publications

The Call electronic, 2x/mo)

Foundation

Holston Conference Foundation
217 S. Rankin Rd.
PO Box 900
Alcoa, TN 37701
Director: **Redding, Roger**, RogerRedding@holston.org
http://www.holston.org/about/agencies-institutions/holston

ILLINOIS GREAT RIVERS (NC, ILLINOIS GREAT RIVERS AREA)

5900 S. 2nd St.
Springfield, IL 62711
PO Box 19207, Springfield, IL 62794-9207
217/529-2040, fax: 217/529-4131
info@igrc.org
http://www.igrc.org/

Episcopal Office

Bishop: **Keaton, Jonathan D.**, 217/529-3820, bishop@igrc.org
Executive Assistant to the Bishop: **Griffith, Janice**, 217/529-3820, jgriffith@igrc.org
Administrative Assistant to the Bishop: **Hammitt, Michelle**, 217/529-3351, mhammitt@igrc.org
Area Office Receptionist: **Schultz, Karen**, 217/529-3820, kschultz@igrc.org

District Superintendents

Russell, Roger W., Cache River District, 618/998-0135, CacheRiver@igrc.org
Reese, Randall W., Embarras River District, 217/347-3915, EmbarrasRiver@igrc.org
Harry, Daniel P., Illinois River District, 309/692-0421, IllinoisRiver@igrc.org
Hwang, In-sook, Iroquois River District, 217/359-0640, IroquoisRiver@igrc.org
Jones, Cynthia A., Kaskaskia River District, 618/242-2817, KaskaskiaRiver@igrc.org
Rorex, C. Douglas, La Moine River District, 217/245-9946, LaMoineRiver@igrc.org
Wilson, Gary J., Mississippi River District, 618/622-3072, MississippiRiver@igrc.org
Harter, Terry P., Sangamon River District, 217/529-3257, sangamonriver@igrc.org
Weatherall, Sylvester, Spoon River District, 309/344-1435, spoonriver@igrc.org
Pogemiller, Leah R., Vermilion River District, 815/844-3530, VermilionRiver@igrc.org

Officers and Leaders

Director of Connectional Ministries: **Lolling, Kent**, 217/529-2442, klolling@igrc.org
Associate Conference Lay Leader: **Graham, Jeff**, jeff_w_graham@yahoo.com
Conference Treasurer: **van Giesen, Richard**, 217/529-2132, rvangiesen@igrc.org
Conference Communications Director: **Black, Paul**, 217/529-2824, pblack@igrc.org

Foundation

United Methodist Foundation of the Illinois Great Rivers Annual Conference, Inc.
PO Box 3487
Springfield, IL 62708-3487
217/529-3217
tfrost@igrc.org
Director: **Frost, Ted**

INDIANA (NC, INDIANA AREA)

301 Pennsylvania Pkwy., Ste 300
Indianapolis, IN 46280-1396
317/924-1321, fax: 317/735-4228
questions@inumc.org
www.inumc.org

Episcopal Office

Bishop: **Coyner, Michael J.**, bishop@inumc.org
Executive Assistant to the Bishop: **Owen, David**, davidvw.owen@inumc.org
Secretary to the Bishop: **Metzler, Edward**, ed.metzler@inumc.org

District Superintendents

Kite, Marion L. III, Central District, 877/791-6707, 317/924-4140, central.district@inumc.org
Byrum, David M., East District, 877/781-6708, 765/282-2322, east.district@inumc.org
Cobb, Michelle A., North Central District, 877/781-6710, 765/319-3704, northcentral.district@inumc.org
Reynolds, Cynthia J., North District, 877/781-6709, 219/575-6235, north.district@inumc.org
Michel, David A., Northeast District, 877/781-6711, 260/482-8494, northeast.district@inumc.org
Lasuer, Craig David, Northwest District, 877/781-6712, 765/807-5619, northwest.district@inumc.org
Wilfong, Charles D., South District, 877/781-6713, south.district@inumc.org
White, Brian Keith, Southeast District, 877/781-6714, 812/418-0950, southeast.district@inumc.org
Purnell, George Anthony, Southwest District, 877/781-6715, southwest.district@inumc.org
Groves, John F., West District, 877/781-6716, 765/276-4797, west.district@inumc.org

Officers and Leaders

Director of Connectional Ministries: **Bushfield, James C.**, jim.bushfield@inumc.org
Co-Conference Lay Leader: **Williams, Ike**, 316/843-9259, ike.williams@att.net
Co-Conference Lay Leader: **Mykrantz, Kayc**, 574/753-7078, kayc@crosswindministries.net
Conference Treasurer: **Gallagher, Jennifer**, jennifer.gallagher@inumc.org
Conference Communications Director: **Gangler, Dan**, dan.gangler@inumc.org

Foundation

United Methodist Foundation of Indiana, Inc.
8401 Fishers Center Dr.
Fishers, IN 46038
317/788-7879, 877/391-8811
foundation@UMFIndiana.org
http://umfindiana.org/
President: **Shettle, Manet**

Iowa (NC, Iowa Area)

2301 Rittenhouse St.
Des Moines, IA 40321-3101
515/283-1991, fax: 515/288-1906
communications@iaumc.org
http://www.iaumc.org/

Episcopal Office

Bishop: **Trimble, Julius C.**, 515/974-8902, dkbrockmeyer@iaumc.org
Assistant to the Bishop for Administration: **Burkhart, J. Robert**, 515/974-8903, bob.burkhart@iaumc.org
Assistant to the Bishop for Connectional Ministries: **Dungan, Karen**, 515/974-8915, karen.dungan@iaumc.org
Executive Secretary to Bishop Trimble: **Brockmeyer, Diane**, 515/974-8902, dkbrockmeyer@iaumc.org

District Superintendents

Weesner, David A., Central District, 515/967-7639, Wendy.Lubkeman@iaumc.org
Crow, David W., East Central District, 319/365-6273, Ann.Zeal@iaumc.org
Tevis, Dennis G., North Central District, 515/832-2784, Alanna.Warren@iaumc.org
Bradford, Jacki L., Northeast District, 319/268-7502, Janet.Condon@iaumc.org
Carver, Thomas L., Northwest District, 712/732-0812, Judi.Calhoon@iaumc.org
Poland, William W., South Central District, 641/342-1644, Sue.Booth@iaumc.org
Gallo-Seagren, Lilian, Southeast District, 319/986-2095, Jean.Carpenter@iaumc.org
Milford, Brian K., Southwest District, 712/243-8573, Shirley.Lewis@iaumc.org

Officers and Leaders

Conference Lay Leader: **Decker, Dave**, 641/494-7663, david.decker@iaumc.org
Conference Treasurer: **Weber, Todd**, 515/974-8919, todd.weber@iaumc.org
Conference Secretary: **LaGree, Patty**, 515/974-8939, patty.lagree@iaumc.org
Conference Communications Director: **McClanahan, Arthur**, 515/974-8906, amcclanahan@iaumc.org

Foundation

Iowa United Methodist Foundation
2301 Rittenhouse St.
Des Moines, IA 50321
515/974-8927

kevin.gowdy@iumf.org
http://iumf.org/
Director: **Gowdy**, **Kevin**

Kansas East (SC, Great Plains Area)
PO Box 4187
Topeka, KS 66604-0187
785/272-9111
office@kansaseast.org
http://www.kansaseast.org

Episcopal Office
Bishop: **Jones**, **Scott J.**, 316/686-0600, bishop@greatplainsumc.org
Assistant to the Bishop: **Beach**, **Gary**, 785/272-9111, gbeach@kansaseast.org
Office Administrator: **Browning**, **Leslie Ann**, 316/686-0600, labrowning@greatplainsumc.org

District Superintendents
Ackerman, **Dennis**, Five Rivers District, 785/841-4804, ds@5riversds.com
Bakely, **Claudia** (as of 7/1/13), Flint Hills District, 785/776-7730, cbakely@kansaseast.org
Chamberlain, **Mike**, Kansas City District, 913/722-4775, ds@kcdistrictumc.org
Kim, **Kibum**, Parsons District, 620/421-9149, kkim@kansaseast.org
Scarbrough, **Kay**, Topeka District, 877/972-9111, kscarbrough@kansaseast.org

Officers and Leaders
Director of Connectional Ministries: **Fisher**, **Evelyn**, 316/684-0266, efisher@kansaseast.org
Conference Lay Leader: **Green**, **Oliver**, 785/273-5593, oliverdeck@aol.com
Conference Treasurer: **Beach**, **Gary**, 785/272-9111, gbeach@kansaseast.org
Conference Secretary: **Robertson**, **Karen**, 785/272-9111, confsec@kansaseast.org
Conference Communications Director: **Diehl**, **Lisa Elliot**, 316/684-0266, ldiehl@kswestumc.org

Publications
Communique (e-newsletter, weekly; www.kansaseast.org/enewsletters)

Foundation
Kansas Area United Methodist Foundation, Inc.
PO Box 605

Hutchinson, KS 67504-0605
620/664-9623
foundation@kaumf.org
www.kaumf.org
Director: **Childs, Steven**

KANSAS WEST (SC, GREAT PLAINS AREA)

9440 E. Boston St., Ste. 110
Wichita, KS 67207
316/684-0266
info@kswestumc.org
http://www.kswestumc.org/

Episcopal Office

Bishop: **Jones, Scott J.**, 316/686-0600, bishop@greatplainsumc.org
Assistant to the Bishop: **Beach, Gary**, 316/686-0600, gbeach@kswestumc.org
Office Administrator: **Browning, Leslie Ann**, 316/686-0600, labrowning@greatplainsumc.org

District Superintendents

Hasty, Don (as of 7/1/2013), Dodge City District, 620/227-2077, dhasty@kswestumc.org
Clayton, Max, Hays District, 785/628-8188, mclayton@kswestumc.org
Livingston, Dennis, Hutchinson District, 620/669-0011, dlivingston@kswestumc.org
Van der Wege, Lew, Salina District, 785/827-5541 x1190, lvanderwege@kswestumc.org
Brooks, Gary, Wichita East District, 316/684-6652, gbrooks@kswestumc.org
Louderback, Linda, Wichita West District, 316/684-6652, llouderback@kswestumc.org

Officers and Leaders

Director of Connectional Ministries: **Fisher, Evelyn**, 316/684-0266, efisher@kswestumc.org
Conference Lay Leader: **May, Carolyn**, 785/443-1223, carolyncollinsmay@yahoo.com
Conference Treasurer: **Beach, Gary**, 316/684-0266, gbeach@kswestumc.org
Conference Secretary: **Dickerson-Oard, Kim**, 316/682-6518, kim@ehumc.org
Conference Communications Director: **Diehl, Lisa Elliot**, 316/684-0266, ldiehl@kswestumc.org

Publications

Kansas West Connection (newspaper, will cease production in December 2013 when Kansas West, Kansas East and Nebraska join to form the Great Plains Annual Conference]
Weekly Update (e-newsletter, weekly, www.kswestumc.org/enewsletters)

Foundation

Kansas Area United Methodist Foundation, Inc.
Address: PO Box 605, Hutchinson, KS 67504-0605
620/664-9623
foundation@kaumf.org
www.kaumf.org
Director: **Childs, Steven**

KENTUCKY (SE, LOUISVILLE AREA)

7400 Floydsburg Rd.
Crestwood, KY 40014-8202
800/530-7236, 502/425-3884, fax: 502/426-5181
jlove@kyumc.org
http://www.kyumc.org/

Episcopal Office

Bishop: **Davis, Lindsey**, 502/425-4240, bishop@kyumc.org
Assistant to the Bishop: **Curry, Rebecca S.**, 502/425-4240, bcurry@kyumc.org
Executive Assistant to the Bishop: **Calvert, Diana**, 502/425-3884, dcalvert@kyumc.org
Episcopal Receptionist: **Starkey, Jill**, 502/425-3884, jstarkey@kyumc.org

District Superintendents

Pillow, C. Gene, Ashland District, 606/836-1095, ashlanddistrict@zoominternet.net
Chapman, Gary A., Bowling Green District, 270/842-5075, bgdist@insightbb.com
Love, Todd B., Columbia District, 270/384-8582, jlmurrell@windstream.net
Stuart, Farley E. III, Corbin District, 606/523-0211, cdist12@newwavecomm.net
Dolin, Owen L., Covington District, 859/442-5444, covdistumc@fuse.net
Brunstetter, J. Paul, Elizabethtown District, 270/769-0453, etowndist@bbtel.com
Hawxhurst, Jean G., Frankfort District, 502/875-2607, jhawxhurst@kyumc.org
Coy, Randall A., 859/299-6260 x107, jwells@lexumc.com

Curry, Rebecca S., 502/425-4240, Louisville@kyumc.org
Smith, Jay Franklin, Madisonville District, mvilledistumc@bellsouth.net
Gibbons, Mark A., Owensboro District, 270/684-3349, odsdcarden@bellsouth.net
Douglas, Charles H., 606/889-0126, prdst@bellsouth.net

Officers and Leaders

Director of Connectional Ministries: **Love, Julie**, 502/425-3884, jlove@kyumc.org
Conference Lay Leader: **Nicholls, Lewis**, lewandbarb@gmail.com
Conference Secretary: **Love, Julie**, 502/425-3884, jlove@kyumc.org
Associate Director of Connectional Ministries for Communications: **Bruce, Cathy**, 502/425-3884, cbruce@kyumc.org

Foundation

Kentucky United Methodist Foundation
921 Beasley St., Ste. 150
Lexington, KY 40509
888/841-7935, 859/977-0400
dbowles@kyumc.org
Director: **Bowles, David**

LOUISIANA (SC, LOUISIANA AREA)

527 North Blvd.
Baton Rouge, LA 70802
225/346-1646
lcumc@bellsouth.net
www.la-umc.org

Episcopal Office

Bishop: **Harvey, Cynthia Fierro**, 225/346-1646, enixmore@bellsouth.net
Assistant to the Bishop: **Moore, Kathy**, 225/346-1646, enixmore@bellsouth.net

District Superintendents

Boyd, Edward, Acadiana, 337/235-2904, acadumc@cox-internet.com
Stinson, Van, Baton Rouge, 225/293-8868, brdistrict@brdistrict.org
Alston, Ellen R., Monroe, 318/387-7364, monroesecretary@bellsouth.net
Edwards, Hadley, New Orleans, 504/835-6330, noladistrict@bellsouth.net
Avery, Donald, Shreveport, 318/869-5729, dravery@hotmail.com
Spurlock, Steven, Lake Charles, 337/439-2982, lcdistrict@lcdumc.com

Officers and Leaders

Director of Connectional Ministries: **Cottrill, Don**, 225/346-1646, DonCottrill@la-umc.org
Conference Lay Leader: **Dove, Carolyn**, 225/931-1666, catdove@soft-spec.com
Conference Treasurer: **Ford, Ralph**, 225/346-1646, RalphFord@la-umc.org
Conference Secretary: **Ford, Ralph**, 225/346-1646, RalphFord@la-umc.org
Conference Communications Director: **Backstrom, Betty**, 225/346-1646, bettybackstrom@la-umc.org

Publications

Louisiana Now! (print, monthly)
Louisiana Now! (e-version, bi-monthly)

Foundation

United Methodist Foundation of Louisiana
8337 Jefferson Highway, Baton Rouge, LA 70809
225/346-1535
information@umf.org
www.umf.org
Director: **Fairly, Robert C. Jr.**

Louisville Area (see Kentucky, Red Bird Missionary)

MEMPHIS (SE, NASHVILLE AREA)

24 Corporate Blvd.
Jackson, TN 38305-2315
731/664-8480, fax: 731/660-5712
communications.mcumc@eplus.net
www.memphis-umc.net

Episcopal Office

Bishop: **McAlilly, William T.**, 615/742-8834, bishop@nashareaumc.org
Assistant to the Bishop: **Hopson, Roger**, roger@nashareaumc.org
Administrative Assistant: **Crew, Gay**, gcrew@nasharea.org

District Superintendents

Clay, Sandra L., Asbury District, 901/590-4820, tcarroll@asburydistrictumc.org
Nation, Harrell A. Jr., Brownsville District, 731/772-9882, bvilledist01@gmail.com

Cavitt, J. Steven, Dyersburg District, 731/285-1066, ddumcds@ecsis.net
Clark, Richard W., Jackson District, 731/660-1376, jaxdist01@gmail.com
David, Cynthia D., McKendree District, 901/590-3588, dspencer@mckendreedistrict.org
McCracken, Sky J., Paducah District, 270/442-0077, padumc@comcast.net
Geary, Joseph A., Paris District, 731/642-9215, parisdist@bellsouth.net

Officers and Leaders

Director of Connectional Ministries: **Bonson, John**, 731/664-8480, director.mcumc@eplus.net
Conference Lay Leader: **Campbell, Gerry**, 731/217-9314, gcampbell@cityofjackson.net
Conference Treasurer: **Finger, James**, 731/664-5540, treasurerm@bellsouth.net
Conference Secretary: **Russell, David**, brodavid53@yahoo.com
Conference Communications Director: **Camp, Lane Gardner**, 731/664-8480, communications.mcumc@eplus.net

Foundation

United Methodist Foundation for the Memphis and Tennessee Conferences
304 S. Perimeter Park Dr., Ste. 3
Nashville, TN 37211
615/259-2008
vwalkup@umfmtc.org
http://www.umfmtc.org/
Director: **Walkup, Vincent**

Michigan Area (see Detroit, West Michigan)

MINNESOTA (NC, DAKOTAS–MINNESOTA AREA)

122 W. Franklin Ave., Ste. 400
Minneapolis, MN 55404
612/870-0058
communications@minnesotaumc.org
www.minnesotaumc.org

Episcopal Office

Bishop: **Ough, Bruce R.**, 612/230-3334, bishop@dkmnareaumc.org
Administrative Assistant: **Kyburz, Sheilah**, 612/230-3334, sheilah.kyburz@dkmnareaumc.org

District Superintendents

Serdar, Pamela, Big Waters District, 612/230-6153, pam.serdar@minnesotaumc.org, minnesotaumc.org/bigwaters

Miller, Mark, North Star District, 320/763-6795, mark.miller@minnesotaumc.org, minnesotaumc.org/northstar

Oglesbee, Clay, River Valley District, 507/263-9221, clay.oglesbee@minnesotaumc.org, minnesotaumc.org/rivervalley

Strom, Philip, Southern Prairie District, 507/723-4860, phil.strom@minnesotaumc.org, minnesotaumc.org/southernprairie

Zabel, Judy, Twin Cities District, 612/230-6146, judy.zabel@minnesotaumc.org, minnesotaumc.org/twincities

Officers and Leaders

Director of Connectional Ministries: **Gregorson, Cindy**, 612/230-6143, cindy.gregorson@minnesotaumc.org

Conference Lay Leader: **TBD**

Conference Treasurer: **Carroll, Barbara**, 612/230-6135, barb.carroll@minnesotaumc.org

Conference Secretary: **Goodwin, Tracy**, 507/263-9221, tracy.goodwin@minnesotaumc.org

Conference Communications Assistant: **Yanchury, Amanda**, 612/230-6139, amanda.yanchury@minnesotaumc.org

Conference Communications Director: **TBD**

Publications

Northern Light (monthly)

Foundation

Minnesota United Methodist Foundation
122 W. Franklin Ave., Ste. 522
Minneapolis, MN 55404
612/230-3337
val.walker@mnumf.org
http://mnumf.org
Director: **Walker, Val**

MISSISSIPPI (SE, MISSISSIPPI AREA)

320 Briarwood Dr.
Jackson, MS 39206

Phone: 601/354-0515
www.mississippi-umc.org

Episcopal Office

Mailing Address: 320-E Briarwood Dr., Jackson, MS 39206
Bishop: **Swanson, James E. Sr.**, 601/354-0515, bishop@mississippi-umc.org
Assistant to the Bishop: **Thompson, Timothy**, 601/345-8211, tim@mississippi-umc.org
Office Administrator: **White, Donna**, 601/345-8212, dwhite@mississippi-umc.org

District Superintendents

Webster, Wayne, Brookhaven, 601/833-1619, brodistumc@bellsouth.net
White, Victoria, East Jackson, 601/944-0776, ejadist@bellsouth.net
Gibson, Mattie, Greenwood District, 662/453-0878, gwddist@bellsouth.net
Cross, Cynthia, Hattiesburg District, 601/264-9181, hatdist@thehour.org
Owen, Billy, Meridian District, 601/483-6221, district@meridianumc.org
Moore, John, New Albany District, 662/534-7733, nadist@bellsouth.net
Hensarling, Heather, Seashore District, 228/604-2300, seashoredistrict@bellsouth.net
Ray, Andy, Senatobia District, 662/562-5865, senatobiadistric@bellsouth.net
Jackson, Embra, Starkville District, 662/323-0198, stkv@bellsouth.net
Barnes, Jimmy, Tupelo District, 662/842-8477, tupdist@gmail.com
Rasberry, Henderson, West Jackson District, 601/944-0776, wjadist@bellsouth.net

Officers and Leaders

Director of Connectional Ministries: **Shelton, Connie**, 601/345-8540, Connie@mississippi-umc.org
Conference Lay Leader: **Crisler, Timothy E.**, 601/857-0401, tcrisler1@hotmail.com
Conference Treasurer: **Stotts, David**, 601/345-8220, david@mississippi-umc.org
Conference Secretary: **Harper, Trey**, 662/392-2010, msconfsecy@gmail.com
Conference Communications Director: **Shelton, Connie**, 601/345-8540, Connie@mississippi-umc.org

Publications

The Circuit Rider (weekly e-newsletter)

Foundation

Mississippi United Methodist Foundation
PO Box 2415

Conferences

Ridgeland, MS 39158-2415
581 Highland Colony Pkwy.
Ridgeland, MS 39157
800/496-0975, 601/948-8845
info@ms-umf.org
Director: **Scarborough, Martha**

MISSOURI (SC, MISSOURI AREA)

3601 Amron Ct.
Columbia, MO 65202-1918
573/441-1770
http://www.moumethodist.org

Episcopal Office

Bishop: **Schnase, Robert C.**, 573/441-1770, bishop@moumethodist.org
Assistant to the Bishop: **Revelle, Elmer**, 573/441-1770, erevelle@moumethodist.org
Office Administrator: **Dunn, Dala**, 573/441-1770, ddunn@moumethodist.org

District Superintendents

Schuermann, Kurt R., Gateway Central District, 636/891-8004, kurt@gatewaydistricts.org
Rathert, Ann, Gateway Regional District, 636/891-8004, revann@gatewaydistricts.org
Villa, Yolanda, Heartland Central District, 816/356-2400, yolanda.villa@swbell.net
Cox, Steve, Heartland North District 816/505-2100, revscox@gmail.com
Collier, Cody, Heartland South District, 816/737-1114, tcodycollier@att.net
Stone, Dale, Mark Twain District, 660/665-8497, mtds@sbcglobal.net
Dyke, Lynn, Mid-State District, 573/441-8878, ldyke@moumethodist.org
Hildreth, Bart, Ozarks North District, 417/869-7878, barthildreth@sbcglobal.net
Hildreth, Bart, Ozarks South District, 417/869-7878, barthildreth@sbcglobal.net
Cox, Steve, Pony Express District, 816/232-6052, revscox@gmail.com
Leist, Fred, Southeast District, 573/334-8723, ds@southeastdistrictumc.org
Nenadal, Sandy, Southwest District, 417/623-2382, snenadal@swdistrict.net

Officers and Leaders

Director of Connectional Ministries: **Habben, Sherry**, 573/441-1770, shabben@moumethodist.org
Conference Lay Leader: **Hammons, Brian**, 417/276-1762, bkhammons@windstream.net
Conference Treasurer: **Waller, Kendall**, 573/441-1770, kwaller@moumethodist.org

Conference Secretary: **Jefferson, Monica**, 314/707-0172, Mjffrsn@aol.com
Conference Communications Director: **Habben, Sherry**, 573/441-1770, shabben@moumethodist.org

Publications

The Missouri Conference Review (every two weeks; http://www.moumethodist.org/enewsletterarchives/type/28)

Foundation

Missouri United Methodist Foundation
111 South 9th, Ste. 230
Columbia, MO 65201
800/332-8238
foundation@mumf.org
http://mumf.org/
Director: **Atkins, David**

Mountain Sky Area (see Rocky Mountain, Yellowstone)

NEBRASKA (SC, GREAT PLAINS AREA)

3333 Landmark Cir.
Lincoln, NE 68504
402/464-5994
http://www.umcneb.org

Episcopal Office

Bishop: **Jones, Scott J.**, 316/686-0600, bishop@greatplainsumc.org
Assistant to the Bishop: **Lambert, Nancy** (as of 7/1/2013), 402/464-5994 x111, nlambert@umcneb.org
Office Administrator: **Browning, Leslie Ann**, 316/686-0600, labrowning@greatplainsumc.org

District Superintendents

Wray, Galen, Blue River District, 402/323-8849, gwray@umcneb.org
Kaye-Skinner, Nan, Elkhorn Valley District, 402/371-1313, nkaye-skinner@umcneb.org
Davis, Alan, Gateway District, 308/234-3098, adavis@umcneb.org
Alnor, Kay, Great West District, 308/284-8922, kalnor@umcneb.org
Flanagan, Dan, 402/898-9862, dflanaga@umcneb.org
Clay, Lance, Prairie Rivers District, 308/384-0603, lclay@umcneb.org

Officers and Leaders

Director of Connectional Ministries: **Lambert**, **Nancy** (as of 7/1/2013), 402/464-5994 x111, nlambert@umcneb.org
Conference Lay Leader: **Watson**, **Tom**, 308/293-1887, tjwatson45@gmail.com
Conference Treasurer: **Kilgore**, **Robin**, 402/464-5994 x117, rkilgore@umcneb.org
Conference Secretary: **Hall**, **Darlene**, 308/546-2350, djhall@nebnet.net
Conference Communications Director: **Witte**, **Kathryn**, 402/464-5994 x113, kwitte@umcneb.org

Publications

Nebraska Messenger (quarterly, http://www.umcneb.org/pages/detail/152)

Foundation

Nebraska United Methodist Foundation
100 W. Fletcher, Ste. 100
Lincoln, NE 68521
402/323-8844
info@numf.org
www.numf.org
Director: **Crisp**, **Anita**

NEW ENGLAND (NE, BOSTON AREA)

276 Essex St.
PO Box 249
Lawrence, MA 01842-0449
978/682-7676
communicate@neumc.org
www.neumc.org

Episcopal Office

Bishop: **Devadhar**, **Sudarshana**, 978/682-7555 x250, bishopsoffice@neumc.org
Assistant to the Bishop: 978/682-7555 x260
Office Administrator: **Borchers**, **Brenda**, 978/682-7555 x250, bishopsoffice@neumc.org

District Superintendents

MacHugh, **Pat**, Northern Maine District, 207/862-8089, revdocpat@gmail.com,
Stenmark, **Beverly**, Mid-Maine District, 207/395-4080, bstenmark@roadrunner.com

Abbott, David, New Hampshire District, 603/225-3455, dabbott@neumc.org
McPhee, James T., Tri-State District, 978/682-7775 x270, mcphee@neumc.org
Chamberland, Heidi, Connecticut/Western Massachusetts District, 860/871-7149, hchamberland@neumc.org
Perez, Rene, Central Massachusetts District, 508/853-1895, rene.a.perez@charter.net
Easterling, LaTrelle Miller, Metro Boston Hope District, 978/682-8055 x200, leasterling@neumc.org
Hong, Seok Hwan, Rhode Island/Southeastern Massachusetts District, 401/246-1100, rimds@neumc.org
Farrell, Brigid, Vermont District, 802/878-1245, bfarr7123@aol.com

Officers and Leaders

Director of Connectional Ministries: **TBD**, 978/682-7555 x260
Conference Lay Leader: **Wilbur, Rene**, 802/446-3953, lwilbur@vermontel.net
Conference Treasurer: **Burnside, William**, 978/682-8055 x111, wburnside@neumc.org
Conference Secretary: **Oduor, Ralph**, 978/682-8055 x130, oduorrr@verizon.net
Conference Communications Director: **Wood, Alexx**, 978/682-8055 x150, communicate@neumc.org

Publications

UMCatalyst News Notes (weekly e-news, www.neumc.org/enewsletterarchives/type/2)
SpiritNet (monthly online printable newspaper, www.neumc.org/spiritnet)

Foundation

United Methodist Foundation of New England
10 Bricketts Mill Rd., Ste. 5, PO Box 370
Hampstead, NH 03841
800/595-4347
info@umfne.org
www.umfne.org
Director: **Mentzer, James**

NEW YORK (NE, NEW YORK AREA)

20 Soundview Ave.
White Plains, NY 10606-3302
914/997-1570
www.nyac.com

Episcopal Office

Bishop: **McLee, Martin D.**, 914/615-2221, fax 914/615-2246, bishop@nyac.com
Assistant to the Bishop: **Walker, Robert**, 914/615-2234, rwalker@nyac.com
Office Administrator: **Fortune, Cheryl**, 914/615-2221, cfortune@nyac.com

District Superintendents

Moore, James W., Catskill Hudson, 845/679-6350, cathudnyac@aol.com
Kieffer, Kenneth J., Connecticut, 203/288-0286, ccnyac@aol.com
Brewington, Adrienne, Long Island East, 631/366-2396, lienyac@aol.com
Yi, Kang (Kenny), Long Island West, 516/333-9868, liwnyac@aol.com
Samueldick St. Clair, Metropolitan, 212/870-2045, mnnyac@aol.com
Ott, Elizabeth, New York/Connecticut, 203/348-9181, nyctnyac@aol.com

Officers and Leaders

Director of Connectional Ministries: **Pearson, Ann A.**, 914/615-2230, apearson@nyac.com
Conference Lay Leader: **Smith, Renata**, 914/664-2622, renata10553@yahoo.com
Conference Treasurer: **Williams, Ross**, 914/615-2212, rwilliams@nyac.com
Conference Secretary: **Jackson, Fredric O.**, 914/615-2231, confsecy@nyac.com
Conference Communications Coordinator: **Utley, Joanne S.**, vision@nyac.com

Publications

The Vision (monthly online only; http://nyac.com/pages/detail/1552)

Foundation

UM Frontier Foundation
20 Soundview Ave.
914/615-2238
muhl1247@gmail.com
Director: **Muhleman, Keith**

NORTH ALABAMA (SE, BIRMINGHAM AREA)

898 Arkadelphia Rd.
Birmingham, AL 35204-3436
205/226-7950
dclifton@northalabamaumc.org
northalabamaumc.org

Episcopal Office

Bishop: **Wallace-Padgett, Debra**, 205/226-7991, dpadgett@umcna.org
Administrative Assistant to the Bishop: **Hulsey, Jilda**, 205/226-7992, jhulsey@umcna.org

District Superintendents

Alford, Bob I., Central District, 205/226-7984, central@northalalbamaumc.org
Clontz, Sherill Ann, Cheaha District, 205/226-7960, cheahadistrict@northalabamaumc.org
Scott, Robin B., Mountain Lakes District, 256/546-7405, mountainlakes@northalabamaumc.org
Cohen, Dale R., Northeast District, 256/536-9451, northeast@northalalbamaumc.org
Stonbraker, Michael P., Northwest District, 256/766-4513, northwest@northalabamaumc.org
Schultz, Ronald E., South Central District, 205/226-7983, southcentral@northalabamaumc.org
Stryker, Richard Lane III, Southeast District, 256/409-9210, southeast@northalabamaumc.org
Thompson, Roger K., Southwest District, 205/752-0414, southwest@northalabamaumc.org

Officers and Leaders

Coordinator of Connectional Ministries and Communication: **Holland, Linda**, 205/226-7954, lholland@umcna.org
Conference Lay Leader: **Lyles, Steve**, 256/234-3400, slyles@umcna.org
Conference Treasurer: **Selman, Scott**, 205/226-7989, sselman@umcna.org
Conference Communications Director: **Clifton, Danette**, 205/226-7973, dclifton@ umcna.org

Foundation

North Alabama United Methodist Foundation
302 Cahaba Valley Cir.
Pelham, AL, 35124
205/503-5650
umcfoundation@aol.com
http://www.themethodistfoundation.org
Executive Director: **Carlton, Charlie**

NORTH CAROLINA (SE, RALEIGH AREA)

700 Waterfield Ridge Pl.
Garner, NC 27529

919/779-6115
communications@nccumc.org
www.nccumc.org

Episcopal Office

Bishop: **Ward, Hope Morgan**, 919/779-6115, bishop@nccumc.org
Assistant to the Bishop: **Russell, Timothy**, 919/779-6115, trussell@nccumc.org
Office Administrator: **Biegger, Becky**, 919/779-6115, beckybiegger@nccumc.org

District Superintendents

Wise, Gil (as of 7/1/2013), Beacon District, 919/779-9435, beacondistrict@nccumc.org
Strother, Jon, Capital District, 919/779-9435, capitaldistrict@nccumc.org
Banks, Donna, Corridor District, 919/779-9435, corridordistrict@nccumc.org
Broadwell, Ray, Fairway District, 919/779-9435, fairwaydistrict@nccumc.org
Wynn, Sam, Gateway District, 919/779-9435, gatewaydistrict@nccumc.org
Daniel, Francis, Harbor District, 919/779-9435, harbordistrict@nccumc.org
Innes, Randy, Heritage District, 919/779-9435, heritagedistrict@nccumc.org, heritagedistrictumc.org
Taylor, Linda, Sound District, 919/779-9435, sounddistrict@nccumc.org, sounddistrictnc.org

Officers and Leaders

Director of Connectional Ministries: **Goehring, Carol**, 919/779-6115, cgoehring@nccumc.org
Conference Lay Leader: **Locklear, Gary**, 910/734-4070, glocklear@nccumc.org
Conference Treasurer: **Dodson, Christine**, 919/779-6115, christine@nccumc.org
Conference Secretary: **Bryan, James "Jerry"**, 919/779-6115, jlbryan@nccumc.org
Conference Communications Director: **Norton, Bill**, 919/779-6115, bnorton@nccumc.org

Publications

North Carolina Conference Christian Advocate (newpaper/online, monthly)
News Brie, (e-newsletter, weekly)

Foundation

United Methodist Foundation, Inc.
700 Waterfield Ridge Pl.
Garner, NC 27529
919/836-0029
ijames@nccumc.org

http://umf-nc.org/
Director: **James, I. Lynn**

NORTH GEORGIA (SE, NORTH GEORGIA AREA)

4511 Jones Bridge Cir.
Norcross, GA 30092
678/533-1399
www.ngumc.org

Episcopal Office

Bishop: **Watson, B. Michael**, 678/533-1360, bishop@ngumc.org
Administrative Assistant to the Bishop: **Selleck, Chris**, 678/533-1360, cselleckat@ngumc.org

District Superintendents

Herzen, Andone, Northwest District, 706/278-3954, herzen.andone@ngumc.net
Whetsone, Gary, Athens Elberton District, 706/549-4915, gary.whetstone@ngumc.net
Hinton, Coy, Atlanta College Park District, 404/209-7990, coy.hinton@ngumc.net
Lewis, Sharma, Atlanta Decatur Oxford District, 770/879-9016, sharma.lewis@ngumc.net
Everhart, Dana, Atlanta Emory District, 770/446-7506, dana.everhart@ngumc.net
Lowry, Jim, Atlanta Marietta District, 770/428-0071, jim.lowry@ngumc.net
Brown, Dan, Atlanta Roswell District, 770/362-1002, dan.brown@ngumc.net
Fleming, Terry, Augusta District, 706/651-8621, terry.fleming@ngumc.net
Chewning, Richard, Gainesville District, 770/536-2586, richard.chewning@ngumc.net
Winn, Richard, Griffin District, 770/227-1074, richard.winn@ngumc.net
Cook, Carol, LaGrange District, 706/882-3343, carol.cook@ngumc.net
Naglee, David, Rome-Carrollton District, 706/291-6113, david.naglee@ngumc.net

Officers and Leaders

Director of Connectional Ministries: **Selleck, Mike**, 678/533-1442, mselleck@ngumc.org
Conference Lay Leader: **Pinson, Mathew**, 404/788-7261, mathewpinson@gmail.com
Conference Treasurer: **Cox, Keith**, 678/533-1393, kcox@ngumc.org
Conference Secretary: **Weber, Donn Ann**, 404/636-9737, donnann.weber@ngumc.net
Conference Communicator: **Davidson, Sybil**, 678/533-1377, sybil@ngumc.org

Director of Ministerial Services: **Brooks, Jane**, 678/533-1366, jane.brooks@ngumc.net

Publications

North Georgia Advocate (twice monthly)

Foundation

Georgia United Methodist Foundation
15 Technology Pkwy. South, Ste. 125,
Norcross, GA 30092
770/449-6726
info@gumf.org
www.gumf.org
Director: **Savage, C.W. "Chuck" II**

NORTH TEXAS (SC, DALLAS AREA)

500 Maplelawn Dr.
Plano, TX 75075
800/815-6690, 972/526-5000, fax: 972/526-5003
ntccommunications@ntcumc.org
www.northtexasumc.org

Episcopal Office

Bishop: **McKee, Michael**, bishop@ntcumc.org
Assistant to the Bishop: **George, Larry**, missions@ntcumc.org
Executive Assistant: **Stanislaus, Joell**, joell@ntcumc.org

District Superintendents

Labarr, Joan Gray, East District, 903/439-1117, janchapman@ntceastdistrict.org
Reed, Clara M., Metro District, 214/942-7712, metro@ntcumc.org
Alegria, Frank, North Central District, 972/788-4114, nc@ntcumc.org
Guier, L. Marvin III, Northwest District, guier@ntcumc.org

Officers and Leaders

Director of Connectional Ministries: **Smith, Jodi S.**, jodi@ntcumc.org
Conference Lay Leader: **Parks, Linda**, ljparks@aol.com
Conference Lay Leader Elect: **Lessner, Henry**, henry@wealthmanagementgroupllc.com
Associate Treasurer: **Cajiuat, Susannah**, 972/526-5026, cajiuat@ntcumc.org
Conference Communications Director: **Patterson, Sheron**, patterson@ntcumc.org

NORTHERN ILLINOIS (NC, NORTHERN ILLINOIS AREA)

77 W. Washington St. Ste. 1820
Chicago, IL 60602
312/346-9766
www.umcnic.org

Episcopal Office

Bishop: **Dyck, Sally**, 312/346-9766 x702, bishop.dyck@umcnic.org
Assistant to the Bishop: **Christopherson, Arlene**, 312/346-9766 x713, achristo@umcnic.org
Office Administrator: **Andrews, Marva**, 312/346-9766 x702, mandrews@umcnic.org

District Superintendents

Zaki, Zaki L., Chicago Northwestern, 312/346-9766 x734, zlzaki@umcnic.org
Malone, Tracy S., Chicago Southern, 312/346-9766 x733, tmalone@umcnic.org
Carrasco, Oscar, Elgin, 847/931-0710 x10 oscarcarrasco24@gmail.com
Wisdom, Dick, Aurora, 847/931-0710 x21 dwisdom@umcnic.org
Kruse-Safford, Lisa, Rockford, 815/561-8285 x12, lksafford@umcnic.org
Park, Young-Mee, DeKalb, 847/931-0710 x11, ypark@umcnic.org

Officers and Leaders

Director of Connectional Ministries: **Pierson, Chris**, 847/931-0710 x15, cpierson@umcnic.org
Conference Lay Leader: **Rivera, Arnold**, 773/794-0082, prariv@yahoo.com
Conference Treasurer: **Chafin, Lonnie**, 312/346-9766 x722, lchafin@umcnic.org
Conference Secretary: **Zink, Lora**, 815/382-1004, lortwin@aol.com
Conference Communications Director: **Gerhardt, Anne Marie**, 847/931-0710 x14, agerhardt@umcnic.org

Publications

Northern Illinois Conference News (monthly)

Foundation

United Methodist Foundation of the Northern Illinois Conference
77 W. Washington St. Ste. 1820
Chicago, IL 60602

312/346-9766 x704
jboryk@umcnic.org
http://www.nicumf.org
President: **Nicol, Harry**

NORTHWEST TEXAS–NEW MEXICO (SC, NORTHWEST TEXAS–NEW MEXICO AREA)

1401 Ave. M
Lubbock, TX 79401-3939
806/762-0201
rprumer@nwtxconf.org
www.nwtxconf.org

Episcopal Office

Bishop: **Bledsoe, W. Earl**, 505/255-8786, bishopbledsoe@nmconfum.com
Assistant to the Bishop: **Lippitt, Diane**, 505/255-8786, dlippitt@nmconfum.com

District Superintendents

Price, George, Abilene District, 325/675-6672, adnwtc.ds@nts-online.net
Bauernfeind, Paul, Amarillo, 806/376-7271, paul@amarillodistrict.org
Patterson, Derrell, Big Spring, 432/263-1259, bigspringds@sbcglobal.net
Edwards, Richard, Lubbock, 806/796-1336, redwards@lubdistumc.com

Officers and Leaders

Director of Connectional Ministries: **Nunn, Jimmy**, 806/762-0201 x11, nunn@nwtxconf.org
Conference Lay Leader: **Murphy, Murray**, 432/816-3477, murraymurphy@att.net
Conference Treasurer: **Andersen, Dave**, 806/762-0201 x12, andersen@nwtxconf.org
Conference Secretary: **Prumer, Rosemary**, 806/762-0201 x11, rprumer@nwtxconf.org
Conference Communications Director: **Williams, Leia Danielle**, 806/762-0201 x23, ldw@nwtxconf.org

Publications

Snapshots of Hope (quarterly)

OKLAHOMA (SC, OKLAHOMA AREA)

1501 N.W. 24th St.
Oklahoma City, OK 73106

405/530-2000
ljohnston@okumc.org
www.okumc.org

Episcopal Office

Bishop: **Hayes, Robert E. Jr.**, 405/530-2025, pweatherford@okumc.org
Assistant to the Bishop: **Harris, Joseph**, 405/530-2077, jharris@okumc.org
Office Administrator: **Weatherford, Pam**, 405/530-2025, pweatherford@okumc.org

District Superintendents

Tener, Greg, Ardmore District, 580/223-2353, revdrgjtener@gmail.com
Warren, George, Bartlesville District, 918/333-1839, umdsbvl@cableone.net
Graves, Charles, Clinton District, 580/323-2703, clindist@swbell.net
Dodson, Donna, Enid District, 580/233-1901, eniddist@sbcglobal.net
Tiger, Chris, Lawton District, 580/248-3343, ldumc1@aol.com
Cates, Darrell, McAlester District, 918/423-0080, mcaldist@allegiance.tv
Mason, Emery, Muskogee District, 918/682-3034, ds@muskogeedistrictumc.org
Johnson, Rockford, North Oklahoma City District, 405/607-2483, nokcdistrict@coxinet.net
Johnson, Frankye, South Oklahoma City District, 405/607-2770, umc1@coxinet.net
Malloy, Patricia, Stillwater District, 405/372-0624, stwdsumc@sbcglobal.net
Peil, Dan, Tulsa District, 918/742-7496, tulsaumc@sbcglobal.net
Burris, David, Woodward District, 580/254-3913, wwds@sbcglobal.net

Officers and Leaders

Director of Connectional Ministries: **Stinson, Craig**, 405/530-2020, cstinson@okumc.org
Conference Lay Leader: **Stewart, Chuck**, 918/797-0932, chuckstewart@windstream.net
Conference Treasurer: **Bakeman, Brian**, 405/530-2067, bbakeman@okumc.org
Conference Secretary: **Harris, Joseph**, 405/530-2077, jharris@okumc.org
Conference Communications Director: **Harris, Joseph**, 405/530-2077, jharris@okumc.org

Publications

The Oklahoma United Methodist Contact (newspaper, every 3 weeks, 17 issues/yr)

Foundation

Oklahoma United Methodist Foundation
4201 N. Classen Blvd.
405/525-6863
www.okumf.org
President: **Junk, Bill**, bjunk@okumc.org

OKLAHOMA INDIAN MISSIONARY (SC, OKLAHOMA AREA)

3020 S. Harvey
PO Box
Oklahoma City, OK, 73109
405/632-2006
dwilson@oimc.org
umc-oimc.org

Episcopal Office

Bishop: **Hayes, Robert E. Jr.**, 405/530-2025
Assistant to the Bishop: **Wilson, David**, 405/632-2006, dwilson@oimc.org
Office Administrator: **Draper, Linda**, 405/632-2006, ldraper@oimc.org

District Superintendents

Johnson, Margaret, Northern, 918/299-2220, anoachi@aol.com
Tecumseh, July, Southern, 580/364-0009, nettvce1@yahoo.com

Officers and Leaders

Director of Connectional Ministries: **Deere, Josephine**, 405/632-2006, jdeere@oimc.org
Conference Lay Leader: **Chalakee, Jim**, 918/224-6080, dgrammieok@yahoo.com
Conference Treasurer: **Galyon, Dennis**, 405/632-2006
Conference Secretary: **Ross, Sunrise**, 405/632-2006, suntiger1@cox.net
Conference Communications Director: **Deere, Josephine**, 405/632-2006, jdeere@oimc.org

Foundation

Indian Missionary United Methodist Foundation, Inc.
Director: **Wahkinney, Kevin**

OREGON IDAHO (W, GREATER NORTHWEST AREA)

1505 S.W. 18th Ave.
Portland, Oregon, 97201
503/226-7931
communications@umoi.org
www.umoi.org

Episcopal Office

Bishop: **Hagiya, Grant J.**, 503/226-1530, bishop@umoi.org
Assistant to the Bishop: **Fields, Kim**, 503/226-1530, kim@umoi.org
Office Administrator: **Delurey, Becky**, 503/226-1530, becky@umoi.org

District Superintendents

Lofsvold, Peg, Cascadia District, 503/581-3969, cascadia@umoi.org
Greathouse, Lowell, Columbia District, 503/249-1851, columbia@umoi.org
Drake, Gwen, Crater Lake District, 541/689-3725, craterlake@umoi.org
Fields, Kim, Sage District, 541/389-1047, sage@umoi.org

Officers and Leaders

Director of Connectional Ministries: **Greathouse, Lowell**, 503/249-1851, lowell@umoi.org
Conference Lay Leader: **Foote, Mary**, 503/648-3072, marycfoote@yahoo.com
Conference Treasurer: **Mullette-Bauer, William**, 503/802-9222, bill@umoi.org
Conference Secretary: **Bartlett, Laura Jacquith**, 503/637-5140, revlaurajbartlett@gmail.com
Conference Communications Director: **Nelson, Greg**, 503/802-9205, greg@umoi.org

Publications

UM Connector (weekly; www.umoi.org/UMConnector)

Foundation

Northwest United Methodist Foundation
203 Mission Ave. Ste. 204,
Cashmere, WA 98815
800/488-4179
tom@nwumf.org
http://www.nwumf.org/
Director: **Wilson, Tom**

Pacific Northwest (W, Greater Northwest Area)

816 S. 216th St. #2
Des Moines, WA 98198-3650
Mailing Address: PO Box 13650, Des Moines, WA 98198-1009
800/755-7710, 206/870-6820, fax: 206/870-6839
dvalera@pnwumc.org
www.pnwumc.org

Episcopal Office

Bishop: **Hagiya, Grant J.**, 206/870-6810, bishop@pnwumc.org
Administrative Administrator: **Engle, Gretchen**, 206/870-6810, gengle@pnwumc.org

District Superintendents

Cockrum, Dale L., Inland District, 800/549-3085, 509/838-3085, inland@pnwumc.org
Foster, L. Daniel, Puget Sound District, 425/267-9010, psdistumc@aol.com
Simpson, Patricia L., Seattle District, 800/755-7710, 206/870-6814, seadist@pnwumc.org
Huycke, Mary K. S., Seven Rivers District, 888/818-4288, sevenrivers@pnwumc.org
Moe, Sharon L., Tacoma District, 800/755-7710, 253/627-5442, tacdist@pwumc.org
Nieda, David K., Vancouver District, 360/695-8598, vancouver@pnwumc.org

Officers and Leaders

Executive Director of Connectional Ministries: **Valera, David**, 206/870-6806, dvalera@pnwumc.org
Conference Treasurer: **Parrish, Craig**, 206/870-6818, cparrish@pnwumc.org
Conference Communications Director: **Scriven, Patrick**, 206/304-9284, pscriven@pnwumc.org

Foundation

United Methodist Foundation of the Northwest
203 Mission Ave. Ste. 204
Cashmere, WA 98815
800/488-4179
tom@nwumf.org

http://nwumf.org/
Executive Director: **Wilson, Tom**

PENINSULA-DELAWARE (NE, PHILADELPHIA AREA)

139 N. State St.
Dover, DE 19901
877/736-3351, 302/674-2626, fax: 302/674-1573
mcleeton@pen-del.org
www.pen-del.org

Episcopal Office

Bishop: **Johnson, Peggy A.**, bshpajohnson@aol.com
Administrative Assistant: **Botti, Amy**, 610/666-9090, abotti@epaumc.org

District Superintendents

Etter, Boyd B., Dover District, 302/674-2626, mgates@pen-del.org
Moore, Gary L., Easton District, 410/770-9673, eastondistrictoffice@goeaston.net
Nicholas, Charlotte A., Salisbury District, 410/749-3331, salisburydistrict@comcast.net
Porter, Derrick, Wilmington District, 302/674-2626, wilmingtondistrict@gmail.com

Officers and Leaders

Director of Connectional Ministries: **Brown, Shirlyn**, 302/674-2626, shirlynbrown@aol.com
Conference Lay Leader: **Gooch, Betty**, 302/344-5478
Conference Treasurer: **Westbrook, William**, 302/674-2626, wwestbrook@pen-del.org

Foundation

Mid-Atlantic United Methodist Foundation, Inc.
Valley Forge, PA and Fulton, MD
800/828-9093 x247
jackbrooks.mafoundation@gmail.com
http://www.midatlanticfoundation.org/
Executive Director: **Brooks, Jack**

Philadelphia Area (see Eastern Pennsylvania, Peninsula–Delaware)

Conferences

RED BIRD MISSIONARY (SE, LOUISVILLE AREA)

54 Queendale Ctr.
Beverly, KY 40913-9607
606/598-5915, fax: 606/598-6405
info@redbirdconference.org
http://www.redbirdconference.org/index.php

Episcopal Office

Bishop: **Davis, Lindsey**

District Superintendents

Stuart, Farley E. III, 606/598-5915, cdist12@newwavecomm.net

Officers and Leaders

Director of Connectional Ministries: **Wiertzema, Ruth A.**
Conference Treasurer: **Fowler, Judith**

RIO GRANDE (SC, SAN ANTONIO AREA)

16400 Huebner Rd.
San Antonio, TX 78248-1693
210/408-4513, fax: 210/408-4515
avega@umcswtx.org
http://www.riograndeconference.org/

Episcopal Office

Bishop: **Dorff, James E.**, 210/408-4502, bishop@umcswtx.org
Administrative Assistant: **Trevino, Dalia**, 210/408-4502, bishop@umcswtx.org

District Superintendents

Campos, Francisco, Central District, 210/408-4514, pasfcamp@yahoo.com
Jara, Nydia I., Northwestern District, nydiayjuanchi@yahoo.com
Jara, Nydia I., Southern District, nydiayjuanchi@yahoo.com

Officers and Leaders

Director of Connectional Ministries: **Vega, Abel Jr**, 210/408-4512, avega@
  umcswtx.org
Conference Treasurer: **Trafton, Margie**, 361/668-6715, rgctreas@att.net
Conference Secretary: **Avitia, Edgar**, 212/870-3828

Rocky Mountain (W, Mountain Sky Area)

6110 Greenwood Plaza Blvd.
Greenwood Village, CO 80111
303/733-3736
http://www.rmcumc.org/new/

Episcopal Office
Bishop: **Stanovsky, Elaine J.W.**
Office Administrator: **Cox, Nancy**, 303/733-0083, execassist@mountainskyumc.org

District Superintendents
Goodier, Steve, Metropolitan District, 303/733-3736, steve@rmcumc.com
Rosa, Melanie, Mile High/Pikes Peak District, 719/481-6448, melanie@rmcumc.com
Strickland, Walter "Skip," Peaks and Plains/Northeast Colorado District, skip@rmcumc.com
Vose, Marvin, Sunshine District, marv@rmcumc.com
Tukutau, Sione, Utah/Western Colorado District, sione@rmcumc.com
Olenyik, Debra, Wyoming District, deb@rmcumc.com

Officers and Leaders
Director of Mission and Ministry: **Kang, Youngsook**, 303/389-9466 x107, youngsook@rmcumc.com
Conference Co-Lay Leader: **Hotze, Margaret**, 970/420-4283, margarethotze.umw@gmail.com
Conference Co-Lay Leader, **Taiwo, Kunle**, 303/745-2938, ktarch@att.net
Conference Treasurer: **Keleshian, Noreen**, 303/325-7051 x151, noreen@rmcumc.com
Conference Communications Director: **Goodier, Steve**, 303/389-9456 x156,. steve@rmcumc.com

Publications
RMC NEWS-WEEKLY

Foundation
Rocky Mountain Conference United Methodist Foundation Inc.
7350 E. Progress Pl. Ste. 205
Greenwood Village, CO 80111
303/778-6370, fax: 303/777-6292
info@rm-umf.org

Conferences

http://www.rm-umf.org
Executive Director: **Kinnison, Kristi**

San Antonio Area (see Rio Grande, Southwest Texas)

SOUTH CAROLINA (SE, COLUMBIA AREA)
4908 Colonial Dr.
PO Box 3787 (zip is 29230)
Columbia, SC, 29203
803/786-9486
website@umcsc.org
www.umcsc.org

Episcopal Office
Bishop: **Holston, L. Jonathan**, 803/786-9486, bishop@umcsc.org
Assistant to the Bishop: **Rivers, Bettye**, 803/786-9486, brivers@umcsc.org

District Superintendents
Leonard-Ray, Susan, Anderson District, 864/226-6649, andist@umcsc.org,
Parrish, Patti, Charleston District, 843/744-0477, chdist@umcsc.org
McClendon, Tim Columbia District, 803/786-9486, codist@umcsc.org, www.coladistumc.org/
Hipp, John, Florence District, 843/669-5992, fldist@umcsc.org
Teasley, Mary, Greenville District, 864/233-3611, gvdist@umcsc.org
Friday, James, Greenwood District, 864/223-2650, gwdist@umcsc.org
Washington, Lillian, Hartsville District, 843/332-1631, hadist@umcsc.org
Knight, Dickie, Marion District, 843/423-1202, madist@umcsc.org
Yebuah, Frederick, Orangeburg District, 803/534-7564, ordist@umcsc.org
Long, Joe Jr., Rock Hill District, 803/328-0218, rhdist@umcsc.org
Harmon, Paul, Spartanburg District, 864/583-5109, spdist@umcsc.org
Peason, Thomas Jr., Walterboro District, 843/549-5441, wadist@umcsc.org

Officers and Leaders
Director of Connectional Ministries: **James, Kathy**, 803/786-9486, kljames@umcsc.org
Conference Lay Leader: **Ware, Barbara**, 864/350-6600, conferencelayleader@umcsc.org
Conference Treasurer: **Prestipino, Tony**, 803/786-9486, aprestipino@umcsc.org
Conference Secretary: **Radcliffe, Karen**, 803/786-9486, khradcliffe@umcsc.org
Conference Communications Director: **Brodie, Matt**, 803/786-9486, mbrodie@umcsc.org

Publications

The South Carolina United Methodist Advocate (Monthly, http://www.advocatesc.org/)
ConnX (Bi-Monthly, http://www.umcsc.org/connx)

Foundation

The South Carolina United Methodist Foundation
2900 Milwood Ave.
803/771-9125
scumf@umcsc.org
http://www.umcsc.org/home/?page_id=355
Director: **Gramling, Roger M.**

SOUTH GEORGIA (SE, SOUTH GEORGIA AREA)

735 Pierce Ave. (31204)
PO Box 7227
Macon, GA 31209
478/475-9286
kelly@sgaumc.com
www.sgaumc.org

Episcopal Office

Bishop: **King, James R. Jr.**, 478/475-9286, jking@sgaumc.com
Assistant to the Bishop for Ministerial Services: **Harris, Jay**, 478/475-9286
Administrative Assistant: **Mathews, Eric**, 478/475-9286, bishopsec@sgaumc.com

District Superintendents

Moseley, Wayne, Americus District, 229/273-3119, americusds@mchsi.com
Cooper, Edwin "Buddy," Columbus District, 706/561-4541, edwincooper52@gmail.com
Tripp, Marcus, Dublin District, 478/272-3371, umcds@sgaumc.com
Martin, Tommy, Macon District, 478/254-6023, tmartin@sgaumc.com
Huling, Mike, Savannah District, 912/352-7867, mhuling@sgaumc.com
Ramsey, Chris, Statesboro District, 912/871-3306
Brantley, Lowery, Thomasville District, 229/228-4081, lowery@sgaumc.com
Bass, Henry, Valdosta District, 229/242-7470, valdist@bellsouth.net
Varnell, Benjy, Waycross District, 912/283-5861, cbv@sgaumc.com

Officers and Leaders

Assistant to the Bishop for Connectional Ministries: **Walton, Denise**, 912/638-8626, denise@sgaumc.com
Conference Lay Leader: **Morgan, Gloria**, 478/272-5320, gmorgan40@bellsouth.net
Conference Treasurer: **Hagan, Miriam**, 478/738-0048, miriam@sgaumcadmin.com
Conference Secretary: **Hutto, Craig**, 706/554-2188, craighuttojr@gmail.com
Conference Communications Director: **Roberson, Kelly**, 912/638-8626, kelly@sgaumc.com

Publications

South Georgia Advocate (twice monthly, www.sgaumc.org/advocate)

Foundation

Georgia United Methodist Foundation
15 Technology Pkwy. S., Ste. 125
Norcross, GA 30092
770/449-6726
info@gumf.org
www.gumf.org
Director: **Savage, C.W. "Chuck" II**

SOUTHWEST TEXAS (SC, SAN ANTONIO AREA)

16400 Huebner Rd.
San Antonio, TX 78248-1694
888/349-4191, 210/408-4500, fax: 210/408-4515
umcenter@umcswtx.org
www.umcswtx.org

Episcopal Office

Bishop: **Dorff, James E.**, bishop@umcswtx.org
Executive Assistant: **Trevino, Dalia**, bishop@umcswtx.org
Assistant to Episcopal Office: **Vázquez-Garza, Virgilio**, wq@umcswtx.org

District Superintendents

Purdy, Steven Mark, Austin District, 512/444-1983, jill@umcad.org
Valverde, Eradio Jr., Corpus Christi District, 361/852-8268, ccdistrict@bizstx.rr.com
Henderson, William Bryan, Kerrville District, 830/896-6400, kdumc@kdumc.org

Merrill, Laura A., McAllen District, 956/428-0200, umcmcallen@sbcglobal.net
Altman, Larry Ray, San Angelo District, 325/486-1500, sangds@suddenlinkmail.com
Rohifs, Carol Walter, San Antonio District, 210/408-4520, carlds@umcswtx.org
Hayes, Terrence K., Victoria District, 361/573-4233, vdsumc@tisd.net

Officers and Leaders

Conference Treasurer/Secretary: **Seilheimer, David**, daseilh@umcswtx.org
Conference Communications Director: **Monahan, Thomas**, tmonahan@umcswtx.org

SUSQUEHANNA (NE, HARRISBURG AREA)

303 Mulberry Dr.
PO Box 2053
Mechanicsburg, PA 17050-2053
800/874-8474, 717/766-7441, fax: 717/766-5976
mike@susumc.org
www.susumc.org

Episcopal Office

Bishop: **Park, Jeremiah J.**, bishoppark@susumc.org
Assistant to the Bishop: **Myers, Greg C.**, gmyers@susumc.org
Executive Administrative Assistant: **Mackey, Christy**, cmackey@susumc.org
Administrative Assistant: **Sample, Kris**, ksample@susumc.org

District Superintendents

Kind, Kathleen, E., Altoona District, 800/842-5923, 814/942-9220, mschnaubelt@susumc.org
Keller, Dennis R., Harrisburg District, 717/766-8124, cshaffer@susumc.org
Salsgiver, Thomas L., Lewisburg District, 800/470-4789, 570/523-9592, debbiejean@susumc.org
Buxton, Jon J., Scranton/Wilkes-Barre District, 570/344-8313, jbuxton@susumc.org
Steffensen, Lori J., State College District, 800/892-4854, 814/237-4365, lmohr@susumc.org
Jones, Beth E., Williamsport District, 800/660-7612, 570/323-0002, jjohnston@susumc.org
Salisbury, Charles W., York District, 800/566-0036, 717/755-8863, evizthum@susumc.org

Officers and Leaders

Director of Connectional Ministries: **Bealla**, **Mike**, 717/766-7441 x3601, mbealla@susumc.org
Conference Treasurer: **Smith**, **Gary**, gsmith@susumc.org
Conference Communications Director: **Wolgemuth**, **Jerry**, 717/766-7441 x3607, jwolgemuth@susumc.org

TENNESSEE (SE, NASHVILLE AREA)

304 S. Perimeter Park Dr., Ste. 1
Nashville, TN, 37211
615/329-1177
admin@tnumc.org
http://tnumc.org

Episcopal Office (Nashville Area)

Bishop: **McAlilly**, **William T.**, 615/742-8834, bishop@nashareaumc.org
Assistant to the Bishop: **Collett**, **John**, 615/742-8834, collett@tnumc.org
Office Administrator: **Crew**, **Gay**, 615/742-8834, gay@nashareaumc.org

District Superintendents

Barrineau, **Karen**, Clarksville District, 931/553-8401, kbarrineau@tnumc.com
Burchfield, **Willie**, Columbia District, 931/381-9558, coldist@tnumc.org
Archer, **Jay**, Cookeville District, 931/526-1343, cookeville@tnumc.org
Halliburton, **Tom**, Columbia District, 615/822-1433, tomehalliburton@hotmail.com
Culbertson, **LeNoir**, Murfreesboro District, 615/893-5886, lenoir.culbertson@tnumc.com
Bryan, **Harriet**, Nashville District, 615/327-3582, harriet.bryan@tnumc.com
Beaty, **Jim**, Pulaski District, 931/363-8981

Officers and Leaders

Director of Connectional Ministries: **Lewis**, **Bettye**, 615/329-1177, bettye.lewis@tnumc.com
Conference Lay Leader: **Neal**, **Holly**, 931/484-4082, hneal56@yahoo.com
Conference Treasurer: **Allen**, **Jim**, 615/327-1162, jim.allen@tnumc.com
Conference Secretary: **Seifert**, **Chris**, 615/585-2530, revchrisseifert@gmail.com
Conference Communications Director: **Sparkman**, **Kevin**, 615/329-1177, communications@tnumc.org

Publications

TNUMConnector (monthly)
TNUMConnects (weekly, eBlast, https://app.e2ma.net/app2/audience/signup/1706480/1703043/)

Foundation

UM Foundation for the Memphis & Tennessee Conferences
304 S. Perimeter Park Dr., Ste. 3
Nashville TN 37211
615/259-2008
sfinger@umfmtc.org
umfmtc.org
Director: **Walkup, Vincent**

TEXAS (SC, HOUSTON AREA)

5215 Main St.
Houston, Texas 77002
713/521-9383
jervin@txcumc.org
www.txcumc.org

Episcopal Office

Bishop: **Huie, Janice Riggle**, 713/521-9383, bishop.huie@txcumc.org
Assistant to the Bishop: **Williamson, B.T.**, 713/521-9383, bt.williamson@txcumc.org

District Superintendents

Matthis Morris, Central North District, 281/895-7700, mmatthis@txcumc.org
Young, Lawrence, Central South District, 713/222-0117, lyoung@txcumc.org
Huffman, Chuck, East District, 936/699-2213, chuffman@txcumc.org
Taylor, Bill, North-Longview District, 903/758-7003 or North-Texarkana, 903/794-6231, btaylor@txcumc.org
Smith, Sandra, Northwest District, 903/593-1861, sandrasmith@tcumc.org
Gilts, Kip, South District, 281/998-8993, kgilts@txcumc.org
White, Dick, Southeast District, 409/833-9510, rlwhite@txcumc.org
Jackson, Jay, Southwest District, 281/499-3700, jjackson@txcumc.org
Fort, Joe Jr., West District, 979/690-5627, jfort@txcumc.org

Officers and Leaders

Director of Connectional Ministries: **Stansell, Elijah**, 713/521-9383, eli@swbell.net
Conference Lay Leader, **Griffin, Stephanie**, 903/882-5484, lesstepgriffin@wildblue.net
Conference Treasurer: **Stansell, Elijah**, 713/521-9383, eli@swbell.net
Conference Secretary, **Brannen, Jesse**, 409/962-5762, jesse@umt.org

Conference Communications Director, **Arnold**, **Paula**, 713/521-9383, parnold@txcumc.org

Publications
Cross Connection (bi-weekly, www.txcumc.org)

Foundation
Heartspring Methodist Foundation
5215 Main St.
Houston, Texas 77002
713/521-9383
heartspringmethodist.org
cjtaylor@heartspringmethodist.org
Director: **Taylor, C. J.**

UPPER NEW YORK (NE, UPPER NEW YORK AREA)
324 University Ave., 3rd Floor
Syracuse, NY, 13210
315/4214-7878
info@unyumc.org
www.unyumc.org

Episcopal Office
Bishop: **Webb**, **Mark J.**, 315/422-5027, bishopwebb@unyumc.org
Assistant to the Bishop: **Doran**, **Christine**, 315/422-5027, executiveassistant@unyumc.org
Office Administrator: **Bradley**, **Mary**, 315/422-5027, bishopsoffice@unyumc.org

District Superintendents
Mudge, **William**, Adirondack District, 518/584-8214 x2, billmudge@unyumc.org
Weihing, **Richard**, Albany District, 518/584-8214 x3, richweihing@unyumc.org
Masland, **David**, Binghamton District, 607/748-0662, davidmasland@unyumc.org
Rood, **Sherri**, Cornerstone District, 716/665-2423, sherrirood@unyumc.org
Barrow, **Darryl R.**, Crossroads District, 315/424-7878 x312, Darryl@unyumc.org
Barton, **Richard**, Finger Lakes District, 315/781-0188, dickbarton@unyumc.org
Anderson, **Theodore**, Genesee Valley District, 585/340-9525, ted@crcds.edu
Ho Lee, **Sung**, Mohawk District, 315/797-1777, sungho@unyumc.org
Stengel, **Cathy**, Mountain View District, 607/962-8047, cathyhallstengel@unyumc.org
Butler, **K. Wayne**, Niagara Frontier District, 716/276-8631, waynebutler@unyumc.org

Sweet, Rebekah, Northern Flow District, 315/535-5149, rebekahsweet@unyumc.org
Rowell, Jan, Oneonta District, 607/441-5102, janrowell@unyumc.org

Officers and Leaders

Director of Connectional Ministries: **Gottschalk-Fielding, William**, 315/424-7878 x316, billg-f@unyumc.org
Conference Lay Leader: **Johnson, Scott**, 716/878-5906, scottjphd@gmail.com
Conference Treasurer: **Mackey, Sherri**, 315/424-7878 x303, sherrimackey@unyumc.org
Conference Secretary: **Hodge, Jeff**, 315/635-6442, jhodge312@yahoo.com
Conference Communications Director: **Mulenga, Maidstone**, 315/424-7878 x307, maidstonemulenga@unyumc.org

Publications

Upper New York Advocate (Monthly)
E-Advocate (2x/Week)

VIRGINIA (SE, RICHMOND AREA)

10330 Staples Mill Rd., Glen Allen, VA 23060
Mailing Address: PO Box 5606, Glen Allen, VA 23058-5606
804/521-1100 or 800/as 768-6040
Communications@vaumc.org
www.vaumc.org

Episcopal Office

Bishop: **Cho, Young Jin**, 804/521-1102, BishopCho@vaumc.org
Assistant to the Bishop: **Joyce, Tom**, 804/521-1103, TomJoyce@vaumc.org
Office Administrator: **Pruden, Estelle**, 804/521-1102, EstellePruden@vaumc.org

District Superintendents (as of July 1, 2013)

Jackson, Kenneth J., Alexandria District, 703/820-7200, AlexandriaDS@novaumc.org
Abbott, Catherine, Arlington District, 703/820-7200, ArlingtonDS@novaumc.org
Kesner, Danny, Charlottesville District, 434/977-4254, CharlottesvilleDS@vaumc.org
Howard, Janine, Danville District, 276/638-2688, DanvilleDS@vaumc.org
Estep, Tammy L., Eastern Shore District, 757/665-6295, esdsumc@verizon.net
Phillips, Bradford, L., Elizabeth River District, 757/473-1592, elizabethriverds@vaumc.org
Parks, Robert J. Jr., Farmville District, 434/392-4687, FarmvilleDS@vaumc.org

Smith, Theodore, Fredericksburg District, 804/448-8326, FredburgDS@gmail.com
Herndon, Ernest T. "Tommy" Jr., Harrisonburg District, 540/433-2382, HarrisonburgDS@vaumc.org
Colwell, Rob, James River District, 804/732-2538, JamesRiverDS@vaumc.org
Davies, Larry E., Lynchburg District, 434/832-0401, LynchburgDS@LynchburgDistrictUMC.org
Jones, Steven, R., Richmond District, 804/521-1100, RichmondDS@vaumc.org
Webster, Kathleen Overby, Roanoke District, 540/989-3335, RoanokeDS@vaumc.org
Rochford, Dave, Staunton District, 540/932-1055, StauntonDS@vaumc.org
Thompson, Lawrence R. Jr., Winchester District, 540/662-7332, WinchesterDS@vaumc.org
Carson, Joseph D., York River District, 757/596-3476, YorkRiverDS@vaumc.org

Officers and Leaders

Director of Connectional Ministries: **Brown, Marc**, 804/521-1133, MarcBrown@vaumc.org
Conference Lay Leader: **Harper, Warren**, 757/258-4498, wrscharper@gmail.com
Conference Treasurer: **Dommisse, David**, 804/521-1109, DavidDommisse@vaumc.org
Conference Secretary: **Blinn, Robert**, 804/991-2291, robert.blinn@trinitydisputanta.org
Conference Communications Director: **Rhodes, Linda S.**, 804/521-1111, LindaRhodes@vaumc.org

Publications

The Virginia United Methodist Advocate (monthly, http://www.vaumc.org/advocate)

Foundation

The Virginia United Methodist Foundation
10330 Staples Mill Rd.
PO Box 5606
Glen Allen, VA 23058-5606
804/521-1120
DaveThompson@vaumc.org
http://vaumfgifts.org/
President: **Thompson, Dave**

West Michigan (NC, Michigan Area)

11 Fuller Ave. SE
PO Box 6247
Grand Rapids, MI 49516-6247
616/459-4503
reception@wmcumc.org
www.westmichiganconference.org

Episcopal Office

2164 University Park, Ste. 250
Okemos, MI 48864
Bishop: **Kiesey, Deborah L.**, 517/347-4030, fax: 517/347-4003, bishop@miareaumc.org
Asstistant to the Bishop: **Dobbs, William D.**, 517/347-4030, bdobbs@miareaumc.org
Administrative Assistant: **Nelson, Deana**, 517/347-4030, dnelson@miareaumc.org

District Superintendents

Williams, Tamara SM, Albion District, 517/629-8150, fax: 517/629-8230, office@albiondistrict.org
Haggard, William, Grand Rapids District, 616/459-4503, fax: 616/459-0242, Grdistrict@wmcumc.org; grsupt@wmcumc.org
Kahn, Anita K., Grand Traverse District, 231/947-5281, fax: 231/947-0181, gtdistrictoffice@tcchrist.com
Hills, David, Heartland District, 989/773-5140, fax: 989/775-6599, office@umcheartland.org
Davis, Neil, Kalamazoo District, 269/372-7525, fax: 269/372-7644, office@kazoodistumc.org
Hundley, Robert L., Lansing District, 517/347-4173, fax: 517/347-4798, lansingdistrict@miareaumc.org

Officers and Leaders

Director of Connectional Ministries: **Heisler, Benton R.**, 616/459-4503, benton@wmcumc.org
Conference Lay Leader: **Soles, Anne**, 231/869-4059, annesoles@charter.net
Conference Treasurer: **Tumonong, Prospero**, 616/459-4503, treas@wmcumc.org
Conference Secretary: **Buchner, Gregory L.**, 989/834-5958, pastorgreg@unitedchurchofovid.com
Director of Communications: **Doyal, Mark**, 517/336-0850, markd@wmcumc.org
Director of New Church Development and Congregational Transformation: **Step, Gary**, 616/459-4503, garys@wmcumc.org

Conference Ministry Consultant: **Garcia**, **Naomi**, 616/459-4503, Naomi@wmcumc.org

Publications
Michigan Area Reporter (monthly, www.westmichiganconference.org/pages/detail/1979

Foundation
United Methodist Foundation
11 Fuller SE, PO Box 6247
Grand Rapids, MI 49516
616/459-4503, 888/217-1905, fax: 616/459-0191
info@umfmichigan.org
www.UMFMichigan.org

WEST OHIO (NC, WEST OHIO AREA)
32 Wesley Blvd.
Worthington, Ohio 43085
614/844-6200; 800/437-0028
westohioumc.org
www.westohioumc.org

Episcopal Office
Bishop: **Palmer**, **Gregory V.**, 614/844-6200, wocbishop@wocumc.org
Assistant to the Bishop: **Sholis**, **Barbara**, 614/844-6200, bsholis@wocumc.org
Executive Secretary to the Bishop: **Corbitt**, **Karen**, 614/844-6200, kcorbitt@wocumc.org
Administrative Coordinator: **McCoy**, **Tim**, 614/844-6200, tmccoy@wocumc.org

District Superintendents
Atha, **Marcus**, Capitol Area North District, 614/222-0602, matha@wocumc.org
Brown, **Kathleen**, Capitol Area South District, 614/222-0600, kbrown@wocumc.org
Mohler, **Dennis**, Foothills District, 740/797-4581, dmohler@wocumc.org
Brown, **Marla**, Maumee Watershed District, 419/897-9770, mbrown@wocumc.org
Heckaman, **Christopher**, Miami Valley District, 937/529-2320, checkaman@wocumc.org
Bennett, **Stephen**, Northwest Plains District, 419/523-9901, sbennett@wocumc.org

Brown, Brian, Ohio River Valley District, 513/421-2057, bbrown@wocumc.org
Watson, Brent, Shawnee Valley District, 740/947-7508, bwatson@wocumc.org

Officers and Leaders

Director of Connectional & Missional Church Initiatives: **Kibbey, Sue Nilson**, 614/844-6200, snkibbey@wocumc.org
Conference Lay Leader: **Slater, Thomas**, 740/398-1690, tslater001@roadrunner.com
Conference Treasurer: **Brownson, Bill**, 614/844-6200, bbrownson@wocumc.org
Conference Secretary: **Aspey, Amy**, 614/844-6200, aaspey@wocumc.org
Conference Communications Director: **Streight, Lisa**, 614/844-6200, lstreight@wocumc.org
Director, Office of Ministry: **Griffin, Wade**, 614/84-6200, wgiffin@wocumc.org
Archivist: **Holliger, Carol**, 740/368-3285, aoum@owu.edu
Chancellor: **Moots, Philip**, 614/255-5441, pmoots@nplmlaw.com

Publications

N*ewsNET*, weekly enewsletter

Foundation

Council on Development
32 Wesley Blvd.
Worthington, Ohio 43085
614/844-6200; 800/437-0028
gcooper@wocumc.org
www.westohioumc.org
Director: **Cooper, George**

WEST VIRGINIA (NE, WEST VIRGINIA AREA)

900 Washington St. E.
Charleston, WV 25301
800/788-3746, 304/344-8331
wvareaumc@aol.com
www.wvumc.org

Episcopal Office

Bishop: **Ball, Sandra Steiner**, 304/344-8330, wvareaumc@aol.com
Assistant to the Bishop: **Wilson, Bill**, drbillwilson@aol.com
Administrative Assistant: **Shafer, Lisa**, wvareaumc@aol.com

District Superintendents

Flynn, Mark W., Greenbrier District, 304/645-1357, greenbrierdistrict@suddenlinkmail.com
Krimmel, Kenneth W., Little Kanawha District, 304/428-6461, office@lkdumc.org
Grant, Edward L., Midland South District, 304/342-8843, office@midlandsouthumc.org
Conley, Ellis E., Monvalley District, 304/366-6811, monvalley@juno.com
Erenrich, David E., Northern District, 304/232-5687, PeggyKlages@comcast.net
Forren, Edwin Dallas, Potomac Highlands, 304/822-4191, potomachighdistrict@yahoo.com
Oates, Helen R., Southern District, 304/252-7985, sdumc@suddenlinkmail.com
Finegan, Mary Ellen, Wesleyan District, 304/472-1095, Wesleyandist@3wlogic.net
Hayes, Gregory L., Western District, 304/736-9962, westernumc@aol.com

Officers and Leaders

Director of Connectional Ministries: **Wilson, William**, 304/344-8331 x31
Conference Lay Leader: **Shaffer, Rich**, 304/428-8536, wv.lay.leader@gmail.com
Conference Treasurer: **Berner, James**, 304/344-8331 x35
Conference Secretary: **Kenaston, Judi**, 304/344-8331 x23
Conference Communications Director: **Allen, Laura Harbert**, 304/344-8331 x22

Foundation

United Methodist Foundation of West Virginia, Inc.
900 Washington St. E. Ste. 203
Charleston, WV 25301
304/342-2113, 800/788-3746
info@umfwv.org
http://www.umfwv.org/
Director: **Taylor, Jeffrey A.**

WESTERN NORTH CAROLINA (SE, CHARLOTTE AREA)

3400 Shamrock Dr.
PO Box 18005
Charlotte, NC 28218
704/535-2260
snimmons@wnccumc.org
www.wnccumc.org

Episcopal Office

Bishop: **Goodpaster, Larry M.**
Assistant to the Bishop: **Langford, Sally O.**, 704/535-2260 x134, slangford@wnccumc.org
Executive Secretary: **Suther, Jane**, 704/535-2260 x138, jsuther@wnccumc.org

District Superintendents

Huffman, Lory Beth, Appalachian District, 704/525-3395, lhuffman@wnccumc.org
Boggs, John, Blue Ridge District, 828/524-8564, jboggs@wnccumc.org
Sorrells, W. Lyn, Catawba Valley District, 704/865-3560, lsorrels@wnccumc.org
Royals, Gary C., Metro District, 704/525-3395, groyals@wnccumc.org
Rankin, Nancy Burgin, Northern Piedmont District, 336/274-2154, nrankin@wnccumc.org
Coles, Amy, Smoky Mountain District, 828/454-6820, acoles@wnccumc.org
Moore, Samuel H. Jr., Uwharrie District, 704/983-1104, smoore@wnccumc.org
Medlin, William T., Yadkin Valley District, 336/725-4502, bmedlin@wnccumc.org

Officers and Leaders

Director of Discipleship Ministry: **Davis, Jennifer**, 704/535-2250 x113, jdavis@wnccumc.org
Conference Lay Leader: **Upchurch, Robert**, 336/431-3821, RUandJU@aol.com
Conference Treasurer: **Burton, Jennifer**, 704/535-2260 x127, jburton@wnccumc.org
Conference Secretary: **Ingram, Kim**, 704/535-2260 x112, kingram@wnccumc.org
Conference Communications Director: **Nimmons, Skyler**, 704/535-2260 x124, snimmons@wnccumc.org

Publications

e-News (every two weeks; wnccumc.org)
The Daily Digest (daily during Annual Conference)

Foundation

United Methodist Foundation of Western North Carolina, Inc.
13816 Professional Center Dr., Ste. 100,
Huntersville, NC 28078
704/817-3990
dsnipes@umfwnc.org
www.umfwnc.org
President: **Snipes, David A.**

Conferences

WESTERN PENNSYLVANIA (NE, PITTSBURGH AREA)

1204 Freedom Rd.
PO Box 5002
Cranberry Township, PA 16066-0002
800/886-3382; 724/776-2300
communications@wpaumc.org
www.wpaumc.org

Episcopal Office

Bishop: **Bickerton, Thomas J.**, 724/776-1499, umbishop@wpaumc.org
Assistant to the Bishop: **Higginbotham Jr., Robert W.**, 724/776-1499, bishopassistant@wpaumc.org
Office Administrator: **Wilson, Tina**, 724/776-1499, Tina.Wilson@wpaumc.org

District Superintendents

Ziegler, Dean D., Butler District, 724/452-0589, butler.district@wpaumc
Blair, William, Connellsville District, 724/628-3453, connellsville.district@wpaumc.org
Patterson, Joseph W., Erie-Meadville District, 814/332-4533, erie-meadville.district@wpaumc.org
Porter, George E. Jr., Franklin District, 814/437-5857, franklin.district@wpaumc.org
Meekins, William B. Jr., Greensburg District, 724/863-5673, greensburg.district@wpaumc.org
Schwab, Sharon, Indiana District, 814/938-1742, indiana.district@wpaumc
Weaver Dunn, Alyce, Johnstown District, 814/361-2464, johnstown.district@wpaumc.org
Strandburg, Thomas Q., Kane District, 814/837-6115, kane.district@wpaumc.org
Scandrol, Donald G., Pittsburgh District, 412/281-7152, pittsburgh.district@wpaumc
Park, Eric, Washington District, 724/225-6632, washington.district@wpaumc.org

Officers and Leaders

Director of Connectional Ministries: **Cox, Gregory D.**, 800/536-9242, dcm@wpaumc.org
Conference Lay Leader: **Gregory, Sharon**, 412/727-1235, conferencelayleader@wpaumc.org
Conference Treasurer: **Morris, Patricia A.**, 412/536-9245, treasurer@wpaumc.org
Conference Secretary: **Wilson, John R.**, 412/767-5646, conference.secretary@wpaumc.org
Conference Communications Officer: **Check, Dawn Lynn**, 724/776-2300 x227, Dawn.Check@wpaumc.org

Publications

InterLink (newspaper, monthly)
Annual Conference Journal (www.wpaumc.org/Journal)
WPAUMC (e-news, weekly, www.wpaumc.org/enews)

Foundation

United Methodist Foundation of Western Pennsylvania
223 Fourth Ave. Ste. 707, Pittsburgh, PA 15222-1713
412/232-0650
info@UMFoundation.org
www.umfoundation.org
Director: **Leasure, Frederick H.**

WISCONSIN (NC, WISCONSIN AREA)

750 Windsor St.
PO Box 620
Sun Prairie, WI 53590-0620
888/240-7328; 608/837-7328, fax: 608/837-8547
mediacontact@WisconsinUMC.org
www.wisconsinumc.org

Episcopal Office

Bishop: **Jung, Hee-Soo**, 608/837-8526, HSJung@wisconsinumc.org
Assistant to the Bishop: **Polster, Steve**, 608/837-8526, spolster@wisconsinumc.org
Administrative Assistant: **Churan, Cindy**, 608/837-8526, cchuran@wisconsinumc.org

District Superintendents

Royappa, Samuel, Capital-Coulee Districts, 607/837-0056, sroyappa@wisconsinumc.org
Spindt Henschel, Ann, Chippewa-Heartland Districts, 715/835-5181, ashenschel@wisconsinumc.org
Thompson, Deborah, Metro Region Districts, 414/271-5080, dthompson@wisconsinumc.org
Lind, Gordon, Nicolet-Winnebago Districts, 920/991-0548, glind@wisconsinumc.org

Leaders and Officers

Director of Connectional Ministry: **Dick, Dan R.**, 608/837-7328, 888/240-7328, ddick@wisconsinumc.org

Conferences

Conference Lay Leader: **Shimko, Deanna**, 262/534-6581, dshimko@wi.rr.com
Conference Secretary: **Wolover, Amber** 608/469-6895, ConfSec@wisconsinumc.org
Conference Treasurer: **King, Lisa**, 608/837-7320 x221 lisaking@wisconsinumc.org
Communications Director: **Virnig, Michele**, 608/837-7328, 888/240-7328 x269, mvirnig@wisconsinumc.org

Publications

ENews (e-newsletter, weekly)
Reflections (quarterly)

Wisconsin United Methodist Foundation

750 Windsor St. Ste. 305
Sun Prairie, WI, 53590
608/938-9582
wumf@wumf.org
http://wumf.org/
President: **Churan, Rick**

YELLOWSTONE (W; MOUNTAIN SKY AREA)

1220 Ave. C Ste. C
Billings, MT 59102-3200
Mailing Address: PO Box 20335, Billings, MT 59104-0335
800/808-0408, 406/256-1385, fax: 406/256-4948
sueking@yacumc.org
http://www.yacumc.org/

Episcopal Office

Bishop: **Stanovsky, Elaine J.W.**
Assistant to the Bishop: **Burt, David**, 406/256-1385, david@yacumc.org

District Superintendents

Morton, Kama Hamilton., Big Horn District (Montana Area), 406/685-3868, kama@yacumc.org
Olenyik, Debra, Big Horn District (Wyoming Area), 406/685-3868, kama@yacumc.org
Morton, Kama Hamilton, Northern Plains District, 406/256-1385 x104, kama@yacumc.org
Daniels, John F., Western Mountains District, 406/896-6396, john@yacumc.org

Officers and Leaders

Conference Treasurer: **Saas**, **Anita**, 406/256-1385, anita@yacumc.org

Foundation

Yellowstone Conference United Methodist Foundation
PO Box 22215
Billings, MT 59104-2215
406/652-1945
sharon@yaumc.org
http://ycumf.org/index.html
President: **Ellis**, **Sharon**

Central Conference Episcopal Areas

Angola East Episcopal Area

Bishop: **Quipungo**, **Jose**
Rua Comandante Dangereux No. 46
Caixa Postal 9
Malange, Angola
Phone/fax: 244/2512 30063, 244/92 354 1594 [cell]
bishopquipungo@yahoo.com

Area Conferences

Eastern Angola Annual Conference

Angola West Episcopal Area

Bishop: **Domingos**, **Gaspar Joao**
Rua de N.S. Da Muxima 12
Caixa Postal 68
Luanda, Angola
244/222 33 2107, fax: 244/222 39 0184
gdomingos61@yahoo.com

Area Conferences

Western Angola Annual Conference

Baguio Episcopal Area

Bishop: **Torio**, **Pedro M. Jr.**
Methodist Mission Center
10 Marcos Highway
PO Box 87
2600 Baguio City, Philippines
63/74 442 2879, fax: 63/74 304 2653
Manila Office and Mailing Address:
United Methodist Headquarters
900 United Nations Ave.
PO Box 756

1000 Ermita, Metro Manila
Philippines

Area Conferences

Central Luzon Philippines Annual Conference
North Central Philippines Annual Conference
Northeast Luzon Phillipines Annual Conference
Northeast Philippines Annual Conference
Northern Philippines Annual Conference
Northwest Philippines Annual Conference
Pangasinan Philippines Annual Conference
Tarlac Phillipines Annual Conference

CENTRAL AND SOUTHERN EUROPE EPISCOPAL AREA

Bishop: **Streiff, Patrick**
Badener Strasse 69
PO Box 2239
CH-8026 Zurich
Switzerland
41/44 299 30 60, fax: 41/44 299 30 69
bischof@umc-europe.org or urs.schweizer@umc-europe.org
http://www.umc-europe.org/

Area Conferences

Austria Provisional Annual Conference
Bulgaria/Romania Provisional Annual Conference
Czech and Slovak Republics Annual Conference
Hungary Provisional Annual Conference
Poland Annual Conference
Serbia-Montenegro-Macedonia Provisional Annual Conference
Switzerland-France Annual Conference

CENTRAL CONGO EPISCOPAL AREA

Bishop: **Yemba, David K.**
2867 Ave Des Ecuries, Ngaliema
B.P. 4727, Kinshasa II
Democratic Republic of Congo
243/810 806 614
bishopccongo@yahoo.com

Area Conferences

Central Congo Annual Conference
Kasai Annual Conference
Western Congo Annual Conference

CÔTE D'IVOIRE EPISCOPAL AREA

Bishop: **Boni, Benjamin**
41 Blvd. de la Republique
01 Bete Postale1282, Abidjan 01
Côte d'Ivoire
West Africa
225/20 21 17 97, fax: 225/20 22 5203
gsuinci@aviso.ci, Bishop's bishopboni@emu-ci.org
http://www.emu-ci.org/

Area Conferences

Côte D'Ivoire Annual Conference

DAVAO EPISCOPAL AREA

Bishop: **Francisco,Ciriaco Q.**
Davao United Methodist Center
104 Recto Ave.
8000 Davao City
Philippines
Phone/fax: 63/82 222 4474
bishopdavao@yahoo.com
umcdea.wordpress.com/
Manila Office and Mailing Address:
United Methodist Headquarters
900 United Nations Ave.
PO Box 756
1000 Ermita, Metro Manila
Philippines

Area Conferences

Bicol Provisional Philippines Annual Conference
East Mindanao Philippines Annual Conference
Mindanao Philippines Annual Conference
Northwest Mindanao Philippines Annual Conference
Visayas Philippines Annual Conference

East Africa Episcopal Area

Bishop: **Wandabula, Daniel**
The United Methodist Church
Plot No.1259, Mukalazi, Bukoto
Next to Trinity Academy
PO Box 12554
Kampala
Uganda
256/41 533978, fax: 256/41 533982
residentbishopeaacumc@gmail.com

Area Conferences

East Africa Annual Conference
  (includes Burundi, Kenya, Rwanda, Sudan and Uganda)

Eastern Congo Episcopal Area

Bishop: **Unda, Gabriel Yemba**
Ave De La Justice 75B
Combe-Kinshasa
Democratic Republic of Congo
243/998127204
gabrielunda@hotmail.com

Area Conferences

Eastern Congo Annual Conference
Kivu Annual Conference
Oriental and Equator Annual Conference

Germany Episcopal Area

Bishop: **Wenner, Rosemarie**
Ludolfusstrasse 2-4
D-60487 Frankfurt, Germany
49/69/24 25 210, fax: 49/69/24 25 2129
sekretariat.bischoefin@emk.de, Bishop: bischoefin@emk.de
http://emk.de/

Area Conferences

East Germany Annual Conference
North Germany Annual Conference
South Germany Annual Conference

LIBERIA EPISCOPAL AREA

Bishop: **Innis, John G.**
Liberia United Methodist Church
Tubman Blvd. at 13th St.
PO Box 10-1010
1000 Monrovia, Liberia
West Africa
231/88 651 7192
Liberiaumc@yahoo.com, Bishop: b.innis123@gmail.com
http://liberiaunitedmethodistchurch.org

Area Conferences
Liberia Annual Conference

MANILA EPISCOPAL AREA

Bishop: **Juan, Rodolfo Alfonso**
United Methodist Headquarters
900 United Nations Ave.
PO Box 756
1000 Ermita, Metro Manila
Philippines
63/2 523 4136, 63/2 521 1114, 63/2 523 0297, fax: 63/2/521 2278

Area Conferences
Bulacan Philippines Annual Conference
Middle Philippines Annual Conference
Palawan Philippines Annual Conference
Pampango Annual Conference
Philippines Annual Conference
Philippines Annual Conference East
Philippines Annual Conference - Cavite
Quezon City Philippines Annual Conference
Southern Tagalog Provisional Annual Conference
Southwest Philippines Annual Conference
West Middle Philippines Annual Conference

MOSCOW EPISCOPAL AREA

Bishop: **Khegay, Eduard**
Khamovnicheskiy Val 24, Stroenie 2

Moscow, 119048
Russia
7/495/961 3458 3
bishop@umc-eurasia.ru
http://www.umc-eurasia.ru

Area Conferences
Central Russia Annual Conference
East Russia and Central Asia Provisional Annual Conference
Northwest Russia Provisional Annual Conference
South Russia Provisional Annual Conference
Ukraine and Moldova Provisional Annual Conference

MOZAMBIQUE EPISCOPAL AREA
Bishop: **Nhanala, Joaquina F.**
Rua da Francisco Barreto 229
Caixa Postal 2640
Maputo, Mozambique
Phone/fax: 258/21 49 3568
Administrative Assistant 258/82 31 6620
umcmho@zebra.uem.mz, Bishop: jnhanala2@yahoo.com

Area Conferences
North Mozambique Annual Conference
South Mozambique Annual Conference
South Africa Provisional Annual Conference

NIGERIA EPISCOPAL AREA
Bishop: **Yohanna, John Wesley**
UMCN Secretariat, Mile Six
Jalingo-Numan Rd.
PO Box 148, Jalingo
Taraba State
Nigeria
234/708 656 9911, 234/806 347 5207
afkulah@yahoo.com

Area Conferences
Gwaten Nigeria Annual Conference
Pero Nigeria Annual Conference
Southern Nigeria Annual Conference

NORDIC-BALTIC EPISCOPAL AREA

Bishop: **Alsted, Christian**
The United Methodist Church
Rigensgade 21A
DK-1316 Copenhagen
Denmark
45/70 20 93 90
office@umc-ne.org
http://www.umc-northerneurope.org/

Area Conferences

Denmark Annual Conference
Estonia Annual Conference
Finland-Finnish Provisional Annual Conference
Finland-Swedish Provisional Annual Conference
Norway Annual Conference
Sweden Annual Conference

NORTH KATANGA EPISCOPAL AREA

Bishop: **Ntambo, Nkulu Ntanda**
PO Box 22037
Kitwe, Zambia
243/81 408 1120, fax: 243/97 108 9792
Bishop@northkatangaumc.org
Street Address:
United Methodist Church
Batiment Mokador Ave. Mobutu
Lubumbashi
Democratic Republic of Congo

Area Conferences

North Katanga Annual Conference
Tanganyika Annual Conference
Tanzania Annual Conference

SIERRA LEONE EPISCOPAL AREA

Bishop: **Yambasu, John K.**
31 Lightfoot Boston St.
PO Box 523

Freetown, Sierra Leone
West Africa
232/22 220212, 232/22 226625, fax: 232/22 224439
bishopyambasu@gmail.com

Area Conferences
Sierra Leone Annual Conference

SOUTHERN CONGO EPISCOPAL AREA

Bishop: **Katembo, Kainda**
United Methodist Church
960 Ave. Mzee Laurent Kabila
Lubumbashi
Democratic Republic of Congo
Mailing Address:
The United Methodist Church
B.P. 20219
Kitwe
Zambia
Satellite: 762/641-651, 762/981-916, 243/88 47256, fax: 243/23 41191 [via Zambia]
akatembokainda@yahoo.fr

Area Conferences
Lukoshi Annual Conference
North-West Katanga Annual Conference
South Congo Annual Conference
South-West Katanga Annual Conference
Zambia Annual Conference

ZIMBABWE EPISCOPAL AREA

Bishop: **Nhiwatiwa, Eben**
163 Chinhoyi St.
PO Box 3408
Harare
Zimbabwe
263/4 751 509, 263/4 751 093
umczim@africaonline.co.zw, Bishop: bishopnhiwatiwa@yahoo.co.uk
http://umczimbabwe.org/

Area Conferences
East Zimbabwe Annual Conference
Malawi Missionary Conference
West Zimbabwe Annual Conference

Groups and Caucuses

Affiliated and Related Groups

Aldersgate Renewal Ministries
(United Methodist Renewal Services Fellowship, Inc.)
http://aldersgaterenewal.org/
Contact: **Dow, Jonathan**, 121 East Ave., Goodlettsville TN 37072, 615/851-9192, fax: 615/851-9372, jdow@aldersgaterenewal.org

Africa University Development Office
http://www.support-africauniversity.org/
Associate Vice-Chancellor for Institutional Advancement: **Salley, James H.**, PO Box 340007, Nashville, TN 37203-0007, 615/340-7438, fax: 615/340-7290, audevoffice@gbhem.org
Affiliation: GBHEM

Appalachian Ministries Network
http://www.appalachia-umc.org/

Appalachia Service Project, Inc.
www.asphome.org
Contact: **Crouch, Walter**, 4523 Bristol Highway, Johnson City, TN 37601, 423/854-8800, walter.crouch@asphome.org

Association for Leaders in Lifelong Learning for Ministry (ALLLM)
http://www.sacem.com/
Formerly known as the Society for the Advancement of Continuing Education for Ministry (SACEM), affiliated with GBHEM
President: **Harewood, Brenda K.**, bkharewood@yahoo.com

Association of Annual Conference Lay Leaders
Contact: **Furr, Steve**, 214 Plantation Trace, Jackson, AL 36545, 251/246-5266, 251/246-4446, furrs@bellsouth.net

Association of United Methodist Conference Pensions & Benefits Officers

http://www.gbophb.org/events_education/AUMCPBO.asp
Affiliation: GBPHB

Better Marriages

http://www.bettermarriages.org/?main
(formerly ACME, Association for Couples in Marriage Enrichment, Inc.)
Contact: **Hunt**, **Priscilla**, PO Box 21374, Winston-Salem, NC 27120, 800/634-8325, acme@BetterMarriages.org

Black Methodists for Church Renewal (BMCR)

http://bmcrumc.org/
Chair: **Bridgeforth**, **Cedrick**, PO Box 561765, Los Angeles, CA 90056, 310/422-9491, pastorcedrick@gmail.com
Manager of Programs & Operations: **Crosby**, **Pamela J.**, 201 8th Ave. So., PO Box 801, Nashville, TN 37203, 615/749-6351 fax: 615/749-6262, pcrosby@umpublishing.org; bmcr@umpublishing.org;

Christian Educators Fellowship (CEF)

http://www.cefumc.org/
Director: **Schleicher**, **Andrew**, PO Box, Nashville, TN 37202, 615/749-6870, director@cefumc.org

Council for Accountable Discipleship

Contact: **Heck**, **Terry**, 47 E. Franklin St., Bellbrook, OH 45305, 937/848-2909, pastor@bellbrookumc.org

Council of Presidents of Historically Black Colleges and Universities

http://www.gbhem.org/education/council-presidents
Affiliation: GBHEM, Contact: **Hopson**, **Cynthia Bond**, 615/340-7378, bcfumc@gbhem.org

Council on Evangelism

http://congressonevangelism.org/
PO Box 1420, Lake Junaluska, NC 28745

Deacons of the Americas and Caribbean

http://www.dotac.diakonia-world.org
President: **Polito**, **Lisa**, lisa.polito@valpo.edu
Affiliation: GBHEM, Contact: **Wood**, **Anita**, awood@gbhem.org

DIAKONIA

(World Federation of Diaconal Associations and Diaconal Communities)

http://www.diakonia-world.org
Secretary: **Kellner**, **Ulrike**, secretary@diakonia-world.org
World President: **Horn**, **Doris**, president@diakonia-world.org
Affiliation: GBHEM

The Disciplined Order of Christ

http://dochr.org/
National President: **Bankson**, **John D.**, 1019 Wisteria Dr., Florence, SC 29501, 843/601-2224, jbankson@sc.rr.com, john.bankson@wellsfargo.com

The Ecumenical Network of the Diaconate

Contact: **Lee**, **Virginia**, Garrett-Evangelical Theological Seminary, 2121 Sheridan Rd., Evanston, IL 60201, virginia.lee@garrett.edu
Affiliation: GBHEM

Educational & Institutional Insurance Administrators (EIIA)

http://eiia.org/
President: **Gadbois**, **Siri S.**, 200 S. Wacker Dr., Ste. 1000, Chicago, IL 60606 312/648-0914, x203 fax: 312/648-5511 sgadbois@eiia.org
Affiliation: GBHEM

Fellowship of UMS in Music and Worship Arts (FUMMWA)

www.fummwa.org
Executive Director: **Bone**, **David**, PO Box 24787, Nashville TN 37202-4787, 800/952-8977, 615/749-6875, David.Bone@UMFellowship.org.

Fellowship of UM Spiritual Directors and Retreat Leaders (FUMSDRL)

President: **Moore, Karen Covey**, 1779 Kirby Pkwy., Ste. 1-100, Memphis, TN 38138-0631, 614/274-4232, fumsdrl@aol.com

The Foundation for Evangelism

http://www.evangelize.org/
125 N. Lakeshore Dr., PO Box 985, Lake Junaluska, NC 28745, 800/737-8333
Executive Director: **Wood, Jane**, 828/454-6800, jwood@foundationforevangelism.org

Hearts on Fire

http://fumsdrl.org/
(formerly: Fellowship of UM Spiritual Directors and Retreat Leaders)

The Historical Society of The United Methodist Church

http://www.historicalsocietyunitedmethodistchurch.org/
President: **Swinson, Daniel**, 223 North Emerson St., Prospect, IL 60056-2509, djswinson@wowway.com
Affiliation: GCAH

International Association of Methodist-related Schools, Colleges and Universities (IAMSCU)

http://www.gbhem.org/education/international-association-methodist-schools-colleges-universities
President: **Brown, Ted**, Martin Methodist College, 433 West Madison St., Pulaski, TN 38478, 931/363-9801 fax: 931/363-9892, tbrown@martinmethodist.edu
Affiliation: GBHEM; Contact: **Lord, Gerald D.**, PO Box 340007, Nashville, TN 37203-0007, 615/340-7399 fax: 615/340-7379, glord@gbhem.org

International Christian Youth Exchange (ICYE)

http://www.icye.org/
Affiliation: GBGM

Legal Services Division of Higher Education
Contact: **Weeks**, **Kent M.**, Weeks &Anderson, 2021 Richard Jones Rd., Ste. 350, Nashville, TN 37215, 615/383-3332 fax: 615/383-3480, kentweeks@comcast.net
Affiliation: GBHEM

Marriage and Engaged Encounter United Methodist
www.encounter.org
Executive Clergy Couple: **White**, **Don & Vivian**, 8306 Heaton Hall St. Humble, TX 77338, 832/794-8162, donvivwhite@juno.com; Executive Lay Couple: **Morris**, **Gary & Lisa**, 145 N. Springs Way, Acworth, GA 30101, 678/819-8885, garylisa@comcast.net

Methodist Hour International
Wolfe, **John L.**, 15770 Birmingham Highway, Alpharetta, GA 30004, 678/488-2162, johnwolfe@mindspring.com

Metodistas Associados Representando la Causa de Hispano-Americanos (MARCHA)
http://www.marchaumc.org/(in Spanish)
Executive Director: **Galván**, **Elías G.**, 9845 E. Desert Cove Ave., Scottsdale, AZ 85260, 480/361-6484 galvin222@msn.com
President: **Alegría**, **Raúl**, 759 Lakeshore Dr., Lake Junaluska, NC 28745 828/454-6712 fax: 828/456-4040 ralegria@lakejunaluska.org

Ministry Development Council
http://www.ministrydevelopment.org/
Chair: **Kron**, **Keith**, Kkron@uua.org
Affiliation: GBHEM

National Association of Annual Conference Treasurers
Affiliation: GCFA, Contact: **Kumar**, **A. Moses Rathan**, 1 Music Cir. N., Nashville, TN 37203-0029, 615/369-2320, fax: 615/369-2321, mkumar@gcfa.org

National Association of Commissions on Equitable Compensation
http://www.gcfa.org/nacec
Contact: **Chambers**, **Laura.**, Senior Researcher, PO Box 340029, 1 Music

Cir. N., Nashville, TN 37203-0029, 615/369-2396, fax: 615/369-2374, lchambers@gcfa.org
President: **Scott**, **Laurel**, New England
Affiliation: GCFA

National Association of Conference Presidents of UM Men
Affiliation: GCUMM

National Association of Directors of Connectional Ministries

National Association of Schools and Colleges of The UMC (NASCUMC)
http://www.gbhem.org/education/national-association-schools-colleges-umc
President: **Simmons**, **Jay K.**, Simpson College, 701 N. C St., Indianola, IA 50125, 515/961-1611, jay.simmons@simpson.edu
Affiliation: GBHEM, nascumc@gbhem.org

National Association of United Methodist Evangelists (NAUME)
http://naume.org/
PO Box 1900, Goodlettsville, TN 37070, 800/658-6569, info@naume.org
Executive Evangelist: **Moore**, **Gary L.**, 1592 Campbell Rd., Goodlettsville, TN 37072, 615/859-9680, 615/519-0085, gary@fanintoflame.org

National Association of United Methodist Foundations (NAUMF)
http://www.naumf.org/
Executive Director: **Marston**, **Tom**, 15530 Waterfront Dr., Huntersville, NC 28028, 704/992-9651, cell: 863/370-0951, naumf2012@gmail.com

National Association of UM Scouters
http://www.gcumm.org/ministries/scouting/
Affiliation: GCUMM

Groups and Caucuses

National Federation of Asian American United Methodists

http://nfaaum.org/
PO Box 18666, Oakland, CA 94619, 925/727-1295, fax: 510/380-6944, nfaaum@gmail.com
President: **Hayashi**, **Donald L.**, Vandalia, OH, hayashidon@aol.com
Affiliation: GCORR

National Fellowship of Associate Members and Local Pastors

http://www.nfamlp.org/
President: **Mahaffey**, **Mike**, Oklahoma, 580/334-9613, mahaffey583@aol.com
Affiliation: GBHEM

National Plan for Hispanic and Latino Ministry

http://new.gbgm-umc.org/plan/hispanic/
Executive Coordinator: **Cañas**, **Francisco**, GBGM, 475 Riverside Dr., Rm. 330, New York, NY 10115, 212/870-3820, 212/870-3693, fax: 212/870-3895, FCanas@gbgm-umc.org

National United Methodist Campers, Inc.

http://www.umcampers.org/
2402 Pinehurst Dr., Monroe, LA 71201-2315, 318/324-8198

National United Methodist Camp and Retreat Committee

http://umcrm.org/
Contact: **Huber**, **Mike**, mikehuber@campsandretreats.org

National UM Native American Center

http://www.cst.edu/academics/research-centers/numnac/
Executive Director: **Noley**, **Homer**, 918/465-5203, numnac@cst.edu
Fiscal Manager: **Hamilton-Allen**, **Robin**, 626/253-1999

Native American International Caucus

http://naicumc.org/
Contact: **Kent**, **Cynthia Ann**, 301 Washington Ave., Belleville, NJ 07109, kent.cy@live.com, NAICCommunications@gmail.com
Affiliation: GCORR

The Order of Saint Luke

http://www.saint-luke.net/
Chancellor: **Alford**, **Scott**, 5330 Park Ave., Memphis, TN 38119, oslchancellor@gmail.com;
Prior-General: **Moore, Elizabeth "Sue,"** 1002 Hunter Ln., Ashland City, TN 37105, esmoore@alum.mit.edu

Pacific Islander National Caucus of United Methodists

http://www.umcmission.org/Connect-with-Us/National-Plans/Pacific-Islander-National-Plan

Professional Association of UM Church Secretaries

http://www.gbgm-umc.org/paumcs/
Affiliation: GCFA
President: **Kingsley**, **Barbara**, PO Box 49, Rush, NY 14543-0049, 585/533-2170, barbing@rochester.rr.com
GCFA Contact: **Haralson**, **Cynthia J.**, PO Box 340029, Nashville, TN 37203-0029 866/367-4232 paumcs@gcfa.org

Saint Brigid of Kildare Monastery

http://www.janrichardson.com/saintbrigidmonastery
Contact: **Stamps**, **Mary E.**, 200 E. Minnesota St., St. Joseph, MN 56374-4620, 320/363-1405, kildaremonastery@yahoo.com

Society of Saint Andrew

http://endhunger.org/
3383 Sweet Hollow Rd., Big Island, VA 24526, 800/333-4597, 434/299-5956, SoSAUSA@EndHunger.org
Executive Director: **Waldmann**, **Mike**
Affiliation: GCUMM

United Christian Ashrams International

http://www.christianashram.org/
Contact: **Escamilla**, **Roberto**, 904 DeVille Ln., Ruston, LA 71270, 318/232-0004, fax: 318/2323-0300, uca@christianashram.org

UM Association of Church Business Administrators

http://www.umacba.org/
President: **King**, **Mark**, 336/724-6311, mking@centenary-ws.org

Affiliation: GCFA, Contact: **Morrison, Alan J.**, PO Box 340029, 1 Music Cir. N., Nashville, TN 37203-0029, 615/369-2350, amorrison@gcfa.org

UM Association of Communicators

http://www.umcommunicators.org/
President: **Caldwell, Neill**, Virginia Annual Conference, NeillCaldwell@vaumc.org
Affiliation: UMCOM

UM Association of Health and Welfare Ministries

http://umassociation.org/
2800 W. Main St., Tupelo, MS 38801, 662/269-2955, fax: 662/269-2956
President/CEO: **Vinson, Stephen L.**
Affiliation: GBGM

UM Association of Scholars in Christian Education (UMASCE)

http://www.umasce.org/
General Inquiries: **Marshall, Ben**, rben@airmail.net
President: **Willhauck, Susan**

UM Campus Ministers Association

Co-chair: **Jeter, Narcie**, winthropwesley@gmail.com
Co-chair: **Shultz, Paul**, paul@iowawesley.org
Affiliation: GBHEM

UM Council on Korean Ministries

http://www.umcmission.org/Connect-with-Us/National-Plans/Korean-Ministry-Plan

UM Higher Education Foundation

https://www.umhef.org/
PO Box 340005, Nashville, TN 37203-0005, 615/649-3990, 800/811-8110
President: **Fletcher, Robert R.**, 615/649-3976, bfletcher@umhef.org
Affiliation: GBHEM

UM Information Technology Association

www.umita.org

Board
President: **Quinn, Chris**, Western North Carolina Conference
Vice President: **Krowl, Ivan**, Texas Conference
Secretary: **Horstman, Jane**, California-Nevada Conference
Treasurer: **Schoeller, David**, Baltimore-Washington Conference
Member: **Minshall, Roland**, Iowa Conference
Member: **Myers, Mary**, Oklahoma Conference
Web Master: **Compton, Bryan**, Virginia Conference
Former President: **Murphy-McCarthy, Michael**, North Georgia Conference
Ex Officio: **Cook, Michael**, GCFA
Ex Officio: **Mai, Danny**, UMCOM

Agencies
General Board of Discipleship: **Johnson, Robert**, 1908 Grand Ave., Nashville, TN 37212, bjohnson@gbod.org
General Board of Pensions & Health Benefits: **Kane, Eileen**, 1201 Davis St., Evanston, IL 60201, ekane@gbophb.org
General Council on Finance and Administration: **Cook, Michael**, Director of Information Technology, 1 Music Cir. N., Nashville, TN 37203-0029, 615/369-2375 fax: 615/369-2374, mcook@gcfa.org
United Methodist Communications: **Mai, Danny**, PO Box 320, Nashville, TN 37202, 615/742-5443 fax: 615/742-5123, helpdesk@umcom.org
General Commission on United Methodist Men: **Davis, Martha**, PO Box 340006, Nashville, TN 37203-0006, mdavis@gcumm.org

UM Men Foundation
http://www.gcumm.org/support/foundation.html
1000 17th Ave. S., Nashville, TN 37212, 615/340-7145, gcumm@gcumm.org
President: **Shytle, Ed**, 606/329-0461, edshytle@roadrunner.com
Affiliation: GCUMM

UM Student Movement
http://www.umsm.org/
Affiliation: GBHEM, Campus Ministry Section, GBHEM, PO Box 340007, 615/340-7415, fax: 615/340-7379, umsm@gbhem.org

UM Single Adult Leaders (UMSAL)
http://www.umsal.org/
Co-president: **Tillman, Jeanie**
Co-president: **Markley, Rene**

University Senate
http://www.gbhem.org/education/university-senate
Affiliation GBHEM, Contact: **Lord**, **Gerald D.**, 615/340-7399, glord@gbhem.org

Wesley Heritage Foundation
http://www.wesleyheritagefoundation.org/; http://www.iew-la.org/(Peru)
President: **Wethington**, **Mark W.**, 910/295-7720, markwhf@gmail.com

The World Methodist Historical Society
www.gcah.org/WMHS.htm
Affiliation: GCAH
President: **Schuler**, **Ulrike**, Memmingerstr. 54, 72762 Reutlingen, Germany, ulrike.schuler@emk.de

Caucuses

(Caucuses are included by their request and publisher's approval)

Affirmation: United Methodist
http://www.umaffirm.org
UMs for Lesbian, Gay, Bisexual, Transgender, and Queer Concerns. Co-spokespersons: Adams, Laci, Atlanta, GA; and Tennant-Jayn, Tim, Minneapolis, MN, umaffirmation@yahoo.com

Good News: Forum for Spiritual Christianity, Inc.
http://goodnewsmag.org/
PO Box 132076, The Woodlands, TX 77393-2076, 832/813-8327
President: **Renfroe, Rob**, rrenfroe@twumc.org
Vice President: **Lambrecht, Thomas**, tlambrecht@goodnewsmag.org

Institute on Religion & Democracy
http://www.theird.org/
President: **Tooley, Mark**, 1023 15th St., NW, Ste. 601, Washington, DC 20005-2601, 202/682-4131 fax: 202/682-4136 info@theird.org

Methodist Federation for Social Action
http://mfsaweb.org
212 E. Capitol St., NE, Washington, DC 20003, 202/546-8806 mfsa@mfsaweb.org
Interim Executive Director: **Pritchett, Chett**, chett@mfsaweb.org

Methodists United for Peace with Justice
http://www.mupwj.org/
Chair: **Hallman, Howard W.**, 1500 16th St. NW, Washington, DC 20036

Mission Society for United Methodists
https://www.themissionsociety.org/
6234 Crooked Creek Rd., Norcross, GA 30092, 800/478-8963, 770/446-1381, fax: 770/446-3044
President/CEO: **McClain, Dick**, 678/542-9021, dick@themissionsociety.org

Reconciling Ministries Network
http://www.rmnetwork.org/
Executive Director: **Oliver, Andy**, 863/397-0678, andy@rmnetwork.org

Southern Asian National Caucus for the United Methodists

http://sancum.org/
1170 E. Main St., Shrub Oak, NY 10580, 914/753-1003, info@sancum.org

Taskforce of United Methodists on Abortion and Sexuality

http://www.lifewatch.org/
Administrator: **Evans**, **Cindy**, Lifewatch/TUMAS, PO Box 306, Cottleville, MO 63338 636/294-2344 cindy@lifewatch.org
Newsletter Editor and President: **Stallsworth**, **Paul T.**, 902 Pinckney St., Whiteville, NC 28472, 910/642-3376

Transforming Congregations Movement

http://www.transcong.org/
Director: **Booth**, **Karen**, 2412 Second St., Monroe, WI 53566, 608/325-5712, 608/426-4337, transcong@aol.com

United Methodist Association of Ministers with Disabilities (AMWD)

http://www.umdisabledministers.org/index.html
Contact: **Vermande**, **Tim**, 3645 Toronto Ct., Indianapolis IN 46268
Co-Chair: **McDonald**, **Evy**, 4514 W. Pyracantha Dr., Tucson, AZ 85741
Co-Chair: **Pridmore**, **J. Eric**

United Methodist Rural Advocates

http://www.umrf.org/
President: **Grace**, **Roger**, 2755 Independence Ct., Grove City, OH 43123 H: 614/871-1083 O: 614/222-0602 C: 614/716-8328 rogergrace@yahoo.com
Contact: **Bastian**, **Dwight**, PO Box 2732, Rancho Mirage, CA 92270 760/328-5105 Dwight@post.harvard.edu

Ecumenical Groups

American Bible Society
http://www.americanbible.org/
1865 Broadway, New York, NY 10023-7505, 212/408-1200, fax: 212/408-1512
President: **Birdsall, S. Douglas**

Associated Church Press
http://www.theacp.org/
924 Woodcrest Way, PO Box 621001, Oviedo, FL 32762-1002, 407/386-3236, fax: 407/341-6615, associatedchurchpress@gmail.com,

The Council of Latin American Evangelical Methodist Churches in Latin America (CIEMAL)
http://gbgm-umc.org/latinam-caribbean/ciemal.html, http://www.ciemal.org/site/ (in Spanish)
President: **Pablo Morales**, Panama

Institute on Religion and Democracy
http://www.theird.org/
President: **Tooley, Mark**, 1023 15th St. NW, Ste. 601, Washington, DC 20005, 202/682-4131 fax: 202/682-4136, info@theird.org,

National Council of the Churches of Christ in the USA
http://www.ncccusa.org/
110 Maryland Ave. NE, Ste. 108, Washington, DC 20002, pjenks@ncccusa.org,
General Secretary: **Birk, Peg J.**, Plymouth Congregational Church, Minneapolis
President: **Lohre, Kathryn Mary**, klohre@fas.harvard.edu, Evangelical Lutheran Church in America

Pan-Methodist Commission
http://www.panmethodist.org/, http://www.gccuic-umc.org/panmeth/index.htm

Project Equality, Inc.
http://www.projectequality.org/
President/CEO: **Perucca, Kirk**, 913/486-7010, kirk@kperuccaasociates.com

World Council of Churches
http://www.oikoumene.org/en
PO Box 2100, CH-1211, Geneva 2, Switzerland +41/22/791-6111, fax: +41/22/791-0361, Charlotte.Vanel@wcc-coe.org,
General Secretary: **Tveit, Olav Fykse**

World Methodist Council
http://worldmethodistcouncil.org/
PO Box 518, 545 N. Lakeshore Dr., Lake Junaluska, NC 28745, 828/456-9432, info@worldmethodistcouncil.org
General Secretary: **Abrahams, Bishop Ivan**
Council President: **Lockmann, Bishop Paulo de Tarso**

Schools, Colleges, Universities, and Seminaries

www.gbhem.org/colleges

SCHOOLS OF THEOLOGY

Boston University School of Theology
Moore, Mary Elizabeth, dean, 745 Commonwealth Ave., Boston, MA 02215, 617/353-3050 fax: 617/353-3061, memoore@bu.edu

Candler School of Theology, Emory University
Love, Jan, dean, 1531 Dickey Dr., Atlanta, GA 30322, 404/727-6322 fax: 404/727-6324, jan.love@emory.edu

Claremont School of Theology
Campbell, Jerry D., president, 1325 N. College Ave., Claremont, CA 91711, 909/447-2552 fax: 909/621-3437, jcampbell@cst.edu

Drew University, The Theological School
Kuan, Kah-Jin Jeffrey, dean, 36 Madison Ave., Madison, NJ 07940, 973/408-3258 fax: 973/408-3534, jkuan@drew.edu

Duke University, The Divinity School
Hays, Richard B., dean, 107 New Divinity, Box 90968, Durham, NC 27708-0968, 919/660-3434 fax: 919/660-3474, rhays@div.duke.edu

Gammon Theological Seminary
Mosley, Albert, president, 653 Beckwith St. SW, Atlanta, GA 30314, 404/581-0300 fax: 404/581-0305, gammonpresident@gmail.com

Garrett-Evangelical Theological Seminary
Amerson, Philip A., president, 2121 Sheridan Rd., Evanston, IL 60201, 847/866-3901 fax: 847/866-3884, philip.amerson@garrett.edu

Iliff School of Theology

Hernandez, Albert, interim president, 2201 S. University Blvd., Denver, CO 80210, 303/765-3183 fax: 303/765-1141, ahernandez@iliff.edu

Methodist Theological School in Ohio

Rundell, Jay, president, 3081 Columbus Pk., Delaware, OH 43015 740/362-3121 fax: 740/362-3135, jrundell@mtso.edu

Perkins School of Theology, Southern Methodist University

Lawrence, William B., dean, PO Box 750133, Dallas, TX 75275-0133 214/768-2534 fax: 214/768-2966, wblawren@smu.edu

Saint Paul School of Theology

McCoy, Myron, president, 5123 Truman Rd., Kansas City, MO 64127 816/483-9600 x101 fax: 816/483-9605, myron@spst.edu

United Theological Seminary

Deichmann, Wendy J., president, 4501 Denlinger Rd., Dayton, OH 45426, 937/529-2201 x3000 fax: 937/529-2345, wjdeichmann@united.edu

Wesley Theological Seminary

McAllister-Wilson, David, president, 4500 Massachusetts Ave. NW, Washington, DC 20016 202/885-8601 fax: 202/885-8605, dwilson@wesleyseminary.edu

PROFESSIONAL SCHOOL

Meharry Medical College

Riley, Wayne J., president/CEO, 1005 Dr. D.B. Todd, Jr. Blvd., Nashville, TN 37208, 615/327-6904 fax: 615/327-6540, wjriley@mmc.edu

SENIOR COLLEGES AND UNIVERSITIES

Adrian College

Docking, Jeffrey R., president, 110 S. Madison, Adrian, MI 49221 517/264-3867 fax: 517/264-3100, jdocking@adrian.edu

Schools, Colleges, Universities, and Seminaries

Alaska Pacific University
Bantz, Don, president, 4101 University Dr., Anchorage, AK 99508, 907/564-8201 fax: 907/562-2337, dbantz@alaskapacific.edu

Albion College
Randall, Donna, president, 611 East Porter St., Albion, MI 49224 517/629-0210 fax: 517/629-0619, drandall@albion.edu

Albright College
McMillan, Lex O., III, president, 13th and Bern St., PO Box 15234, Reading, PA 19612-5234, 610/921-7600 fax: 610/921-7737, lmcmillan@alb.edu

Allegheny College
Mullen, James H., president, 520 N. Main St., Meadville, PA 16335 814/332-5380 fax: 814/724-6032, james.mullen@allegheny.edu

American University
Kerwin, Cornelius, president, 4400 Massachusetts Ave. NW, Washington, DC 20016-8060 202/885-2121 fax: 202/885-3265, president@american.edu

Baker University
Long, Patricia N., president, PO Box 65, Baldwin City, KS 66006-0065 785/594-8311 fax: 785/594-8425, president@bakeru.edu

Baldwin-Wallace University
Helmer, Robert C., president, 275 Eastland Rd., Berea, OH 440172088 440/826-2424 fax: 440/826-3777, rhelmer@bw.edu

Bennett College for Women
Terry, Esther, interim president, 900 E. Washington St., Greensboro, NC 27401, 336/517-2155 fax: 336/370-8653, eterry@bennett.edu

Bethune-Cookman University
Jackson, Edison O., interim president, 640 Dr. Mary McLeod Bethune Blvd., Daytona Beach, FL 32114, 386/481-2004 fax: 386/481-2010, jackson@cookman.edu

Birmingham-Southern College

Krulak, Charles, president, Box 549002, 900 Arkadelphia Rd., Birmingham, AL 35254, 205/226-4620 fax: 205/226-7020, ckrulak@bsc.edu

Boston University

Brown, Robert A., president, One Silber Way, 8th Floor, Boston, MA 02215, 617/353-2200 fax: 617/353-3278, rabrown@bu.edu

Brevard College

Joyce, David O., president, One Brevard College Dr., Brevard, NC 28712, 828/884-8264 fax: 828/884-3790, president@brevard.edu

Centenary College

Lewthwaite, Barbara-Jayne, president, 400 Jefferson St., Hackettstown, NJ 07840, 908/852-1400 fax: 908/850-9508, lewthwaiteb@centenarycollege.edu

Centenary College of Louisiana

Rowe, B. David, president, 2911 Centenary Blvd., Shreveport, LA 71104, 318/869-5101 fax: 318/869-5010, president@centenary.edu

Central Methodist University

Inman, Marianne E., president, 411 Central Methodist Square, Fayette, MO 65248, 660/248-6221 fax: 660/248-2287, minman@centralmethodist.edu

Claflin University

Tisdale, Henry N., president, 400 Magnolia St., Orangeburg, SC 29115, 803/535-5412 fax: 803/535-5402, president@claflin.edu

Clark Atlanta University

Brown, Carlton E., president, 223 James P. Brawley Dr., SW, Atlanta, GA 30314, 404/880-8566 fax: 404/880-6315, caupresident@cau.edu

Columbia College

Dinndorf, Beth, president, 1301 Columbia College Dr., Columbia, SC 29203, 803/786-3178 fax: 803/754-3178, bdinndorf@columbiasc

Schools, Colleges, Universities, and Seminaries

Cornell College
Brand, Jonathan, president, 600 First St. SW, Mount Vernon, IA 52314-1098, 319/895-4000 fax: 319/895-5237, lgarner@cornellcollege.edu

Dakota Wesleyan University
Duffett, Robert G., president, 1200 W. University Ave., Mitchell, SD 57301, 605/995-2601 fax: 605/995-2723, roduffett@dwu.edu

DePauw University
Casey, Brian W., president, PO Box 37, Greencastle, IN 46135-0037, 765/658-4220 fax: 765/658-4224, president@depauw.edu

Dickinson College
Durden, William G., president, PO Box 1773, Carlisle, PA 17013-2896, 717/245-1322 fax: 717/245-1941, durden@dickinson.edu

Dillard University
Kimbrough, Walter, president, 2601 Gentilly Blvd., New Orleans, LA 70122, 504/571-2170 fax: 504/654-1815, wkimbrough@dillard.edu

Drew University
Bull, Vivian, president, 36 Madison Ave., Madison, NJ 07940, 973/408-3100 fax: 973/408-3080, vbull@drew.edu

Duke University
Brodhead, Richard H., president, 207 Allen Bldg., Box 90001, Durham, NC 27708-0001, 919/684-2424 fax: 919/684-3050, president@duke.edu

Emory & Henry College
Reichard, Rosalind, president, PO Box 947, Emory, VA 24327-0947, 276/944-6107 fax: 276/944-6598, rreichard@ehc.edu

Emory University
Wagner, James W., president, 408 Administration Bldg., Atlanta, GA 30322, 404/727-6013 fax: 404/727-5997, wagner@emory.edu

Ferrum College
Braaten, Jennifer L., president, PO Box 1000, Ferrum, VA 24088, 540/365-4202 fax: 540/365-4269, jbraaten@ferrum.edu

Florida Southern College
Kerr, Anne B., president, 111 Lake Hollingsworth Dr., Lakeland, FL 33801, 863/680-4100 fax: 863/680-5096, akeer@flsouthern.edu

Green Mountain College
Fonteyn, Paul J., president, One Brennan Cir., Poultney, VT 05764, 802/287-8201 fax: 802/287-8097, fonteynp@greenmtn.edu

Greensboro College
Czarda, Lawrence D., president, 815 W. Market St., Greensboro, NC 27401-1875, 336/272-7102 fax: 336/217-7230, lczarda@greensboro.edu

Hamline University
Hanson, Linda N., president, Hamline University MS-C1914, 1536 Hewitt Ave., St. Paul, MN 55104, 651/523-2202 fax: 651/523-2030, president@hamline.edu

Hendrix College
Arnold, Ellis III, president, 1600 Washington Ave., Conway, AR 72032, 501/450-1351 fax: 501/450-3821, Arnold@hendrix.edu

High Point University
Qubein, Nido R., president, 833 Montlieu Ave., High Point, NC 27262, 336/841-9201 fax: 336/841-5123, nqubein@highpoint.edu

Hiwassee College
Tricoli, Robin J., president, 1225 Hiwassee College Dr., Madisonville, TN 37354, 423/420-1225 fax: 423/420-1929, rjt@hiwassee.edu

Huntingdon College
West, J. Cameron, president, 1500 E. Fairview Ave., Montgomery, AL 36106-2148, 334/833-4409 fax: 334/833-4485, camwest@huntingdon.edu

Huston-Tillotson University
Earvin, Larry L., president/CEO, 900 Chicon St., Austin, TX 78702-2795, 512/505-3003 fax: 512/505-3195, llearvin@htu.edu

Illinois Wesleyan University
Wilson, Richard F., president, PO Box 2900, Bloomington, IL 61702-2900, 309/556-3151 fax: 309/556-3970, president@iwu.edu

Iowa Wesleyan College
TBD, president, 601 N. Main St., Mount Pleasant, IA 52641, http://www.iwc.edu/

Kansas Wesleyan University
Lowen, Wayne, interim president, 100 E. Claflin Ave., Salina, KS 67401-6196, 785/827-5541, x1225 fax: 785/827-0927, wayne.lowen@kwu.edu

Kentucky Wesleyan College
Turner, W. Craig, president, 3000 Frederica St., Owensboro, KY 42301, 270/852-3104 fax: 270/852-3190, cturner@kwc.edu

LaGrange College
McAlexander, Dan, president, 601 Broad St., LaGrange, GA 30240, 706/880-8230 fax: 706/880-8358, dmcalexander@lagrange.edu

Lebanon Valley College
Thayne, Lewis Evitts, president, 101 N. College Ave., Annville, PA 17003, 717/867-6211 fax: 717/867-6910, thayne@lvd.edu

Lindsey Wilson College
Luckey, William T., Jr., president, 210 Lindsey Wilson St., Columbia, KY 42728, 270/384-8001 fax: 270/384-8009, luckeyw@lindsey.edu

Lycoming College
Douthat, James E., president, 700 College Pl., Williamsport, PA 17701-5192, 570/321-4101 fax: 570/321-4307}, douthat@lycoming.edu

MacMurray College
Hester, Colleen, president, 447 E. College Ave., Jacksonville, IL 62650, 217/479-7025 fax: 217/479-7201, colleen.hester@mac.edu

Martin Methodist College
Brown, Ted, president, 433 W. Madison St., Pulaski, TN 38478, 931/363-9801 fax: 931/363-9892, tbrown@martinmethodist.edu

McKendree University
Dennis, James M., president, 701 College Rd., Lebanon, IL 62254, 618/537-6936 fax: 618/537-6417, jdennis@mckendree.edu

McMurry University
Russell, John H., president, 1400 Sayles Blvd., Abilene, TX 79697-0098, 325/793-3801 fax: 325/793-4628, jrussell@mcm.edu

Methodist University
Hancock, Ben E. Jr., president, 5400 Ramsey St., Fayetteville, NC 28311-1498, 910/630-7005 fax: 910/630-7317, bhancock@methodist.edu

Millsaps College
Pearigen, Robert W., president, 1701 N. State St., Jackson, MS 39210, 601/974-1001 fax: 601/974-1004, rob.pearigen@millsaps.edu

Morningside College
Reynders, John C., president, 1501 Morningside Ave., Sioux City, IA 51106, 712/274-5100 fax: 712/274-5358, reynders@morningside.edu

Nebraska Methodist College
Joslin, Dennis A., president, 720 N. 87th St., Omaha, NE 68114, 402/354-7257 fax: 402/354-7090, dennis.joslin@methodistcollege.edu

Nebraska Wesleyan University
Ohies, Frederik, president, 5000 Saint Paul Ave., Lincoln, NE 68504-2794, 402/465-2217 fax: 402/465-2537, president@nebrwesleyan.edu

North Carolina Wesleyan College
Gray, James A., president, 3400 N. Wesleyan Blvd., Rocky Mount, NC 27804, 252/985-5140 fax: 252/985-5199, jgray@ncwc.edu

Schools, Colleges, Universities, and Seminaries

North Central College
Hammond, Troy, president, 30 N. Brainard St., Naperville, IL 60540, 630/637-5454 fax: 630/637-5457, tdhammond@noctyri.edu

Ohio Northern University
DiBiasio, Daniel, president, 525 S. Main St., Ada, OH 45810, 419/772-2030 fax: 419/772-1932, d-dibiasio@onu.edu

Ohio Wesleyan University
Jones, Rock, president, 61 S. Sandusky St., Delaware, OH 43015, 740/368-3000 fax: 740/368-3007, rfjones@owu.edu

Oklahoma City University
Henry, Robert H., president, 2501 N. Blackwelder, Oklahoma City, OK 73106-1493, 405/208-5032 fax: 405/208-5264, rhenry@okcu.edu

Otterbein University
Krendl, Kathy, president, One South Grove St., Westerville, OH 43081, 614/823-1420 fax: 614/823-3114, kkrendl@otterbein.edu

Paine College
Bradley, George C., president, 1235 Fifteenth St., Augusta, GA 30901-3182, 706/821-8230 fax: 706/821-8333, gbradleyg@paine.edu

Pfeiffer University
Miller, Michael C., president, PO Box 960, Misenheimer, NC 28109-0960, 704/463-3030 x2050 fax: 704/463-1363, mike.miller@pfeiffer.edu

Philander Smith College
Moore, Johnny, president, 900 Daisy Bates Dr., Little Rock, AR 72202, 501/370-5275 fax: 501/370-5277, jmoore@phiilander.edu

Randolph College
Klein, John E., president, 2500 Rivermont Ave., Lynchburg, VA 24503, 434/947-8140 fax: 434/947-8139, jklein@randolphcollege.edu

Randolph-Macon College

Lindgren, Robert R., president, PO Box 5005, Ashland, VA 23005-5505, 804/752-7211 fax: 804/752-3129, rlindgren@rmc.edu

Reinhardt College

Isherwood, J. Thomas, president, 7300 Reinhardt College Cir., Waleska, GA 30183-2981, 770/720-5502 fax: 770/720-5887, jti@reinhardt.edu

Rocky Mountain College

Wilmouth, Robert president, 1511 Poly Dr., Billings, MT 59102, 406/657-1015 fax: 406/238-7253, bob.wilmouth@rocky.edu

Rust College

Beckley, David L., president, 150 Rust Ave., Holly Springs, MS 38635, 662/252-2491 fax: 662/252-8863, dlbeckley@rustcollege.edu

Shenandoah University

Fitzsimmons, Tracy, president, 1460 University Dr., Winchester, VA 22601, 540/665-4505 fax: 540/665-5481, tfitzsim@su.edu

Simpson College

Byrd, John W., president, 701 North C St., Indianola, IA 50125-1264, 515/961-1566 fax: 515/961-1623, presidents.office@simpson.edu

Southern Methodist University

Turner, R. Gerald, president, PO Box 750100, Dallas, TX 75275, 214/768-3300 fax: 214/768-3844, mjj@smu.edu

Southwestern College

Merriman, W. Richard, Jr., president, 100 College St., Winfield, KS 67156-2499, 620/229-6223 fax: 620/229-6224, dick.merriman@sckans.edu

Southwestern University

Schrum, Jake B., president, PO Box 770, Georgetown, TX 78627-0770, 512/863-1454 fax: 512/819-9911, schrum@southwestern.edu

Schools, Colleges, Universities, and Seminaries

Syracuse University
Cantor, **Nancy**, chancellor and president, 900 S. Crouse Ave., Crouse-Hinds Hall, Ste. 600, Syracuse, NY 13244-2130, 315/443-2235 fax: 315/443-3503, chancellor@syr.edu

Tennessee Wesleyan College
Knowles, **Harvey**, president, PO Box 40, Athens, TN 37371-0040, 423/746-5201 fax: 423/746-5302, hknowles@twcnet.edu

Texas Wesleyan University
Slabach, **Frederick G.**, president, 1201 Wesleyan St., Fort Worth, TX 76105, 817/531-4401 fax: 817/531-4496, fslabach@txwes.edu

Union College
Hawkins, **Marcia A.**, president, 310 College St., Barbourville, KY 40906, 606/546-1211 fax: 606/546-1609, president@unionky.edu

University of Denver
Coombe, **Robert D.**, chancellor, 2199 S. University Blvd., Denver, CO 80208-2111, 303/871-2111 fax: 303/871-4101, chancellor@du.edu

University of Evansville
Kazee, **Thomas A.**, president, 1800 Lincoln Ave., Evansville, IN 47722, 812/488-2151 fax: 812/488-4017, tkl@evansville.edu

University of Indianapolis
Manuel, **Robert L.**, president, 1400 E. Hanna Ave., Indianapolis, IN 46227, 317/788-3211 fax: 317/788-6152, manuel@uindy.edu

University of Mount Union
Giese, **Richard F.**, president, 1972 Clark Ave., Alliance, OH 44601, 330/823-6050 fax: 330/829-8725, gieserf@mountunion.edu

University of Puget Sound
Thomas, **Ronald R.**, president, 1500 N. Warner St., #1094, Tacoma, WA 98416-1094, 253/879-3201 fax: 253/879-3938, president@pugetsound.edu

University of the Pacific
Eibeck, Pamela A., president, 3601 Pacific Ave., Stockton, CA 95211, 209/946-2222 fax: 209/946-2652, peibeck@pacific.edu

Virginia Wesleyan College
Greer, William T., Jr., president, 1584 Wesleyan Dr., Norfolk, VA 23502-5599, 757/455-3204 fax: 757/455-3139, wtgreer@vwc.edu

Wesley College
Johnston, William N., president, 120 N. State St., Dover, DE 19901, 302/736-2508 fax: 302/736-2312, william.johnson@wesley.edu

Wesleyan College
Knox, Ruth A., president, 4760 Forsyth Rd., Macon, GA 31210-4462, 478/757-5212 fax: 478/757-2485, rknox@wesleyancollege.edu

West Virginia Wesleyan College
Balch, Pamela, president, 59 College Ave., Buckhannon, WV 26201, 304/473-8181 fax: 304/473-8187, balch@wvwc.edu

Wiley College
Strickland, Haywood L., president, 711 Wiley Ave., Marshall, TX 75670, 903/927-3200 fax: 903/938-8100, hstrickland@wileyc.edu

Willamette University
Thorsett, Stephen E., president, 900 State St., Salem, OR 97301, 503/370-6209 fax: 503/370-6148, president@willamette.edu

Wofford College
Dunlap, Benjamin B., president, 429 N. Church St., Spartanburg, SC 29303-3663, 864/597-4010 fax: 864/597-4018, president@wofford.edu

Young Harris College
Cox, Cathy, president, PO Box 98, Young Harris, GA 30582, 706/379-5137 fax: 706/379-4319, ccox@yhc.edu

Schools, Colleges, Universities, and Seminaries

Two-Year Colleges

Andrew College
Seyle, David, president, 413 College St., Cuthbert, GA 39840-1395, 229/732-5928 fax: 229/732-2176, DavidSeyle@andrewcollege.edu

Lon Morris College
TBA, president, 800 College Ave., Jacksonville, TX 75766-2923, 903/589-4012 fax: 903/586-8562, _____@lonmorris.edu

Louisburg College
LaBranche, Mark D., interim president, 501 N. Main St., Louisburg, NC 27549, 919/497-3226 fax: 919/496-0247, mdl@Louisburg.edu

Spartanburg Methodist College
Keith, Colleen Perry, president, 1000 Powell Mill Rd., Spartanburg, SC 29301-5899, 864/587-4236 fax: 864/587-4379, keithc@smcsc.edu

College Preparatory Schools

Carrollton Christian Academy
Culpepper, David, head of school, 2205 E. Hebron Pkwy., Carrollton, TX 75010, 972/242-6688 x1450 fax: 972/245-0321, david.culpepper@ccasaints.org

Kents Hill School
LaCasse, Jeremy, head of school, PO Box 257, Kents Hill, ME 04349-0257, 207/685-4914 x120 fax: 207/685-9529, jlacasse@kentshill.org

Lydia Patterson Institute
de Anda, Socorro Brito, president, PO Box 11, El Paso, TX 79940, 915/533-8286 fax: 915/533-5236, sdeanda@lydiapattersoninstitute.org

McCurdy Ministries
Alvarado, Patricia, interim superintendent, 261 McCurdy Rd., Española, NM 87532, 505/753-7221 x210 fax: 505/753-7830, pialvarado@mccurdy.org

The Pennington School
Townsend, Stephanie G., head of school, 112 W. Delaware Ave., Pennington, NJ 08534, 609/737-6111 fax: 609/737-9269, ptownsend@pennington.org

Randolph-Macon Academy
Hobgood, Henry M., president, 200 Academy Dr., Front Royal, VA 22630, 540/636-5201 fax: 540/636-5344, hobgood@rma.edu

Red Bird Mission School
Collins, O. Taylor, president, 70 Queendale Center, Beverly, KY 40913, 606/598-3155 fax: 606/598-3151, exec@rbmission.org

Robinson School
Hildebrand, Dan, head of school, #5 Calle Nairn, San Juan, Puerto Rico 00907, 787/999-4611 fax: 787/999-4616, dhildebrand@robinsonschool.org

Tilton School
Saliba, Peter, head of school, 30 School St., Tilton, NH 03276, 603/286-1710 fax: 603/286-1709, psaliba@tiltonschool.org

Wyoming Seminary College Preparatory School
Nygren, Kip, president, 201 N. Sprague Ave., Kingston, PA 18704-3593, 570/270-2150 fax: 570/270-2154, knyren@wyomingseminary.org

UNIVERSITY SENATE OF THE UNITED METHODIST CHURCH APPROVED GRADUATE THEOLOGICAL SEMINARIES

Note: Unless specifically noted, only main campus programs of these schools are approved. July 1, 2012 through June 30, 2013 (¶ 1417.2, *2012 Book of Discipline*)

Asbury Theological Seminary (Florida Dunnam Campus)
8401 Valencia College Ln. Orlando, FL 32825, 407/482-7500, www.asburyseminary.edu

Schools, Colleges, Universities, and Seminaries

Asbury Theological Seminary (Kentucky Campus)
204 N. Lexington Ave., Wilmore, KY 40390, 859/858-3581, www.asburyseminary.edu

Asbury Theological Seminary (Online Campus)
ExL (Extended Learning Program), 800/2-ASBURY, www.asburyseminary.edu

Ashland Theological Seminary
910 Center St., Ashland, OH 44805, 866/287-6446 or 419/289-5166, www.ashland.edu/seminary

Austin Presbyterian Theological Seminary
100 East 27th St., Austin, TX 78705-5797, 512/472-6736, www.austinseminary.edu

*Boston University School of Theology
745 Commonwealth Ave., Boston, MA 02215, 617/353-3050, www.bu.edu/sth

Brite Divinity School
Texas Christian University, 2925 Princeton St., Ft. Worth, TX 76129, 817/257-7575, www.brite.tcu.edu

*Candler School of Theology
Emory University, 1531 Dickey Dr., NE, Atlanta, GA 30322, 404/727-6123, www.candler.emory.edu

Chicago Theological Seminary
1407 E. 60th St., Chicago, IL 60637, 773/896-2400, www.ctschicago.edu

Christian Theological Seminary
1000 W. 42nd St., Indianapolis, IN 46208, 317/924-1331, www.cts.edu

*Claremont School of Theology
1325 N. College Ave., Claremont, CA 91711-3199, 909/447-2500, www.cst.edu

Colgate Rochester Crozer Divinity School
1100 S. Goodman St., Rochester, NY 14620, 585/271-1320, www.crdcs.edu

*Drew University Theological School
36 Madison Ave., Madison, NJ 07940, 973/408-3000 www.drew.edu/theo

*Duke Divinity School
Box 90968, Durham, NC 27708, 919/660-3400 www.divinity.duke.edu

Eastern Mennonite Seminary
1200 Park Rd., Harrisonburg, VA 22802, 540/432-4000 www.emu.edu/seminary

Eden Theological Seminary
475 E. Lockwood Ave., St. Louis, MO 63119, 800/969-3627 or 314/961-3627 www.eden.edu

Evangelical Seminary
121 S. College St., Myerstown, PA 17067, 800/532-5775 or 717/866-5775 www.evangelical.edu

Fuller Theological Seminary
135 N. Oakland Ave., Pasadena, CA 91182, 800/235-2222 or 626/584-5200 www.fuller.edu

*Gammon Theological Seminary
653 Beckwith St., S.W., Atlanta, GA 30314, 404/581-0300 www.gammonseminary.org

*Garrett-Evangelical Theological Seminary
2121 Sheridan Rd., Evanston, IL 60201, 800-SEMINARY or 847/866-3900 www.garrett.edu

Harvard Divinity School
45 Francis Ave., Cambridge, MA 02138, 617/495-5761 www.hds.harvard.edu

Hood Theological Seminary
1810 Lutheran Synod Dr., Salisbury, NC 28144, 704/636-7611 www.hoodseminary.edu

*Iliff School of Theology
2201 S. University Blvd., Denver, CO 80210, 800/678-3360 or 303/744-1287 www.iliff.edu

Interdenominational Theological Center (Gammon Theological Seminary only)
700 Martin Luther King, Jr., Dr. SW, Atlanta, GA 30314, 404/527-7700 www.itc.edu

Lancaster Theological Seminary
555 W. James St., Lancaster, PA 17603, 800/393-0654 or 717/393-0654 www.its.org

Louisville Presbyterian Theological Seminary
1044 Alta Vista Rd., Louisville, KY 40205, 800/264-1839 or 502/895-3411 www.lpts.edu

Luther Seminary
2481 Como Ave., St. Paul, MN 55108, 651/641-3456 www.luthersem.edu

Lutheran Southern Theological Seminary
4201 N. Main St., Columbia, SC 29203, 803/786-5150 www.ltss.lr.edu

Lutheran Theological Seminary at Philadelphia
7301 Germantown Ave., Philadelphia, PA 19119-1794, 800/286-4616 or 215/248-7302 www.ltsp.edu

Memphis Theological Seminary
168 E. Pkwy. S., Memphis, TN 38104, 901/458-8232 www.memphisseminary.edu

*Methodist Theological School in Ohio
3081 Columbus Pk., Delaware, OH 43015-0931, 740/363-1146 www.mtso.edu

Moravian Theological School
60 W. Locust St., Bethlehem, PA 18018, 610/861-1516 www.moravianseminary.edu

New York Theological Seminary
475 Riverside Dr., Ste. 500, New York, NY 10115, 212/870-1211 www.nyts.edu

Pacific School of Religion
1798 Scenic Ave., Berkeley, CA 94709, 510/848-0528 www.psr.edu

Palmer Theological Seminary
588 N. Gulph Rd., King of Prussia, PA 19406, 1/800/220-3287 or 610/896-5000 www.palmerseminary.edu

*Perkins School of Theology
Kirby Hall, 5915 Bishop Blvd., Dallas, TX 75275, 1/888/THEOLOGY or 214/768-8436 www.smu.edu/theology

Phillips Theological Seminary
901 N. Mingo Rd., Tulsa, OK 74116, 918/610-8303 www.ptstulsa.edu

Pittsburgh Theological Seminary
616 N. Highland Ave., Pittsburgh, PA 15206, 412/362-5610 www.pts.edu

Presbyterian School of Christian Education (see Union Presbyterian Seminary)

Princeton Theological Seminary
PO Box 821, 64 Mercer St., Princeton, NJ 08542-0803, 609/921-8300 www.ptsem.edu

*Saint Paul School of Theology (Kansas City Campus)
5123 Truman Rd., Kansas City, MO 64127, 816/483-9600 www.spst.edu

*Saint Paul School of Theology (Oklahoma City University Campus)
2501 N. Blackwelder Ave., Okalhoma City, OK 73106, 405/208-5757 www.spst.edu/ok

Samuel Dewitt Proctor School of Theology
1500 N. Lombardy St., Richmond, VA 23220, 804/257-5715 www.vuu.edu/samuel_dewitt_proctor_school_of_theology.aspx

Seattle Pacific University
3307 Third Ave. W, Seattle, WA 98119-1997, 206/281-2342 www.spu.edu/academicsschool-of-theology/seattle-pacific-seminary

Seattle University School of Theology and Ministry
901 12th Ave., PO Box 222000, Seattle, WA 98122, 206/296-5330 www.seattleu.edu/STM/

Seminario Evangélico de Puerto Rico
77 Ponce de León Ave., San Juan, PR 00925, 787/763-6700 www.se-pr.edu/portal/

Sioux Falls Seminary
2100 S. Summit Ave., Sioux Falls, SD 57105, 1/800/440-6227 or 605/336-6588 www.sfseminary.edu

Union Presbyterian Seminary (Charlotte Campus)
5141 Sharon Rd., Charlotte, NC 28210, 1/800/229/2990 or 980/636-1700 www.upsem.edu/admissions/charlotte_campus/

Union Presbyterian Seminary (Richmond Campus)
3401 Brook Rd., Richmond, VA 23227, 1/800/229/2990 or 804/355-0671 www.upsem.edu/admissions/richmond_life/

Union Theological Seminary in the City of New York
3041 Broadway at 121st St., New York, NY 10027, 212/662-7100 www.utsnyc.edu

*United Theological Seminary
4501 Denlinger Rd., Dayton, OH 45426, 937/529-2201 www.united.edu

United Theological Seminary of the Twin Cities
3000 Fifth St., N. W., New Brighton, MN 55112, 651/633-4311 www.unitedseminary-mn.org

University of Dubuque Theological Seminary
2000 University Ave., Dubuque, IA 52001, 800/369-8387 or 563/589-3000 www.uhdts.dbq.edu

University of the South School of Theology
335 Tennessee Ave., Sewanee, TN 37383-0001, 931/598-1000 www.theology.sewanee.edu

Vanderbilt University Divinity School
411 21st Ave. S., Nashville, TN 37240, 615/322-2776 www.vanderbilt.edu/divinity

*Wesley Theological Seminary
4500 Massachusetts Ave., N.W., Washington, DC 20016, 202/885-8600 www.wesleyseminary.edu

Yale Divinity School
409 Prospect St., New Haven, CT 06511, 203/432-5303 www.yale.edu/divinity

*United Methodist School

MEMBERS OF THE COMMISSION ON THEOLOGICAL EDUCATION

The Rev. Dr. **Kah-Jin Jeffrey Kuan**, Chair, Madison, NJ
The Rev. Dr. **Bill T. Arnold**, Wilmore, KY
The Rev. **Beth Downs**, Glen Allen, VA
Bishop **Larry M. Goodpaster**, Charlotte, NC
The Rev. Dr. **Rock Jones**, Delaware, OH
Dr. **Jan Love**, Atlanta, GAbold
The Rev. Dr. **David McAllister-Wilson**, Washington, DC
The Rev. Dr. **Myron McCoy**, Kansas City, MO
Dr. **Helene Slessarev-Jamir**, Claremont, CA
The Rev. Dr. **David F. Watson**, Dayton, OH
The Rev. Dr. **J. Cameron West**, Montgomery, AL
Dr. **Phyllis Whitney**, Mount Pleasant, IA

Staff
The Rev. Dr. **Gwen Purushotham**, GBHEM, associate general secretary, Division of Ordained Ministry

Index

A

Abarca, David, 40
Abbott, Catherine, 144
Abbott, David, 122
Abdon, Reynaldo V., 70
Abrahams, Ivan, 179
Abrams, Cynthia J., 35
Acevedo-Delgado, German, 45
Ackerman, Dennis, 111
Adair, Steven, 66
Adamson, Georgia, 98
Agtarap, Bener, 96
Agtarap, Sophia, 66
Ahn, Sung Hoon, 32, 105
Aichele, Frank, 43
Akuamoah, Donna, 82
Albin, Tom, 40, 84
Alegria, Frank, 127
Alegría, Raúl, 169
Alegria, Richard, 78
Alexander, Neil M., 54, 56, 72
Alford, Bob I., 124
Alford, Scott, 172
Allen, Emily, 64
Allen, Eydie, 48
Allen, Helen, 66, 68
Allen, Jim, 141
Allen, Laura Harbert, 149
Alnor, Kay, 120
Alschwede, Stephanie M., 76
Alsted, Christian, 5, 15, 31, 71, 161
Alston, Ellen R., 54, 114
Altland, Sheri, 68
Altman, Larry Ray, 140
Alvarado, Patricia, 193
Amerson, Philip A., 181

Andersen, Dave, 129
Anderson, Christopher J., 63
Anderson, Ruby D., 43
Anderson, Theodore, 143
Andone, Herzen, 126
André, Manuel João, 38
Andrews, Marva, 128
Angoran, Yed, 36
Archer, Jay, 141
Argue, James, 25, 94
Arichea, Daniel C., Jr., 5
Arieux, Lauren, 28
Armistead, Kathy, 58
Armstrong, Holly, 57
Arnold, Bill T., 200
Arnold, Ellis, III, 186
Arnold, Greg, 79
Arnold, Paula, 143
Arroyo, Giovanni, 74
Askew, Sally Curtis, 30
Aspey, Amy, 148
Atha, Marcus, 147
Atkins, David, 120
Atnip, Scott D., 43, 44
Austin, Sharon G., 104
Avery, Donald, 114
Avitia, Edgar, 135

B

Backstrom, Betty, 115
Bailey, Marshall, 64
Bakely, Claudia, 111
Bakeman, Brian, 130
Bakker, Shawn, 45
Balasundaram, Praveena, 81
Balch, Pamela, 192

Index

Balisi, Eliseo C., 54
Ball, Ronald T., 92
Ball, Sandra Steiner, 148
Ballard, Thomas T., 106
Bank, Wayne, 101
Banks, Donna, 125
Bankson, John D., 167
Bankston, L. James, 38
Bantz, Don, 183
Barker, Amy Valdez, 23
Barnes, Jeffrey R., 57
Barnes, Jimmy, 118
Barnes, Tara, 81
Barrineau, Karen, 141
Barrow, Darryl R., 143
Barrow, Ricky, 69
Barry, Kathleen, 67
Bartelt, Joanne, 101
Bartle, Naomi, 72
Bartlett, Laura Jacquith, 132
Barton, Carol A., 81
Barton, Richard, 143
Bashore, George W., 9
Bass, Henry, 138
Bass, Patrick, 39
Bass, Tracy, 51
Bassford, Virginia O., 98
Bastian, Dwight, 177
Bauernfeind, Paul, 129
Bautista, Liberato C., 35
Beach, Demetrio, 47
Beach, Gary, 111, 112
Bealla, Mike, 141
Beard, Frank J., 70
Beaty, Jim, 141
Bechtold, Steve G., 105
Beckett, David, 93
Beckley, David L., 47, 190
Bell, David, 101
Bender, Charles, 105
Bennett, Stephen, 147
Berner, James, 51, 149
Berquist, Greg, 96
Bess, David, 57
Bickerton, Thomas J., 5, 17, 78, 88, 151
Biegger, Becky, 125
Bigach, Sheila, 56

Biler, Brenda, 51
Bilog, Francisco, 36
Bindl, Helene, 70
Birdsall, S. Douglas, 178
Birk, Peg J., 178
Bishop, John W., 25, 27
Bjornevik, Per Endre, 25
Black, Paul, 108
Blackwell, Dennis L., 30
Blair, Alan, 57
Blair, Karen, 68
Blair, William, 151
Blake, Bruce P., 9
Blakeney, Rori, 42
Blankenship, Tina, 38
Bledsoe, W. Earl, 5, 18, 31, 89, 129
Blinn, Robert, 145
Bloom, Linda, 30
Boesch, Jim, 79
Boggs, John, 150
Boigegrain, Barbara A., 53
Bolleter, Heinrich, 9
Bone, David, 167
Boni, Benjamin, 5, 14, 157
Bonner, Bruce, 69
Bonner, Byrd, 28
Bonner, Hannah, 41
Bonner, John H., 92
Bonson, John, 116
Booher, Jody, 57
Booth, Karen, 177
Borchers, Brenda, 121
Botti, Amy, 103, 134
Bouknight, Jeanette, 20
Bowles, David, 114
Bowman, Randy, 100
Boyd, Edward, 114
Braaten, Jennifer L., 186
Brackey, Donald, 51
Braddon, David V., 54
Bradford, Jacki L., 110
Bradley, George C., 189
Bradley, Joanna, 40
Bradley, Mary, 143
Brand, Jonathan, 185
Brandyberry, Donna, 35
Brannen, Jesse, 142

Index

Brantley, Lowery, 138
Bray, Adam B., 85
Breeden Andrew, 40
Brewer, Scott, 27
Brewington, Adrienne, 123
Bridgeforth, Cedrick, 51, 97, 166
Broadwell, Ray, 125
Brockmeyer, Diane, 110
Brockus, Sarah, 80
Brodhead, Richard H., 185
Brodie, Matt, 137
Brooks, Gary, 112
Brooks, Jack, 96, 103, 134
Brooks, Jane, 127
Brooks, Lonnie, 93
Brooks, Philip, 38
Brower, Charles, 20
Brown, Angela, 30
Brown, Brian, 148
Brown, Carlton E., 184
Brown, Dan, 126
Brown, David L., 73
Brown, Jay W., 43, 44
Brown, Kathleen, 147
Brown, Kelly, 26
Brown, Marc, 145
Brown, Marla, 147
Brown, Olu, 36
Brown, Robert A., 184
Brown, Shirlyn, 134
Brown, Ted, 47, 168, 188
Brown, Warner H., Jr., 5, 19, 91, 96
Browning, Leslie Ann, 111, 112, 120
Brownson, Bill, 148
Bruce, Cathy, 114
Brumbaugh, Susan, 71
Bruner, Linda, 57
Brunstetter, J. Paul, 113
Bruster, Timothy Keith, 30
Bryan, Harriet, 141
Bryan, James "Jerry," 125
Bryan, Robert Lawson, 51
Bryant, Dan C., 44, 102
Bryant, Stephen D., 37
Bryant, Vonzella, 38
Buchner, Gregory L., 146
Bull, Vivian, 185

Bulmer, Bruce, 99
Burchfield, Willie, 141
Burkhart, J. Robert, 72, 110
Burns, Robert, 100
Burnside, William, 122
Burris, David, 130
Burris, Todd, 54, 94
Burt, David, 153
Burton, Jennifer, 51, 52, 150
Burton, Susan, 35
Burton-Edwards, Taylor W., 39
Busbia, Mark, 53
Bush, Elizabeth, 25
Bushart, Hannah, 64
Bushfield, James C., 54, 109
Butler, Joey, 67
Butler, K. Wayne, 143
Buxton, Jon J., 140
Byrd, Jeff, 68
Byrd, John W., 190
Byrum, David M., 109

C

Cabrera, Bridget, 82
Cage, John Bright, 78
Cajiuat, Susannah, 127
Calderon, Chelsea C., 31, 32
Calderon, Lourdes, 36
Caldwell, Cindy, 69
Caldwell, Linda, 72, 96
Caldwell, Neill, 173
Calentine, Raggatha, 64
Calvert, Diana, 113
Camp, Lane Gardner, 116
Campbell, Gerry, 116
Campbell, Jerry D., 181
Campbell, Scott, 32
Campos, Francisco, 135
Cañas, Francisco, 171
Cantor, Nancy, 191
Cape, Kim, 48
Capen, Beth, 30
Carcaño, Minerva G., 5, 19, 71, 73, 90, 97
Carder, Kenneth, 9
Cardillo, John, 105
Carey, Lladale, 69

Index

Carey, Melanie, 101
Carlton, Charlie, 124
Carmichael, Dan, 52
Carnahan, Charles, 36, 37
Carrasco, Oscar, 128
Carroll, Barbara, 117
Carson, Joseph D., 145
Carter, Brenda, 36
Carter, Kenneth H., Jr., 6, 18, 90, 104
Carter, Tom, 49
Carter-Rimbach, Joan E., 44
Carver, Thomas L., 110
Casey, Brian W., 185
Cashion, Steve, 57
Cataldo, Jodi, 47
Cates, Darrell, 130
Caudill, Roy, 99
Cavitt, J. Steven, 116
Cazombo, Elvira Moises, 44
Chafin, Lonnie, 31, 32, 128
Chalakee, Jim, 131
Chamberlain, Mike, 111
Chamberlain, Ray W., 9
Chamberland, Heidi, 122
Chambers, Laura, 169
Chamness, Benjamin, 9
Chapman, Gary A., 113
Charley, Francis B., 70
Cheatham, Dena, 49
Check, Dawn Lynn, 151
Cherry, F. Richard, 107
Chesser, Dawn, 39
Chewning, Richard, 126
Childs, Steven, 112, 113
Cho, Young Jin, 6, 19, 31, 90, 144
Choi, Thomas S., 97
Choy, Wilbur W. Y., 9
Christian, Monica S., 54
Christian, Solomon, 32
Christie, Annaleigh, 57
Christie, Neal, 35, 84
Christopher, Sharon A. Brown, 9
Christopherson, Arlene, 128
Chumley, Maddie, 36
Chun, Young-Ho, 54
Churan, Cindy, 152
Churan, Rick, 153

Clark, Connie, 54
Clark, Philip Jayphen, 32
Clark, Richard W., 116
Clark, Roy C., 9
Clark, Scott, 69
Clay, Lance, 120
Clay, Sandra L., 115
Claycomb, Judy Wismar, 102
Clayton, Max, 112
Clements, Pamela, 58
Clifton, Danette, 124
Clontz, Sherill Ann, 124
Clymer, Wayne K., 9
Cobb, Michelle A., 109
Cockrum, Dale L., 133
Cody, Ebony, 82
Cohen, Dale R., 124
Colaw, Emerson S., 9
Coles, Amy, 150
Collett, John, 141
Collett, Rita B., 40
Collier, Cody, 119
Collier, T. Cody, 70
Collins, O. Taylor, 194
Collinsworth, Allyson, 50
Colvin, Eleanor F., 64
Colwell, Rob, 145
Compton, Bryan, 174
Congdon, Caitlin, 66
Conley, Ellis E., 149
Conley, Sharon, 40
Conover, Matt, 27
Cook, Carol, 126
Cook, Karen, 32
Cook, Michael, 28, 174
Coombe, Robert D., 191
Cooper, Edwin "Buddy," 138
Cooper, George, 148
Cooper, Kurt J., 32
Cooper, Michelline, 76
Copan, Lil, 58
Copeland, Jennifer, 47
Coppedge, Archer I., 106
Coppock, Diane, 41
Coppock, Larry, 79
Corbin, Ivan, 61
Corbitt, Karen, 147
Costello, Robert E., 105

Index

Cotto, Irving, 103
Cottrill, Don, 115
Court, Steven, 102
Cox, Cathy, 192
Cox, Gregory D., 64, 151
Cox, Keith, 126
Cox, Nancy, 136
Cox, Steve, 119
Coy, Randall A., 113
Coyner, Michael J., 6, 16, 25, 26, 87, 109
Crabtree, Tamara, 58
Craddock, Rashida, 80
Craig, Judith, 9
Crane, David, 55
Crawford, Susan, 66
Crew, Gay, 115, 141
Crisler, Timothy E., 43, 44, 118
Crismo, Phebe, G., 76
Crisp, Anita, 121
Cropsey, Marvin W., 71
Crosby, Pamela J., 166
Cross, Cynthia, 118
Cross, Randolph M., 99
Crossman, Bob, 38, 94
Crouch, Walter, 165
Crow, David W., 110
Crowe, Joseph A., 58
Crowell, Linda Johnson, 55
Crutchfield, Charles N., 9
Culbertson, Barry, 47
Culbertson, LeNoir, 141
Culpepper, David, 193
Cunningham, Elsie, 67
Cunningham, Mike, 57
Curry, Jodi, 26
Curry, Rebecca S., 113, 114
Czarda, Lawrence D., 186

D

Dandridge, Carolyn W., 38
Dang, Bau N., 97
Daniel, Francis, 125
Daniel, Gary A., 92
Daniels, John F., 153
Daniels, Joseph, 95
Daugherty, Ruth, 87

David, Cynthia D., 116
David, Wes, 97
Davidson, Sybil, 126
Davies, Larry E., 145
Davis, Alan, 120
Davis, G. Lindsey, 6, 19, 90
Davis, Jennifer, 150
Davis, Lindsey, 113, 135
Davis, Martha, 79, 174
Davis, Neil, 146
Davis, Ryan C., 25
Dawson, Tangi, 68
Day, Alfred, III, 61
Dayap, Efraim A., 44
Day-Lewis, Kimberly G. W., 84
de Anda, Socorro Brito, 193
De Carvalho, Emilio J. M., 9
Dean, Mary Catherine, 59, 72
Dean, Sharon, 27
DeBlaker-Gebhard, Kyra, 74
Debree, Susan K., 90
Deckard, Stephanie, 70
Decker, Dave, 110
Deere, Josephine, 131
Degnan, Diane, 69, 72
Dehority, Mark, 79
Deichmann, Wendy J., 182
"Del," James D., 107
del Rosario, DJ, 47
DeLaunay, Janine, 55
Dellinger, Lisa A., 76
Delurey, Becky, 132
Deming, Lynne, 40
Denmark, John A., 32
Dennis, James M., 188
Denson, Lane, 69
Devadhar, Sudarshana, 6, 17, 20, 88, 121
DeVine, Jerome, 101
DeWitt, Jesse R., 9
Diaz, Olga, 20
DiBiasio, Daniel, 189
Dick, Barbara, 72
Dick, Dan R., 32, 152
Dickerson-Oard, Kim, 112
Diehl, Lisa Elliot, 111, 112
Dilmore, Pamela, 41, 58
Dinndorf, Beth, 184

205

Dinofia, Peter T., 103
Dixon Hall, Maria, 64
Dobbs, David, 101
Dobbs, William D., 100, 146
Docking, Jeffrey R., 182
Dodge, David, 104
Dodson, Christine, 25, 26, 125
Dodson, Donna, 130
Doepken, Jim, 93
Dolin, Owen L., 113
Domingos, Gaspar Joao, 6, 13, 20, 51, 155
Domingues, Jorge, 45
Dommisse, David, 145
Donley, Lee, 78
Dopke, Cynthia, 23
Doran, Christine, 143
Dorff, James E., 6, 18, 47, 89, 135, 139
Douglas, Charles H., 114
Douglas, Linda C., 80
Douthat, James E., 187
Dove, Carolyn, 115
Dow, Jonathan, 165
Downs, Beth, 47, 200
Doyal, Mark, 146
Dozier, Larry, 78
Drake, Gwen, 132
Draper, Linda, 131
DuBose, Mike, 67
Duffett, Robert G., 185
Dulworth, Elbert, 101
Dungan, Karen, 110
Dunlap, Benjamin B., 192
Dunlap, Nancy, 39
Dunlap-Berg, Barbara, 67
Dunn, Dala, 119
Dunnewind, Frank, 92
Durden, William G., 185
Dwyer, Tatiana, 81
Dyck, Sally, 6, 16, 64, 87, 128
Dyke, Lynn, 119

E

Earvin, Larry L., 187
Easterling, LaTrelle Miller, 122
Easto, Laura, 95
Eberhart, Diane Wasson, 70
Edgar, David N., 32
Edin, Jean, 52
Edwards, Hadley, 114
Edwards, Richard, 129
Ehrman, James W., 31, 32
Eibeck, Pamela A., 192
Eichelberger, Paul, 95
Eidson, Joshua, 79
Elias, Joao Damiao, 70
Elliott, Sherry, 40
Ellis, Claudia, 57
Ellis, Sharon, 154
Elmore, Tonya L., 92
Emmert, Don, 52
Engle, Gretchen, 93, 133
Engroff, Greg, 40
Enstine, Ed, 78
Entwistle, Dan, 36
Epler, Neil, 92
Epperson, Mark, 94
Erbele, Terrence, 93
Erenrich, David E., 149
Erin Kane, 77
Erlandsson, MaryAnna, 68
Escamilla, Roberto, 172
Escobar, Pax, 38
Eshleman, Julie, 101
Estep, Tammy L., 144
Etter, Boyd B., 134
Eutsler, R. Kern, 10
Evans, Cashar, Jr., 64, 65
Evans, Cindy, 177
Evans, Emily Rogers, 43, 44
Everhart, Dana, 126
Ewing, Selby T., 81

F

Fairly, Robert C., Jr., 115
Fannin, Robert E., 10
Farnell, Emily, 32
Farrell, Brigid, 122
Fenner, Bruce, 49
Fenstermacher, Ed, 36
Fergus, Judi, 61
Ferguson, Sandra, 95
Fernandes, Moises Domingos, 10

Index

Fernandes, Roland, 28, 43, 46
Fick, Corey, 63
Fields, Kim, 132
Figueredo, Mary, 53
Finau, Sela E., 73
Finegan, Mary Ellen, 149
Finger, James, 116
Fisher, Evelyn, 111, 112
Fisher, Violet, 10
Fitzsimmons, Tracy, 190
Flanagan, Dan, 120
Fleming, Terry, 126
Fletcher, Robert R., 50, 173
Flick, Christine, 70
Flippen, Laura, 49
Flores, Daniel F., 62
Floyd, Joan, 40
Flynn, Mark W., 149
Flynn, Rachel, 52
Fogle-Miller, Carlene R., 76
Fonteyn, Paul J., 186
Foote, Mary, 132
Ford, Ralph, 115
Forren, Edwin Dallas, 149
Fort, Joe, Jr., 142
Fortune, Cheryl, 123
Foster, L. Daniel, 133
Foust, Robert, 28
Fowler, Judith, 135
Francisco, Ciriaco Q., 157
Franklyn, Paul, 58
Frazier, Carl, 54
Frazier, R. Carl, Jr., 55
Friday, James, 137
Frost, Ted, 108
Fryer, Christine, 48
Fukumoto, JoAnn Yoon, 73
Fullerton, Heather, 105
Furr, Steve, 92
Furtado, Jefferson, 69
Fusco, John, 69

G

Gadbois, Siri S., 167
Gadit, Farhan, 82
Gaines, Tammy, 57

Gaither, Stacy, 39
Gallagher, Jennifer, 109
Gallo Seagren, Lilian, 76
Gallo-Seagren, Lilian, 110
Galván, Elias G., 10, 169
Galyon, Dennis, 131
Gamboa, José C., Jr., 10
Gangler, Dan, 109
Garcia, Edward, 55
Garcia, Naomi, 147
Garibay, Haniel Robles, 32
Garvin, Lisa, 32
Gary, Dan, 28
Gearhart, Amy, 48
Geary, Joseph A., 116
Gentzler, Richard H., 39
George, Gary, 51, 52, 101
George, Larry, 127
Gerhardt, Anne Marie, 128
Gibbons, Mark A., 114
Gibbs, Laurina, 81
Gibbs, Robert, 104
Gibson, Mattie, 118
Giese, Richard F., 191
Gilbert, Kathy L., 67
Gilliam, Lynn, 40
Gilliam, W. Craig, 85
Gilpin, M. Scott, 38
Gilts, Kip, 142
Gittens, Betty E., 82
Gladstone, Carl, 41
Glass, Laurens, 69
Godfrey, Jay, 83
Godwin, Gregory, 78
Goehring, Carol, 125
Goldman, LeeAnn, 77
Gong, Leigh Ann, 35
Gonzales, Vince, 73
Gooch, Betty, 134
Goodier, Steve, 136
Gooding, Anthony, 66
Goodpaster, Larry M., 5, 6, 18, 72, 89, 150, 200
Goodwin, John, 52
Goodwin, Kevin, 52
Goodwin, Tracy, 117
Goolsbey, John T., 27, 28

Index

Gordon, Melanie, 39
Gosmire, Doreen, 99
Goto, Shinya, 55
Gottschalk-Fielding, William, 144
Gowdy, Kevin, 111
Grace, Roger, 177
Graham, Jeff, 108
Gramling, Roger M., 138
Grant, Edward L., 149
Grant, Reginald, 78
Graves, Charles, 130
Graves, David W., 106
Graves, Gary W., 72
Graves, Russ, 104
Gray, James A., 188
Gray, Lindsay, 40
Greathouse, Lowell, 132
Green, Joseph S., 106
Green, Oliver, 111
Greenwaldt, Karen, 37
Greer, Chari, 56
Greer, William T., Jr., 192
Gregorson, Cindy, 117
Gregory, Debbie, 40
Gregory, Sharon, 151
Griffin, Stephanie, 142
Griffin, Wade, 148
Griffith, Janice, 52, 107
Grossman, Gail, 36
Grove, William Boyd, 10
Groves, John F., 109
Guier, L. Marvin, III, 127
Guy, Nichea VerVeer, 80
Gwinn, Alfred Wesley, Jr., 10

H

Habben, Sherry, 119, 120
Haden, William R., 70
Hagan, Miriam, 52, 139
Haggard, William, 146
Hagiya, Grant J., 6, 19, 47, 90, 93, 132, 133
Hahn, Heather, 67
Hahn, Wesley, 65
Haigler, Anne, 72
Hall, Betsy, 58

Hall, Darlene, 121
Halliburton, Tom, 141
Hallman, Howard W., 176
Hamdorff, Sara, 38
Hamilton-Allen, Robin, 171
Hammitt, Michelle, 107
Hammond, Troy, 189
Hammons, Brian, 119
Hancock, Ben E., Jr., 188
Hancock, Charles W., 10
Handy, Stephen E., 73
Hanke, Gilbert C., 79
Hanshew, Don, 32
Hanson, Linda N., 186
Haralson, Cynthia J., 27, 172
Hardt, John Wesley, 10
Harewood, Brenda K., 165
Harmon, Paul, 137
Harper, Trey, 118
Harper, Warren, 145
Harris, Jay, 138
Harris, Joseph, 73, 130
Harrison, Mark, 35
Harrison, Sheila, 66
Harry, Daniel P., 108
Harter, Terry P., 108
Harvey, Cynthia Fierro, 6, 18, 89, 114
Hassinger, Susan W., 10
Hastings, Gretchen, 104
Hasty, Don, 112
Haugh, Thomas C., 103
Haupert-Johnson, Sue, 104
Hauser, Joshua, 72
Haverstock, Zedna, 51, 52
Hawkins, Erin, 74
Hawkins, Marcia A., 191
Hawxhurst, Jean G., 113
Hayashi, Donald L., 171
Hayes, Gregory L., 149
Hayes, Robert E., Jr., 5, 6, 18, 25, 26, 89, 130, 131
Hayes, Terrence K., 140
Hays, Richard B., 181
Hearn, J. Woodrow, 10
Hearne, Richard, 32
Heavner, Betsey, 39
Heck, Terry, 166

Index

Heckaman, Christopher, 147
Heile, Dan, 57
Heisler, Benton R., 146
Heist, Linda, 49
Helmer, Robert C., 183
Henderson, Gary, 66, 68
Henderson, William Bryan, 139
Henry, Robert H., 189
Henry, Tyler A. R., 32
Hensarling, Heather, 118
Herity, Sheila, 68
Hernandez, Albert, 182
Hernandez, Rini, 104
Herndon, Ernest T. "Tommy," Jr., 145
Hestand, Joshua, 49
Hester, Colleen, 187
Hicks, Kenneth W., 10
Hicks, Neelley, 66
Hiers, Terri J., 50
Higginbotham, Robert W., Jr., 55, 151
Hildebrand, Dan, 194
Hildreth, Bart, 119
Hill, A. Lynn, 70
Hill, John S., 35
Hillery, Maggie, 67
Hills, David, 146
Hinton, Coy, 126
Hipp, John, 137
Hirsen, Sarah, 53
Hixon, Stephanie Anna, 85
Ho Lee, Sung, 143
Hobgood, Henry M., 194
Hodge, Jeff, 144
Hodges-Batzka, John, 42
Holland, Linda, 124
Holliger, Carol, 148
Hollon, Larry, 66, 67
Holloway, Robert W., 98
Holly, Mary Lynn, 68
Holston, L. Jonathan, 6, 18, 89, 137
Holt, Andrew, 69
Holt, Gloria E., 70
Homitsky, Larry, 61, 62
Hong, Seok Hwan, 122
Hooker, David Anderson, 85
Hoosier, Regina, 59
Hopkins, John L., 6, 17, 31, 87, 101

Hopson, Cynthia Bond, 50, 166
Hopson, Roger, 115
Horn, Doris, 167
Horstman, Jane, 174
Horswill-Johnston, Steve, 38
Horton, Anne, 36
Hoshibata, Robert T., 6, 19, 31, 91, 99
Hotchkiss, Sara, 28, 71
Hotze, Margaret, 136
Howard, George, 45
Howard, Janine, 144
Howell, James, 33
Hubble, R. Michael, 106
Huber, Mike, 171
Huff, A. V., III, 61, 62
Huffman, Chuck, 142
Huffman, Lory Beth, 150
Huffman, Tracy, 101
Hughes, H. Hasbrouck, Jr., 10
Huie, Janice Riggle, 6, 18, 89, 142
Huling, Mike, 138
Hulsey, Jilda, 124
Humper, Joseph C., 10
Humphrey, James, 102
Hundley, Robert L., 146
Hundley, Stephen, 26, 27
Hunt, Priscilla, 166
Hupp, Michael, 57
Hustedt, Steve, 100
Hutchinson, William W., 10
Hutto, Craig, 139
Huycke, Mary K. S., 133
Hwang, In-sook, 108
Hygh, Larry R., Jr., 97

I

Iannicelli, Rebecca, 95
Iliya, Eunice Musa, 76
Ingram, Kim, 48, 150
Inman, Marianne E., 184
Innes, Randy, 125
Innis, John G., 6, 15, 159
Irons, Neil L., 10
Isherwood, J. Thomas, 190
Ives, S. Clifton, 10
Ivey, Dorothy, 31, 33

Index

J

Jacinto, Ranny, 33
Jackson, Edison O., 183
Jackson, Embra, 118
Jackson, Fredric O., 123
Jackson, Jay, 142
Jackson, Kenneth J., 144
Jackson, Sandy, 39
Jacob, Ann, 37
Jaffary, Syed I., 80
James, I. Lynn, 126
James, Kathy, 137
James, Royya, 66
Janoe, Rhonnie, 68
Jara, Nydia I., 135
Jarrett, Deborah, 66
Jefferson, Monica, 120
Jenkins, Elaine, 50
Jerusalem, Rose Beverly, 26
Jeter, Narcie, 173
Jett-Roberts, Frances, 75
Job, Rueben P., 10
Johnson, Alfred, 10
Johnson, Cynthia A., 33
Johnson, Frankye, 130
Johnson, Margaret, 131
Johnson, Peggy A., 6, 17, 31, 88, 103, 134
Johnson, Robert, 38, 174
Johnson, Rockford, 130
Johnson, Sandra G., 106
Johnson, Scott, 144
Johnson, Susie, 81, 84
Johnston, Mada, 59
Johnston, William N., 192
Jolly, Donovan C., 82
Jones, Beth E., 140
Jones, Cynthia A., 108
Jones, L. Bevel, III, 11
Jones, Richard A., 33
Jones, Rock, 189, 200
Jones, Scott J., 6, 18, 73, 89, 111, 112, 120
Jones, Steven, R., 145
Jones, Zelda C., 82
Jordan, Charles Wesley, 11
Joslin, Dennis A., 188
Joyce, David O., 184

Joyce, Tom, 144
Joyner, F. Belton, Jr., 30
Juan, Rodolfo Alfonso, 6, 15, 36, 159
Jung, Hee-Soo, 7, 17, 43, 84, 87, 152
Junk, Bill, 52, 131
Justo, Benjamin A., 11

K

Kahn, Anita K., 146
Kaleuati, Kaleuati, 76
Kamara, Yeabu, 44
Kammerer, Charlene P., 11
Kane, Eileen, 174
Kang, Youngsook, 136
Karandy, Kurt, 31, 33
Karges, Cynthia B., 33
Karima, Chilima, 69
Kashala, Mujinga, 70
Kassongo Ka Suedi, Stanislas, 70
Katembo, Kainda, 7, 16, 61, 162
Kaye-Skinner, Nan, 120
Kazee, Thomas A., 191
Keaton, Jonathan D., 7, 16, 87, 107
Keaton, Susan, 77
Keenan, Suzy, 103
Keene, Gary, 98
Keese, Teresa, 52
Keith, Colleen Perry, 193
Kelemeni, Tupou Seini, 44, 80
Keleshian, Noreen, 136
Keller, Dennis R., 140
Kellner, Ulrike, 167
Kemper, Thomas, 45
Kenaston, Diane M., 76
Kenaston, Judi, 70, 71, 149
Kendall, Gail, 97
Kennedy, Gary, 100
Kent, Cynthia Ann, 171
Kerr, Anne B., 186
Kerwin, Cornelius, 183
Kesner, Danny, 144
Khegay, Eduard, 15, 54, 159
Kibbey, Sue Nilson, 148
Kiboko, Jeanne Kabamba, 30
Kidd, Audrey, 57
Kidd, Ron, 41, 59

Index

Kieffer, Kenneth J., 123
Kiesey, Deborah L, 7, 16, 87, 100, 146
Kilgore, Robin, 121
Kilpatrick, Joe W., 55
Kim, David, 39
Kim, Heasun, 82
Kim, Jeehye, 74
Kim, Joseph, 35
Kim, Kibum, 111
Kim, Myungim, 74
Kim, Young Joo, 67
Kimball, Kathryn, 40
Kimbrough, Walter, 185
Kind, Kathleen E., 33, 140
King, James R., Jr., 7, 19, 90, 138
King, Joyce, 95
King, Lisa, 153
King, Mark, 172
King, Susan, 40
Kingsley, Barbara, 172
Kinnison, Kristi, 137
Kite, Marion L., III, 109
Klaiber, Walter, 11
Klein, John E., 189
Knight, Dickie, 137
Knight, Jefferson, 31, 33
Knight, Martha S., 81
Knowles, Harvey, 191
Knox, J. Lloyd, 11
Knox, Jean, 49
Knox, Ruth A., 192
Knudsen, Diane, 96
Koch, Rankin H., 98
Koch, Tim, 53
Kohler, Rebecca, 72
Kowalski, Edward, 57
Krau, Carol, 39
Kraybill, Ron, 84
Krendl, Kathy, 189
Krimmel, Kenneth W., 149
Kris, Mary Ellen, 46
Kroger, Greg, 99
Kron, Keith, 169
Krowl, Ivan, 174
Krulak, Charles, 184
Krumbach, Audrey, 77
Kruse-Safford, Lisa, 128

Kuan, Kah-Jin Jeffrey, 181, 200
Kuch, Marie, 43, 44
Kulah, Arthur F., 7
Kumar, A. Moses Rathan, 25, 27, 71, 169
Kuonen, Rose, 94
Kurien, Christopher Jacob, 73, 103
Kwak, Jisun, 105
Kyburz, Sheilah, 99, 116
Kymn, Gloria, 52

L

Labarr, Joan Gray, 127
LaBranche, Mark D., 193
LaCasse, Jeremy, 193
Laferty, Matthew A., 61, 62
LaGree, Patty, 110
Lakatos, Judit, 62
Lambert, Nancy, 120, 121
Lambrecht, Thomas, 176
Langford, Sally O., 150
Lansberry, Candace, 100
Larson, Alex, 33
Lasuer, Craig David, 109
Lauber, Melissa, 65, 95
Lawrence, William B., 30, 182
Le, Truong, 41
Leake, Harry, 69
Lear, Heather, 39
Leasure, Frederick H., 152
Leath, Jennifer, 20
Ledbetter, Susan, 94
Lee, Clay F., Jr., 11
Lee, Jacob, 67
Lee, Linda, 11
Lee, Sung-ok, 81
Lee, Sunyoung, 54
Lee, Sunyoung "Sunnie," 54, 55
Lee, Virginia, 167
Leeland, Paul L., 7, 18, 51, 89, 92
Leist, Fred, 119
Leonard-Ray, Susan, 33, 137
Lesesne, John, 49
Lessner, Henry, 127
Lewis, Bettye, 141
Lewis, Candace, 38
Lewis, Dan, 98

Lewis, Julie, 69
Lewis, Sharma, 126
Lewis, William B., 11
Lewthwaite, Barbara-Jayne, 184
Leyva, Elizabeth, 76
Lilleoja, Tarmo, 78
Lind, Gordon, 152
Lindgren, Robert R., 190
Lindley, Gary A., 98
Lindsey, Allison Ross, 44
Link, Conrad, 95
Lippitt, Diane, 129
Livingston, Dennis, 112
Lockhart, Brenda, 37
Locklear, Gary, 125
Locklear, Neffie Connie, 73
Lockmann, Paulo de Tarso, 179
Lockward, Jorge A., 71
Lofsvold, Peg, 132
Logan, Rhodes, 28
Lohre, Kathryn Mary, 178
Lolling, Kent, 108
Loney, Carlton, 68
Long, Joe, Jr., 137
Long, Patricia N., 183
Long, Robert, 52
Looney, Richard C., 11
Lord, Gerald D., 49, 168, 175
Lord, Kimberly, 48
Louderback, Linda, 112
Louter, Doris R. [Becky], 82
Love, Jan, 181, 200
Love, Julie, 114
Love, Todd B., 113
Lowen, Wayne, 187
Lowery, J. Michael, 7, 18, 54, 88, 98
Lowery, Trip, 49
Lowry, Jim, 126
Lowry, Robby, 52
Loyer, Matthew J., 62
Lubbock, Mark, 79
Luckey, William T., Jr., 187
Ludlum, Beth, 50
Luna, Pat, 33
Lusk, Bettie, 62
Lutz, Sandra W., 30
Lux, David, 70, 71

Lyght, Ernest S., 11
Lyles, Steve, 124
Lyon, Louie, 100
Lyons-Bristol, Frances, 63

M

Mabry, Tim, 56
Machado, João Somane, 11
MacHugh, Pat, 121
MacKendree, Bob, 57
Mackey, Christy, 140
Mackey, Sherri, 144
Mackinstosh, Hugh, 37
Maenzanise, Beauty, 61, 62
Maguiraya Acdal, Rodel, 73
Mahaffey, Mike, 171
Mahaney, Deborah, 45
Mahle, Kathi Austin, 30
Mai, Danny, 69, 174
Maldonado, Carmilla, 55
Maliel, Paul, 105
Malloy, Patricia, 130
Malone, Nathan A., 106
Malone, Tracy S., 74, 128
Maloney, Diane, 68
Managuelod, Narciso Immanuel, 79
Mangiduyos, Gladys, 20
Mann, Karon, 94
Manning, Allison, 65
Manskar, Steven, 39
Manuel, Robert L., 191
Mapoissa, Armindo, 42
Mariano, Feliza, 52
Markley, Rene, 174
Marshall, Ben, 173
Marston, Tom, 170
Martin, Delores, 95
Martin, Laurene, 59
Martin, Tommy, 138
Martinez, Joel N., 11
Martinez, Luisa C., 33
Masland, David, 143
Mason, Emery, 130
Mathews, Eric, 138
Matonga, Forbes, 48
Matthews, Marcus, 7, 17, 88, 95

Index

Matthis, Morris, 142
Mawokomatanda, Shandirai, 84
Maxwell, Jeffreyl, 101
May, Carolyn, 112
May, Felton Edwin, 11
Mayfield, Sheila, 69
Maynard, Charles W., 106
Maynard, Phil, 38
McAlexander, Dan, 187
McAlilly, William T., 7, 19, 90, 115, 141
McAllister-Wilson, David, 182, 200
McCallum, Jennifer, 83
McClain, Dick, 176
McClain, Jo Ann, 5
McClain, William Bobby, 62
McClanahan, Arthur, 110
McClendon, Tim, 74, 137
McCleskey, J. Lawrence, 11
McConnell, Calvin D., 11
McCord, Michael, 50
McCoy, Myron, 182, 200
McCoy, Tim, 147
McCracken, Sky J., 116
McCrae, Darlynn, 20
McCray, Marian B., 74
McDavid, Robert Neil, 92
McDonald, Evy, 177
McGhee, Delaine, 74
McIntyre, Dean, 39
McIntyre, Ingrid, 84
McKee, Adam, III, 106
McKee, Larry Michael, 17, 88
McKee, Michael, 7, 127
McKinney, Eric, 55
McKinney, Sarah, 20
McLee, Martin D., 7, 17, 88, 123
McLoud, Kevin, 57
McMillan, Lex O., III, 183
McMillan, Samuel D., IV, 71
McPhee, James T., 122
McPherson, David, 100
McVay, Philip E., 92
Meadors, Alyce, 56
Meadors, Marshall L., Jr., 11
Medlin, William T., 150
Meekins, William B., Jr., 151
Mefford, Bill, 35

Mentzer, James, 122
Merkel-Brunskill, Michelle K., 63
Merrill, Laura A., 140
Merriman, W. Richard, Jr., 190
Merritt, Frances, 58, 59
Metzler, Edward, 109
Mhone, Daniel Levson Ion, 44
Michel, David A., 109
Middleton, Jane Allen, 11
Milford, Brian K., 55, 110
Miller, Craig, 39
Miller, Diana, 61, 62
Miller, Emily R., 81
Miller, Mark, 117
Miller, Michael C., 189
Miller, Randall, 31, 33
Miller, Sandy, 40
Mills, Ianther Marie, 47, 48
Minnick, C. P., Jr., 11
Minor, Ruediger R., 11
Minshall, Roland, 174
Minthorn, Robin, 48
Minton, Kenneth, 104
Mitchell, Cathy D., 76
Moe, Sharon L., 133
Mohler, Dennis, 147
Monahan, Thomas, 140
Monroe, Walter, 104
Moore, Charles E., 26
Moore, Cynthia, 95
Moore, Elizabeth "Sue," 172
Moore, Gary L., 134, 170
Moore, James W., 123
Moore, John, 118
Moore, Johnny, 189
Moore, Karen Covey, 168
Moore, Kathy, 114
Moore, Mary Elizabeth, 181
Moore, Samuel H., Jr., 150
Moore, Susan, 27
Moore, Yvette L., 81
Moots, Philip, 26, 148
Morales, Pablo, 178
Moreno Jackson, María, 48
Morey, Mike, 94
Morgan, Gloria, 139
Morgan, Hope, 125

Index

Morgan, Robert C., 11
Morris, Daniel W., 92
Morris, Gary & Lisa, 169
Morris, Patricia A., 52, 151
Morris, William W., 11
Morrison, Alan J., 28, 173
Morrison, Susan Murch, 12
Morton, J. Vance, 98
Morton, Kama Hamilton, 153
Moseley, Wayne, 138
Mosley, Albert, 181
Mowery, Don, 65
Moy, Elaine, 77
Mudambanuki, Tafadzwa, 67
Mudge, William, 143
Mueller, Gary E., 7, 17, 88, 94
Muhleman, Keith, 123
Muhota, Joseph Mazawu, 33
Mui, Halina, 82
Mulenga, Maidstone, 55, 95, 144
Mullen, James H., 183
Mullette-Bauer, William, 132
Mulligan, Nicola, 105
Mulongo, Ndala Joseph, 71
Murphy, Marsha, 57
Murphy, Murray, 129
Murphy, Tonya, 44
Murphy-McCarthy, Michael, 174
Museu, Joseph Tunda, 26
Mutombo, Stanislas Ilunga, 44
Mutti, Albert Frederick, 12
Myers, Greg C., 55, 140
Myers, Mary, 174
Myers, Ron, 44
Mykrantz, Kayc, 109

N

Nacpil, Emerito P., 12
Naglee, David, 126
Nakanishi, Leanne, 98
Nascimento, Amos, 48
Nation, Harrell A., Jr., 115
Natt, Ellen J., 71
Nausner, Asa Helene, 74
Neal, Holly, 141
Nedderman, Leslie, 82

Neely, Janice, 39
Nelson, Craig, 104
Nelson, Deana, 100, 146
Nelson, Greg, 132
Nelson, Keith F., 99
Nelson, Kenneth L., 33
Nenadal, Sandy, 119
Nesbitt, Claretta, 82
Nessler, Paul, 52
Newell, Kelly, 42
Nhanala, Joaquina F., 7, 15, 76, 160
Nhiwatiwa, Eben, 16, 64, 162
Nibbelink, Jim, 33, 100
Nicholas, Charlotte A., 134
Nicholls, Lewis, 114
Nichols, Richard, 105
Nicholson, Gary L., 103
Nicol, Harry, 129
Nieda, David K., 133
Niederer, Jörg, 33
Niedringhaus, Charles, 69
Niedziela, Dana, 28
Nies, Colette, 53
Niethammer, Hans-Martin, 48
Nimmons, Skyler, 150
Nixon, Paul, 38
Nkonge, Jean-Marie, 44
Noble, Kathy, 67
Noley, Homer, 171
Noll, Fran Lawrie, 105
Norris, Alfred L., 12
Norton, Bill, 125
Nowling, Lisa Schubert, 33
Ntambo, Nkulu Ntanda, 7, 16, 161
Nunn, Jimmy, 129
Nurse, Denise, 80
Nygren, Kip, 194

O

Oates, Helen R., 149
Obergfell, Daniel, 33
Oden, William B., 12
Odland, Tove, 43, 44
Oduor, Ralph, 122
Oehl, Karen, 102
Oglesbee, Clay, 117

Oglesby, Dennis M., Jr., 55
Ohies, Frederik, 188
Olah, Kristie L., 96
Olenyik, Debra, 136, 153
Oliphint, Clayton, 20
Oliver, Andy, 176
Olsen, Øystein, 12
Olson, Deena, 27
Olson, Harriett Jane, 80
O'Neil, Julie, 99
Onema, Fama, 12
Orman, Gail, 56
Ott, Donald A., 12
Ott, Elizabeth, 123
Ough, Bruce R., 7, 16, 21, 87, 99, 116
Overton, Melanie, 50
Owen, Billy, 118
Owen, David, 109
Owens, Dale, 28
Owens, Regina D., 35

P

Page, Jonathan, 65
Palmer, Gregory V., 7, 17, 54, 87, 147
Palomo, Manuel G., Sr., 62
Panovec, Kay, 66, 69
Paparella, Amee, 35
Park, Eric, 36, 37, 151
Park, HiRho, 49
Park, J. W., 95
Park, Jeremiah J., 7, 17, 61, 88, 140
Park, Joon-Sik, 20
Park, Young-Mee, 128
Parker, Abby, 41
Parker, Michael A., II, 33
Parks, Linda, 127
Parks, Robert J., Jr., 144
Parris, Mark D., 33
Parrish, Craig, 84, 93, 133
Parrish, Patti, 137
Paschke, Ruth, 38
Patterson, Cynthia, 102
Patterson, Derrell, 129
Patterson, J. Liz, 34
Patterson, Joseph W., 151
Patterson, L. Dale, 63

Patterson, Sheron, 127
Pearigen, Robert W., 188
Pearson, Ann A., 123
Peason, Thomas, Jr., 137
Peck, Rich, 79
Pederson, Michelle, 50
Peil, Dan, 130
Pendergrass, Annette, 104
Pennel, Joseph E., Jr., 12
Perez, Migdiel, 40
Perez, Rene, 122
Perry, Ronny, 69
Perucca, Kirk, 178
Peters, Susan, 97
Peterson, Brian T., 82
Phillips, Bradford, L., 144
Phillips, Clarenda, 31, 34
Phillips, Mary Catherine, 92
Pierce Norton, MaryJane, 38
Pierre-Okerson, Judith, 80
Pierson, Chris, 31, 34, 128
Pillow, C. Gene, 113
Pinkerton, Jerry, 51, 52
Pinson, Mathew, 126
Plumbstead, Wayne J., 105
Pogemiller, Leah R., 108
Poland, William W., 110
Polito, Lisa, 167
Polster, Steve, 152
Pon, Marjorie M., 41, 58
Porter, Derrick, 65, 134
Porter, George E., Jr., 151
Porter, Thomas W., 85
Pospisil, Jeff, 99
Powell, Anita Adams, 103
Powers, John, 104
Prestipino, Tony, 137
Preston, James, 55
Price, George, 129
Price, Larry, 79
Pridgeon, Jeremy Kimble, 92
Pridmore, J. Eric, 177
Pritchard, Donna, 71
Pritchett, Chett, 176
Proferes, Joanna, 104
Pruden, Estelle, 144
Prumer, Rosemary, 129

Index

Purdy, Steven Mark, 139
Purnell, George Anthony, 109
Purushotham, Gwen, 49, 84, 200
Purushotham, Samuel, 55

Q

Qubein, Nido R., 186
Quick, Beth, 34
Quinn, Chris, 174
Quipungo, Jose, 8, 13, 155

R

Radcliffe, Karen, 137
Rader, Sharon Z., 12
Ragland, Sharon, 26
Rambach, Barbara, 105
Ramsey, Chris, 138
Ramsey, Dan, 78, 79
Randall, Donna, 183
Rankin, Nancy Burgin, 150
Ransom, Opal G., 76
Rasberry, Henderson, 118
Rasing, Mighty, 42
Rathert, Ann, 119
Ratliff, Mike, 41
Ray, Andy, 118
Ray, Natasha, 55
Raynor, Shane, 58
Redding, Elizabeth, 27
Redding, Roger, 107
Redman, Elizabeth, 39
Reece, Emily, 38
Reed, Clara M., 127
Reese, Randall W., 108
Reeves, Bud, 94
Refsdal, Knut, 20
Reichard, Rosalind, 185
Reid, Debbie, 53
Reisman, Kimberly, 64, 65
Reist, Fitzgerald, 71, 72
Renfroe, Rob, 176
Rentsch, Greg, 102
Rettberg, Richard, 28, 85
Revelle, Elmer, 119
Revels, Akwiasdi K., 55

Reyes, Ruben T., 30
Reynders, John C., 188
Reynolds, Cynthia J., 109
Rhodes, Linda S., 145
Rhodes, Schuyler, 96
Rhodes, Wayne, 35
Rice, Lee Ann, 41
Richards, Ramona, 58
Richards, Yvette K., 43, 44, 80
Richardson, Beth, 40
Riddle, W. Zac, 26
Riley, Wayne J., 182
Riss, Timothy, 43, 44
Rivera, Arnold, 128
Rivera, Edgardo, 95
Rivera-Báez, Glorymar, 37
Rivers, Bettye, 137
Roberson, Kelly, 139
Roberson, Laura, 96
Roberts, Dede, 94
Roberts, Frances J., 35
Robertson, Karen, 111
Robinson, Cathy, 58
Robinson, Delmar, 26
Rochford, Dave, 145
Rodia, Jennifer, 66
Rodriguez, Samuel, 38
Rogers, Alice, 65
Rogers, Cornish, 62
Rogers, Leigh M., 81
Rohifs, Carol Walter, 140
Rollins, Benita, 102
Rood, Sherri, 143
Rooks, Jessica, 65
Rorex, C. Douglas, 108
Rosa, Melanie, 136
Rosario, Ileana, 71
Rosheuvel, Janis, 81
Ross, Sunrise, 131
Roth, Meghan, 31, 34
Rowe, B. David, 184
Rowell, Jan, 144
Royals, Gary C., 150
Royappa, Samuel, 152
Ruffle, Douglas, 38
Ruiz-Millan, Ismael A., 44
Rundell, Jay, 182

Index

Runyan, Jeff, 40
Ruof, Klaus Ulrich, 55
Russell, David, 116
Russell, John H., 188
Russell, John W., 12
Russell, Roger W., 108
Russell, Ryan M., 76
Russell, Timothy, 125
Ruth, Barbara J., 55

S

Saas, Anita, 153
Sachen, Kristin, 96
Saliba, Peter, 194
Salisbury, Charles W., 140
Salley, James H., 50, 165
Salley, Susan, 58
Salsgiver, Thomas L., 56, 140
Salter, Andris Y., 82
Samelson, David, 96
Sample, Kris, 140
Sanders, Janet, 56
Sano, Roy I., 12
Sansone, Amanda, 57
Santiago, Ali, 74
Santiago, Maria Teresa, 34
Saufferer, Cindy, 45
Saunders, Linda, 66
Savage, C. W. "Chuck" II, 127, 139
Scandrol, Donald G., 151
Scarborough, Martha, 119
Scarbrough, Kay, 111
Scavuzzo, David, 102
Schäfer, Franz W., 12
Schenk, Carl, 72
Schleicher, Andrew, 166
Schnase, Robert C., 8, 18, 51, 89, 119
Schoeller, David, 174
Schol, John R., 8, 64, 105
Schramm, Linda, 62
Schrum, Jake B., 190
Schuermann, Kurt R., 119
Schuette, Natalie, 27
Schuler, Ulrike, 175
Schultz, Karen, 107
Schultz, Ronald E., 124

Schwab, Sharon, 151
Schwaller, Tyler M., 76
Scott, Alvin, 56
Scott, Donald F., 98
Scott, George "Doug," 62
Scott, Laurel, 170
Scott, Marvlyn B., 35
Scott, Robin B., 124
Scriven, Patrick, 133
Sears, Denise Smartt, 123
Sears, Johnny, 40
Seifert, Chris, 141
Seilheimer, David, 140
Selleck, Chris, 126
Selleck, Mike, 126
Selman, Scott, 52, 124
Serdar, Pamela, 117
Serdyukov, Pavel, 65
Severe, David L., 88
Sewell, Peggy, 27
Seyle, David, 193
Shafer, Lisa, 148
Shaffer, Rich, 149
Shamana, Beverly, 12
Sharpe, Calvin, 84, 85
Sharpe, Dwayne, 38
Sharpe, Sally, 59
Shaver, Kim, 57
Shearman, Gayle, 96
Sheetz, Brian, 102
Shelton, Connie, 118
Shenise, Mark C., 63
Sherer-Simpson, Ann B., 12
Shettle, Manet, 109
Shimko, Deanna, 152
Sholis, Barbara, 147
Shownes, Patrick, 66
Shultz, Paul, 173
Shytle, Ed, 79, 174
Sidorak, Stephen, Jr., 20
Siemens, Stan, 85
Sim, Sam, 37
Simmons, Jay K., 170
Simpson, Kim, 37, 71, 98
Simpson, Patricia L., 133
Sims, Mary Jo, 95
Sison, Vida Grace, 65

Sit, Tyler, 48
Skeete, F. Herbert, 12
Slabach, Frederick G., 191
Slater, Thomas, 148
Slessarev-Jamir, Helene, 200
Sloan, Barry, 37
Sloane, Ken, 39
Sluder, Lori L., 106
Smiley, Tim, 104
Smith, Amy C., 56
Smith, Bobby L., 28
Smith, Brent, 27
Smith, Cory R., 92
Smith, Deb, 39
Smith, Gary, 141
Smith, Jay Franklin, 114
Smith, Jodi S., 26, 127
Smith, Lanella, 30
Smith, Renata, 123
Smith, Sandra, 142
Smith, Theodore, 145
Smith, Wilma, 35
Snider, Jan, 69
Snipes, David A., 150
Soles, Anne, 146
Solomon, Dan E., 12
Solomon, Lindsey, 66
Soriano, Leo A., 8
Sorrells, W. Lyn, 150
Southern, Gray, 53
Spain, Robert H., 12, 56
Sparkman, Kevin, 141
Spaw, Mark, 101
Spencer, Gary, 104
Spencer, Wanda, 82
Spindt Henschel, Ann, 152
Sprague, C. Joseph, 12
Spurlock, Steven, 114
Spurrell, Marilyn, 99
Squires, Jessica, 45
Stacker, Cheryl, 49
Staempfli, Andreas C., 45
Stafford, James, 40
Stallsworth, Paul T., 177
Stamps, Mary E., 172
Stanislaus, Joell, 127
Stanovsky, Elaine J. W., 8, 19, 36, 91, 136, 153

Stansell, Elijah, 26, 142
Stanton, Nathan D., 45
Stapleton, Amy, 74
Starkey, Jill, 113
Stead, Jerre, 85
Steele, Rodney, 65
Steffensen, Lori J., 140
Steiner Ball, Sandra L., 8, 17, 88
Stella, Connie, 58
Stengel, Cathy, 143
Stenmark, Beverly, 121
Step, Gary, 146
Stephens, Darryl W., 77
Stephens, Michael, 58
Sterling, Lucille, 100
Stevens, Willard R. "Buzz," 97
Stewart, Chuck, 130
Stewart, Sharon S., 34
Sticher, Hermann L., 12
Stickler, LeeDell, 41, 58
Stickley-Miner, Deanna, 45
Stikes, Bill, 34
Stinson, Craig, 130
Stinson, David, 98
Stinson, Van, 114
Stith, Forrest C., 13
Stockton, Thomas B., 13
Stokes, Mack B., 13
Stokes, Martha, 37
Stonbraker, Michael P., 124
Stone, Dale, 119
Stone, Kathleen, 81
Stotts, David, 26, 118
Stowe, Marc, 79
Strandburg, Thomas Q., 151
Strausbaugh, Joseph, 79
Streiff, Patrick, 8, 14, 156
Streiff, Peggy, 102
Streight, Lisa, 148
Strickland, Daphine, 34
Strickland, Haywood L., 192
Strickland, Walter "Skip," 65, 136
Strom, Philip, 117
Strother, Jon, 125
Stryker, Richard Lane, III, 124
Stuart, Farley E., III, 113, 135

Index

Stultz, Valerie, 102
Sturdivant, Sue, 49
Sumner, Shannon, 26
Suther, Jane, 150
Sutton, Tara, 101
Swanson, James E., Sr., 8, 19, 78, 90, 118
Sweet, Rebekah, 144
Swenson, Mary Ann, 5, 13, 20
Swetman, Michael, 37
Swinson, Daniel, 168

T

Tabor, J. David, 106
Taiwo, Kunle, 136
Talbert, Melvin G., 13
Tan, Wee-Li, 105
Tang, Anthony, 61, 62
Tanton, Tim, 66, 67
Tatem, Dorothy Watson, 103
Taylor, Bill, 142
Taylor, C. J., 143
Taylor, Daniel H., Jr., 107
Taylor, Jeffrey A., 149
Taylor, Julie, 81
Taylor, Linda, 125
Taylor, Mary Virginia, 8, 19, 90, 106
Taylor, Meg, 106
Teasley, Mary, 137
Tecumseh, July, 131
Teel, David, 58
Tello, Michelle, 75
Tener, Greg, 130
Terry, Carol, 69
Terry, Esther, 183
Tevis, Dennis G., 110
Thayne, Lewis Evitts, 187
Thiel, Sherri, 66, 68
Thomas, Ronald R., 191
Thompson, Becky, 80
Thompson, Brenda A., 80
Thompson, Dave, 145
Thompson, Deborah, 152
Thompson, Lawrence R., Jr., 145
Thompson, Roger K., 124
Thompson, Timothy, 118
Thornell, Blake, 41

Thorpe, Robbie, 57
Thorsett, Stephen E., 192
Tielke, Kenneth, 79
Tiger, Chris, 130
Tillman, Jeanie, 174
Tinker, Kelsey, 41
Tinley, Josh, 58
Tisdale, Henry N., 184
Tobey, Briana Nicole, 34
Todd, James B., 103
Tomlinson, Ed, 51, 53
Tooley, Mark, 176, 178
Toquero, Solito K., 13
Torio, Pedro M., Jr., 14, 155
Tournoux, Joy, 23
Townsend, Stephanie G., 194
Trafton, Margie, 135
Trammell, Ben, 79
Travis, Anne S., 56, 89, 107
Trefz, Rebecca, 65
Trent, Cheryl E., 80
Trevino, Dalia, 135, 139
Tricoli, Robin J., 186
Trimble, Julius C., 8, 16, 87, 110
Trinidad, Saul C., 34
Tripp, Marcus, 138
Tritle, Barrie, 48
Tuell, Jack M., 13
Tukutau, Sione, 136
Tulloch, Julia R., 83
Tumblin, Thomas F., 56
Tumonong, Prospero, 146
Turner, R. Gerald, 190
Turner, Rachel, 41, 58
Turner, W. Craig, 187
Tveit, Olav Fykse, 179
Tweh, N. Oswald, Sr., 30
Tyrell, Hortense A., 82

U

Unda, Gabriel Yemba, 8, 14, 158
Upchurch, Robert, 150
Urda, Ana-Haydee, 76
Usher-Kerr, Marva D., 83
Utley, Joanne S., 123

Index

V

Valera, David, 133
Valverde, Eradio, Jr., 139
Van der Wege, Lew, 112
van Giesen, Richard, 108
Van Gorp, Carol, 82
Vannoy, Karen, 100
Vargo, Jessica, 25, 26, 102
Varnell, Benjy, 138
Vaughan, Jackie, 66
Växby, Hans, 8
Vázquez-Garza, Virgilio, 64, 65, 139
Vega, Abel, Jr., 135
Velander, Peter, 40
Vermande, Tim, 177
Vetter, Molly E., 31, 34
Vianese, Carmen, 45
Vickery, Scott, 82
Villa, Yolanda, 119
Villareal, Marisa, 83
Vinson, Stephen L., 173
Viuya, Priscilla, 48
Virnig, Michele, 153
Vogt, Amanda, 79
Vonner, Sally L., 83
Vose, Marvin, 136

W

Wagner, James W., 185
Wahkinney, Kevin, 131
Waldmann, Mike, 172
Walker, Cheryl L., 39
Walker, James, 62
Walker, Robert, 123
Walker, Val, 117
Walkup, Vincent, 116, 142
Wallace, Larry L., 56
Wallace, Vicki, 68
Wallace, William T., 76
Wallace-Padgett, Debra, 8, 18, 76, 89, 124
Waller, Kendall, 119
Walsh, Fran, 69
Walton, Denise, 139
Wandabula, Daniel, 8, 73, 158
Ward, Hope Morgan, 8, 19, 43, 84, 90

Ware, Barbara, 137
Warren, George, 130
Washington, Lillian, 137
Watkins, Nancy, 61, 62
Watson, B. Michael, 8, 19, 90, 126
Watson, Brent, 148
Watson, David F., 200
Watson, Michael, 20
Watson, Tom, 121
Watts, Michael B., 56
Waymack, Dale, 40
Weatherall, Sylvester, 108
Weatherford, Pam, 130
Weatherspoon, Dale, 74
Weaver, Peter D., 5, 13
Weaver, Sandra Long, 68
Weaver Dunn, Alyce, 151
Webb, Mark J., 8, 17, 88, 143
Weber, Donn Ann, 126
Weber, Todd, 110
Webster, Kathleen Overby, 145
Webster, Wayne, 118
Weeks, Kent M., 169
Weesner, David A., 110
Weihing, Richard, 143
Weikel, Walter P., 106
Wenner, Rosemarie, 5, 8, 15, 158
Wertz, Frederick, 13
West, J. Cameron, 186, 200
Westad, Anne, Berit, 76
Westad, Audun, 71
Westbrook, William, 134
Wethington, Mark W., 175
Whitaker, Timothy W., 13
White, Brian Keith, 109
White, C. Dale, 13
White, Deborah, 57
White, Dick, 142
White, Don & Vivian, 169
White, Donna, 118
White, Justin, 73, 74
White, Mary, 26, 27, 85, 103
White, Paul, 102
White, Sara Ann, 43, 45
White, Victoria, 118
White, Woodie W., 13
Whitlatch, Cathy, 45

Index

Whitney, Phyllis, 200
Whittaker, Michelle C., 35
Wiatt, Wayne, 56
Wiblin, Maria D., 87
Wiertzema, Ruth A., 135
Wiggins Hare, Dawn, 77
Wilborn, Kathey Michelle, 97
Wilbur, Margaret, 81
Wilbur, Rene, 122
Wiley, David E., III, 105
Wilfong, Charles D., 109
Wilke, Richard B., 13
Wilke, Sarah, 39
Willhauck, Susan, 173
Williams, Andrew Ponder, 34
Williams, Heather, 56
Williams, Ike, 109
Williams, Kathryn A., 20
Williams, Leia Danielle, 129
Williams, Marti, 40
Williams, Rick, 28
Williams, Robert J., 63
Williams, Rosa, 105
Williams, Ross, 123
Williams, Tamara SM, 146
Williamson, B. T., 142
Willimon, William H., 13
Willis, Valarie, 26
Wills, Richard J., Jr., 13
Wilmouth, Robert, 190
Wilson, Bill, 148
Wilson, Carol E., 65, 106, 107
Wilson, David, 131
Wilson, Gary J., 108
Wilson, Jennifer A., 79
Wilson, Joe A., 13
Wilson, John R., 151
Wilson, Melba, 53
Wilson, Milton "Mickey," 104
Wilson, Richard F., 187
Wilson, Robin, 37
Wilson, Thomas B., 93
Wilson, Tina, 151
Wilson, Tom, 132, 134
Wilson, William, 149
Wilterdink, Chris, 41
Winegar, Grady C., 62

Wingfield, Myron, 49
Winkler, James, 35, 102
Winn, Richard, 126
Winton, Suzanne, 37
Wisdom, Dick, 128
Wise, Gil, 125
Witt, Kevin, 39
Witte, Kathryn, 121
Wolcott, Richard, 102
Wolf, Christina, 63
Wolf, Janet, 85
Wolf, Susie, 56
Wolfe, John L., 169
Wolgemuth, Jerry, 141
Wolover, Amber, 153
Wood, Alexx, 122
Wood, Anita, 49, 167
Wood, Jane, 168
Wood, Pattie, 98
Wood, Steve Doyle, 26
Woods, Carol, 98
Worsham, Sonia, 58
Wray, Galen, 120
Wright, Doug, 79
Wright, Rachel, 47, 48
Wright, Varlyna D., 105
Wynn, Sam, 125

X, Y

Yambasu, John K., 9, 16, 43, 161
Yanchury, Amanda, 117
Yeakel, Joseph H., 13
Yebuah, Frederick, 137
Yebuah, Lisa, 34
Yeh, Mark, 58
Yemba, David K., 9, 14, 47, 156
Yi, Kang (Kenny), 123
Yin, Burt, 96
Yocom, Rena, 49
Yohanna, John Wesley, 15, 78, 160
Yokem, Mackey, 94
Yoshino, Mariellen, 96
Young, Evan, 95
Young, Lawrence, 142
Youngquist, Patricia H., 27, 28
Young-Ross, Bridgette, 50

Index

Z

Zabel, Judy, 117
Zaki, Zaki L., 128
Zeh, Katey, 35
Zellner, Dave, 53
Ziegler, Dean D., 151
Zink, Lora, 128

www.ingramcontent.com/pod-product-compliance
Lightning Source LLC
Chambersburg PA
CBHW050557170426
43201CB00011B/1728